CONTENTS.

CHAPTER I.

A Word to my Class 1
Importance of a beggar's history—Biography—Retrospective and prospective glances.

CHAPTER II.

Early Days 26
Author's birth—First recollection of external objects—Kingstone-upon-Hull—Father's departure to sea, and the Author given up to the care of grandsire—Sent to a "Dame's school"—School mistress's stock of ghost stories—Elevated to the Free School of Sculcoates—A holiday in the fields—Gathering Easter Dues at Hull—Father's return—Press-gang and blood money—Author "put out" as a linen draper's errand boy—Discharged therefrom as incorrigible—Goes to work in a brick yard—Leaves the brick yard—Engages at a pottery—Afflicted with chilblains—Kindness of the foreman, and advantages derived from his intelligence—Necessity of youth being instructed in the moral and commercial value of labour—Leaves the "pot house" to prepare for an apprenticeship.

CHAPTER III.

Apprenticeship.......................... 57
Apprenticeship the April of life—Shipwright—Cogan's charity—Mr. Thompson a benevolent man—Circulating library—Affray with press gang, and demoralizing effects of war.

CHAPTER IV.

Things that I Remember 77
Religious prejudice—Cobbett's Register—Wooller's Black Dwarf—Rottenborough elections—Election at Hull—Andrew Marvell—Strawberry gardens—First visit to a Theatre—Private theatricals—"Wise men."

CHAPTER V.

A Voyage to Greenland 116

Departure—Sea sickness—Greenland sailors—Shetland Isles—Seal fishing—May-day in Greenland—Whale fishing—Superstition of sailors, &c.

CHAPTER VI.

Beginning the World 159

Embarks for Calcutta—Marriage—Commences the trade of a sawyer—Saw-mills—The mission of machinery—York—Impression on visiting the Cathedral—Yorkshire Thompson and theatricals

CHAPTER VII.

The Strolling Player 185

Resolves upon taking to the stage—General Jarvis—Templeton—Clarke—F. D. Campbell—Tickhill—Bolsover—A manager's room—Derbyshire—W—r D—n, a Quack Doctor—Different degrees of morals in the people—S. and K. managers, and a manageress—Kimberley—Batty's circus—Sets up strolling manager on his own account—Strolling reminiscences—Shakspeare almost unknown in the rural districts—Rustics heard of Indian jugglers, Tom Cribb, and Tom Thumb, but never heard of Shakspeare.

CHAPTER VIII.

Our Village 295

Settles at Edwinstowe as a painter—Studies—Countess of Scarbrough—Ancient privileges of the villagers—Church yard—What may be expected from an ignorant and enslaved labour class—Characteristics of Robin Hood and the Forest Outlaws—"His Honor," an eccentric character—Odd Fellows' Lodges—Establishment of an Artisans' Library—Sherwood Gatherings—Spencer T. Hall—Miss E. S. Carey—Millhouse's stone of Memorial—Pemberton, the "Wanderer"—Association of Self-Help.

CHAPTER IX.

Birkland and Bilhagh 388

Study of Nature profitable—Edwinstowe Church—Birkland and Bilhagh—Remarkable Oaks: Major's, Millhouse, Greendale, Parliament, and Shambles' Oaks—Birches and Sherwood Forest.

THE AUTOBIOGRAPHY OF AN ARTISAN.

CHAPTER I.

A WORD TO MY CLASS.

I HAVE somewhere read, that the moral history of a beggar, fully and honestly given, might greatly enlarge and enlighten the views of a philosopher. It has not been the fashion hitherto to trouble the philosophers of our country with the moral history of beggars, simply because they were the despised class, and consequently too mean to teach a lesson; and if views cannot be enlarged by the history of wealth, they stand a narrow chance of extension from the beggar class. No; the " poor beggar" receives taunts enow from haughty pride, without writing himself down a son of poverty. The conventionalisms of to-day require, that if you would "rise in the world," you must be rich; and if you are not in reality wealthy, then it behoves you to do all in your power to make people believe you are so, and the kind world will bid you "good morning." Only proclaim to them that you are "poor and honest," and, as surely as darkness follows the decline of day, so surely will the everyday world sink you a fathom deeper in the slough of contempt, every time they meet you, or hear your name repeated. Amongst my earliest lessons, I can remember the money lessons: "Get money—honestly, if you can. If you have not wealth, try a foreign surname—talk of genealogical trees—coming over with the Conqueror—your ancestors—how many men your father slew—or any other of the ready-made sentences miscalled 'respectable;' and, as certainly as thousands before you have 'made men of themselves,' so surely will you 'get on in the world.'" Our literature teems with the histories of wealth-made men; and if the means of their accumulating wealth were "as fully and honestly given," as the parading of its power is humiliating, it would "point a moral" that might "greatly enlarge the views" of the artisan and peasant wealth-producing class.

We have the lives of statesmen, many of whom have devoted their time to the framing of one-sided laws, whose object has been to enslave the artisan, and make him "a beggar" indeed;—to allow the "taskmaster" to blaze in Courts, bedecked in blue ribbons, buckled in garters, feed upon dainty viands, and leave a new generation to devise fresh means to swell the family treasure—to look down upon the poor "unwashed" as mere animals, whose aspirings soar no higher than the felling of timber or the constructing of palaces, fortifications, and war ships—"born thralls," to bow down to those in high places, and labour from early morn to gloomy night. "Flesh and blood" is cheap enough—work on until the grey twilight make blade and weft one dunny mass—and thus the round of toil goes on, and on, and on. Soon his toil-riven frame breaks beneath the task, and after repeated applications, he is elevated to the Union house, separated from his wife, little ones, all that made life worth living for. There he can rest. Rest! the last dregs of the oil of life are nearly burnt out; even now the flame flickers from the old lamp—it flares and pales out; he dies in quiet—no crowd throng around his couch. What need of mourners? we "still fill up our numbers." Now he is honoured with the pomp befitting a "pauper's grave:" packed in a shell, where no black cloth or gaudy tinsel decorates his "last jacket." No! the beauty of saw-tooth texture and natural fibre are all visible; no mock attempt is made with "baked meats" to mar the sad solemnity—no coach does he need, or trail of mourners; four attenuated serge-clad spectres, fit emblems of the pauper's fate, "hoist him on their shoulders," and bear him to his "freehold," where he can lay in peace, and feed the worms.

> "Oh! where the mourners? alas! there are none!
> —He has left not a gap in the world now he's gone,—
> Not a tear in the eye of child, woman, or man—
> To the grave with his carcass as fast you can,
>   Rattle his bones over the stones,
>   He's only a pauper whom nobody owns."
>
> THE PAUPER'S FUNERAL.

We have the histories of heroes, who see nothing to care for in the artisan class, until their trade of blood has inflamed the angry passions of (miscalled) rival nations; then, for the moment, the mob rise into "likely young men," and they are depraved by the offer of a paltry bribe, "to cut foreign throats" or stop a breach—excellent targets for the assailants' balls to centre in; the legal murder over, they are demoralized by being let loose upon a conquered people, dignified by the name of foes—a pack of human blood-hounds, devouring them by "sack and pillage." When they have won laurels for heroes, and dominion for princes, the artisan soldiers are discharged with a centesimal portion of "prize money," to batten upon glory! I do not under-value the labours of the statesman, or have any desire to dim the so-called glory that wreathes the brows of the hero; they were necessary in the old war-days—they may be wanted again. Many of them have perilled their lives in the field, and braved the storm-vexed ocean for country and fame; but the sooner their swords are beaten into ploughshares, the better for the cupboards of the artisans and the cause of humanity. The diplomacy of statesmen has been necessary in the half-civilized strife of nations; many of them have dignified humanity, nevertheless they have not troubled themselves about the elevation of the working classes.

We have the histories of philosophers, from the ancient sage to the modern philosopher; we have the histories of the sculptors and painters who have strown the wilderness of the world with precious flowers; we have the poets—those "laurelled prophets of future good:" all have been written—from the depopulators of countries to the insane ravings of "unknown tongues;" they have all been worthy of a place in undying pages—all, save the wealth-producer. There is no master-chiselling in his bust, to recommend it to a niche in the world's gallery. Oh, no! The artisan! what does he want with literature?—what has he to do with mind? Let the horny-handed labourer, by inadvertence, drop the two short words "I think," and every "Jack in office," by virtue of his one step upward, is in a fever. Yes! he fears the contagion engendered by the march of intellect will kill his occupation. The tyrant whipper reminds the luckless wight who prates of thinking, "He has no right to think; let those think who are paid for thinking." Mark ye— the *pay* for thinking! Such has been the every ready reply to him who dared to utter "I think." As to the matter of the pay, the toiler is not overburdened with that; it is usually scanty indeed, and more particularly if he enjoys the rural blessing of being a ploughman. But if he be so cared for by the parish authorities as to be honoured with a stone bench and hammer—how then? Oh! his progression to the stone heap does not require intense thought. No; he can enjoy that luxury without thinking; and in *some* parishes, it is considered a luxury to break stone—albeit not an over-paid one: if it were, the trade would soon be ruined by competition. I have heard the humanity-mongers declare, that if they were allowed to earn above seven shillings for the six days' work at stone-breaking, all the farms would be deserted, and the "greasy rascals" would run a tilt at the stone benches. What need ye, then, of learning? "'Tis folly to be wise."

I hear a burly, wine-flushed farmer, who resides some two miles from my cottage, exclaiming, "What do these working men want with learning?" Yes, the good easy man wonders! That round face, and beef, bacon, and partridge-fed stomach, that never feels the want of a crust, except as a pleasant contrast to the products of his luxury-stored larder and cellars—this poor man, who is for ever preaching poverty, because corn will not fetch "eighty-six," wonders what the sun-burnt sons of labour want with learning. He declares that the repeal of the "famine laws" will ruin the country. Alas, poor country! you bleed at every vein, when any thing to benefit the poor man is agitated. This farmer, who has made a fortune by his trade, despite his whine of ruin, has leisure to look at all the attempts that have been made in his time to make men of the rascals. Hear his cogitations: "What," says he, "have all these schools done for them? Fifty years ago, a labourer never troubled his head about schools. What need is there of learning to hold the handles of a plough, or whop a flail upon a thrashing floor? Men could work then. Now, if you lay down a newspaper, and turn your back, the servant takes it up and reads it, and thus neglects his or her work. If you leave an unsealed letter, 'tis ten to one but the servant reads it. All this is the result of the schools, and the bother about reading and moralizing with the working men." Will you believe it? this man blusters about humanity, employing the people, and fox-hunting! Oh, these far-seeing friends of the people! More brick, ye knaves! what need ye of straw? More brick! more brick! Yet this reviler of the poor man's school might as well whistle to the winds as attempt to stop the progress of mind—aye, of mind, even amongst the thrashers and hedge-plashers. He cannot understand this march of mind. No! Mammon hath blinded him; the metal-god hath given him a gilt-edged banking book; and instead of plenty making him the poor man's benefactor, prejudice has sealed up the eyes of his humanity, and he thirsts for more human sweat and blood—for the means to forge new fetters to manacle the labourer who dares to think. Is this tyrant an exception? Alas! no. Would he were! He is one of a large class. "Fifty years ago," says he, "there was no bother about the schools." It is indeed a glorious thing to know, that in the year one thousand eight hundred and forty-six, the schools are multiplying—the murky clouds are breaking, that overspread the earth a generation ago, when boys were taught to handle swords of lath, to dress in lines, and charge in companies, at a bed of nettles, and cut off their heads, as I was taught, and have so charged, in order that, when a grown baby, I might not depart from my early lessons of how good and loyal a thing it was to cut a Frenchman's throat!

Why wonder that the lower orders have been poachers, and tainted with crime? They saw no evil in taking a luxury when they could catch one. How should the "ignorant creature" who was forbidden the exercise of thought, save how to thrash the greatest quantity of corn for the least reward—how could such an one understand the social relation of classes, and shrink from the commission of a law-made crime?

Wonder, that the poor man takes no heed for the future, when he was taught to revel for a season in war-created wealth—to cry "Ne'er heed! when I can work no longer, there is the parish for me! what do I pay the rates for? enough for the day is the evil thereof." He was forbidden to think! Why? Oh, the free exercise of thought would have taught him to scan the war debt—prevented his clamouring for the "heaven-born minister"—have given him a perspective view of the skilly and separation-cemetery—would have taught him to calculate taxes on food, and the blessings flowing from the rights of commerce, property taxes, pensions, high-priced legislation, the debasing system of place-making—to assert his right of citizenship—his duty to control the law-makers who contrive the statutes that are to feed or starve, reward or punish him—would have taught him self-dependance and moral elevation, instead of serfish cringing crumb-picking—the free exercise of thought would have taught him the advantage of sobriety over the debasing sensuality that sinks the man beneath the level of the brute—would have taught him *that* true wisdom which alone makes man the noblest work of God!

Have not the people paid the penalty of prisons, transportations, and the like punishments, for listening to, and being led by, the demagogues who promised them food, and leisure to enjoy an hour in the fields? This is visited against them by the class who care just as much for them as they do for their cart-horses and the other labour machines upon their domains. Amongst the clamourers for freedom who belong to the working classes, whether Radicals, Democrats, Chartists, Complete Suffragists, Free Traders, or by whatever name they may be called—how many of them, who have been favoured with a "little learning," have signed the dagger and torch warrant? How many out of the few who dared to think were found amongst the physical force corps? Yet the cry is, the "mob," coupled with the epithet "ignorant." Wonder, indeed! that the hungry, over-wrought, hovel-huddled, ill-clad, straw-bedded slave class, were ready, at any risk, to carry the link or beard a tyrant, at the nod of any man who pledged himself to lead them to bread loaves, homes, and liberty! Think the matter over, ye who affect to love the poor! and ask yourselves what ignorance may not do?

Give the artisans and peasantry food, and leave to study political economy, with occasional leisure to wander in the fields and lanes—to trace the river's banks—there to read the revelations of Universal Goodness—there to feel the loving care of the Great Father for every plant, and flower, and creeping thing—to hear the humanising music of the song birds—to listen the wild winds antheming their joy, as they kiss the tree tops, and fan the mountain's brow in their aerial course. Educate them—and trust me, for I have had six-and-forty years' close communion with them—educate them, and you need not dream of mobs, daggers, or Captain Swing!

"Educate them!" I hear some timid one exclaim. "Have they not been bidden to go to the church on Sundays, and taught the catechism?" Yes! Nevertheless you cannot be blind to the fact, that however useful in their place catechisms and church extensions may be, creeds and forms are but chaff for the young and growing mind to feed upon, and have done very little for the education and moral elevation of the masses. They ask, "Was not the pastor regular in the pulpit? did he not visit the National School at stated periods? did he not send the curate, or, still better, did he not go himself to the cottages, and exhort, baptize, and give the sacrament when needed?" Yes; all this, and more, has been done. But too often the end of this is frequently to have a "full church," and keep a perfect surveillance over the poor. The spirit—the humble desire to make "the salt of the earth" happy—has, in too many cases, the least to do with these visits. Too often, if the poorest of the poor be regular at church, and can repeat the catechism, then he is a candidate for the charities of the district, and a good Christian; but let him profess dissent, and he may expect to be despitefully used. For instance: let his pig die, or a similar calamity befal him; then, confiding as the poor always are, his first essay is to solicit the assistance of his neighbours to repair a heavy loss, and his poverty prompts him to take his petition to the pastor, who every Sunday professes his love for the very worst of his flock; and what is the result? "I am sorry for your loss, but I cannot relieve you; I never see you at the church, and I contrive to know all who are there." And now the blush purples the cheek of the slave-beggar all despised. He feels he is not even allowed the right of thought upon so vital a point as the mode in which he shall worship his God, and seek for Heaven; and with struggling shame and indignation, he answers, "True,

Sir, I am seldom at your church, but I am frequently at the chapel." "Oh, that does not matter! You know the church is the appointed place. What do you expect at the chapel, where bricklayers, joiners, and tinkers get up to expound the Scriptures? Where do they get their 'sign and seal?' Who laid hands on them?" Oh, this imposing of hands!

> "So easily are bishops made,
> By man or woman's whim,
> That Wesley hands on Coke hath laid,
> But who laid hands on him?"

Notwithstanding, the poor man finds life and spirituality in the blood-warm inspirations of the chapel preachers; he is punished with neglect because he dared to prefer the licensed conventicle, and listened to the man who called sinners to repentance in the by-paths of society.

How antagonistic are our practices! While our laws proclaim toleration in religion, and issue licenses where the preachers are to exhort, we pay an orthodox hierarchy millions per annum to preach exclusion, and punish with contempt the poverty, or inclination, that enters the licensed house.

So it is with our chapel suppliant. As a consequence he gets no pig charity from the High Church "successor of the Apostles;" he keeps it for fine linen and pliant claimants. But the evil seldom ends here: the curate, 'squire, and other "respectables" follow the Christian pastor's example. Then their visits: they are not always acceptable to the cottagers. They are too inquisitive sometimes—too much of "How much does your husband earn? where does he work? Ten shillings per week! why you must be well off!" So annoying have such visits been occasionally, as to have caused more than one housewife, as she watched the pastor's approach from her casement, to lock her door, and go out "a-neighbouring," and her neighbour, in turn, to lock all within, draw close the calico window-curtain, and each assume the stillness of night, until the visitor is assured, or fancies he has cheated himself into the assurance, that the housekeepers are abroad. I ask, does not such visiting produce mischief, tainting the mind, and preparing it for the easy commission of falsehood, wherever interest points the course?

I have seen the poor dissenting ministers, after a fourteen miles' walk, propping up a weak side with a walking-stick or umbrella (lacking a cushioned carriage), visiting the abodes of the poor, and their coming anticipated, their arrival welcomed with repeated greetings. They are welcomed by the poor, because they mingle with, and are of, the poor; they preach for the people; all their labours are to refine and elevate the people, endeavouring to win them to a sense of duty by acts of loving-kindness, charity, and mercy. For such labours the people are ever ready to tender their whole, as their appreciation of services so valuable. They remember and reverence them as the first " home missionaries," who sought up the alleys, into the hovels, into every place where despised humanity was huddled up in ignorance, and having found it, they dragged it forth, and bathed it in the light of Heaven. They established the Sunday Schools, where reading, writing, and arithmetic have been taught, and which have proved far more Christianising than all the lectures ever delivered upon Catechisms and the authority of State Churches. They appeal to the sympathies of their flocks for support to their churches; they have no faith in compulsory rates, High Court citations, and dungeon payments for God's revelations.

I claim no especial favour for professions, and have no kinship with the bigots who arrogate to themselves all purity for any particular church; nor do I condemn the sincerity of those who differ from me. It is my boast to be a Christian—love to God and to man are the articles of my creed. I believe, that wherever "two or three are gathered together in God's name," no matter about the form of the temple, or the materials thereof; whether it be brick, stone, or an altar of turf—whether under a groined, ribbed, and open-timbered roof—a plaster ceiling, or the azure vault of Heaven;—I have a lively faith that God will be there to bless them; and there He may be "worshipped in spirit and in truth."

Then, as it is desirable that the people should be honest—untainted by hypocrisy—true to God, and true to themselves—again I say, EDUCATE THEM! encourage the poor to THINK. Tell them of a verity, that God made of one flesh all the dwellers upon earth—open their hearts and minds, and assuredly you will have their love and esteem. Why "kick against the pricks?" Why should man rebel? God is indeed true; we now live in the transition from heart-hardening ignorance, to soul-blessing enlightenment.

How long do you expect the people to read the "contrasts," that so often figure in the public prints, and fancy they will believe that the poor alone must have the penny loaf doled out to them by the churchwardens from the church steps, on the morning of St. Thomas's day, and stand shivering in the biting breeze, until the "fat churchwarden" shall have arrived to serve out " the dole;" and the Right Reverend giver of the penny loaf, "faring sumptuously every day," and laying up to himself "treasures upon earth," to the amount of hundreds of thousands of pounds in cash, besides land and other valuables? If the poor are indeed poverty-stricken, the God of Creation, who "made nothing in vain," has endowed them with reason, and sooner or later they will exercise it.

I know I shall be censured for this blunt truth-speaking. Be it so; there is some advantage in being used to it. All people profess to love the truth, but they sometimes give queer rewards to the man who dares to speak out the whole truth. If the wound require the probe, before a healthy course can be prescribed, let us at once bear the smart, and speak the truth, and "shame the devil."

It requires but little acquaintance with the world, to learn that in our villages generally, the poor man dares not speak out, unless his words be of the honied class; the fear of discharges, and want, are the lessons ever teaching the working man sullenness and deceit; for if the truth be unpalateable, it will find little favour from the simple fact of its being the truth. In the rural districts there is always to be found one, at least, of those scandal-mongers who are ever sniffing in the gale of envy, and ready to launch their envenomed shafts at the poor man who dares to speak fearlessly. Hence

I have had the lash of their scandal-thongs across my broad shoulders. In my village obscurity I have been denounced as a Jacobin, because I have been heard to pronounce the names of Lord John Russell, Thomas Duncombe, or some score of similar Radicals; have been branded an infidel, because I choose to worship God in a temple of my own selecting; taunted, too, with epithets not fit for tender ears, by those " wha are sae guid theirsels."

How far a portrait of " our village" Puffin will be interesting, my readers must decide; doubtless there is one to be found in every town or village. It is said that every man is " the phase of a class;" if so, strange things may be interesting. Here is a " full length" of our busy-body. A biped, with a huge stomach and little brains, one who believes himself to be of vast importance, fancies he has done mankind some service, and wonders they do not know it. At every step, he gives his body a pompous, but ingenious twist; had he lived a century sooner, it is probable we should have had the advantage of the Archimedean screw, for such an eccentric spiral movement could not have been observed without giving an useful hint. He is ignorant enough to imagine that those who hear his tales, believe any more of them than is necessary for their purpose. Our mountain of gross flesh grows four inches at a tangent, when you question his epithets; do but dispute his right to call you an infidel, and he swells enormously, resembling an air balloon, his short thick legs and splayed feet answering for the car. He plumes himself upon his wealth. Wealth alone can make a man, according to his views; hence his hand flies instinctively to the canvas bag in his right-hand breeches pocket, and, with the assurance of a nabob, he will wager you five sovereigns that he knows the meaning of that word, infidel, which plays upon his lips. Yes; he can tell you the identical dictionary he saw it in before Tom Paine was forced to run away! If you are rich enough to accept his wager, or learned enough to argue upon his assertion, the scene soon becomes laughable: speedily the two balls in the creature's head start forward, until they are as prominent as the delph-ware knob on the lid of my tea-pot; his fleshy lips open, and, with a whizz like the noise of steam rushing from the valve, his gas evaporates, and amidst the fizzing you hear him bellowing, "Yes, Sir, I *do* know what an infidel means: it means a man, Sir, that believes the Bible, but not the Testament." Ay, and our village Daniel is not the less learned upon other points, political and moral. He can make you mischief by the hour; and, what is of greater consequence, he can be believed, when it serves the purpose of those who listen to him.

To keep this excrescence moist, it is now and then whetted with a patronizing nod, or "Good morning," and occasionally rewarded with a place in the village offices, by the village law-givers; and upon the report of this ready-to-say-anything sort of gentleman, the "dangerous character" is too often sentenced. It may be advanced that this is a morbid sketch, and if not so, that no sensible person would believe such a tale-bearer. The picture is a true one, and I have nothing to do with the perception or sensibility of those who believe him; if they do not believe him, they act as if they did, and to the poor wight who is arraigned by him the consequences are equal.

How can we expect a healthy tone of morality to dwell around the artisan and labour classes, if we subject them to such degradations? Often has my heart bled to hear the poor wretch, whose wife and children were pining in rags, forced to utter, with a tongue of oil, words which his conscience abhorred, merely to keep the "half loaf," which presumptuous tyranny threw to him, as a sufficient reward for his labour. Thus forced to play the hypocrite, to "keep soul and body together," what need, then, of wonderment that the labourers are always hoping for some change—they care not what—to force the heartless ones to a reckoning—believing that any change must bring advantage to those thus sunk in the scale of humanity? It may be—it is—morally wrong, but who is to blame for it?

Ignorance is a fearful thing; and if ye still war against God's will, and attempt to chain down this unlettered and squalid poverty—this thousand a day increase in our numbers—the retribution will be fearful. Cannot you perceive it is in vain? Will not the very increase work its own redemption, by becoming too bulky for you to wield with success?

The safety valve is education, and the consequences will fall upon the heads of those who try to stem its current. Can there be no helps, save by the profession of Act of Parliament creeds—by the tossing-up of caps for one-sided laws—by the exhibiting of well-starved specimens of the genus *homo* at agricultural meetings? Ask conscience this question: Will the God who watches the fall of a sparrow to the ground, allow his vengeance long to slumber, if his poverty children are to be thus mocked? It must not continue. Look into the world's history book, and read the progression: it was written in heaven at the world's birth, and has been too long despised by the tyrant and bigot! Learn that there is no standing still, and that as generation succeeds to generation, the blessings of wisdom and truth shall prevail.

Who, that looks abroad into the world, and will look with other than the sickly lights of prejudice, can fail to observe, that on every side the struggle is for enlightenment? The poor do feel that their Creator has given them aids to make even labour light; and yet they are forbidden the exercise of them, for very fear that well-taught men will not do the drudgery of labour; as if the command to labour, given to us in the world's morning, was intended only to apply to those sunk in mental degradation. We know that labour is our wealth, hence we welcome it. We would not be idlers, even if we were better paid for trifling with time than we are for working. No, we had rather

"Rub, than rust."

But this we have also learned: that although destined to earn our bread by the sweat of our brow, we were "created in God's image," and endowed with reason; and we cannot longer be persuaded to insult our Father by letting his best gift lie uncultured.

Hence, then, our resolve—as the schools, so called, have shut us out, because our poverty could not furnish a *golden key* to unlock their brazen gates, lest, if admitted there, we should assert our right to the learned professions, and claim a share of learning's fees.

Seeing that our poverty has been an insuperable bar to admission into any school, save the so-called charity schools, and a mere apology for learning doled out to us—just allowed to learn enough to "get the catechism," some to write their own names, few to learn the simple elements of accounts—then, with such acquirements, early in life, started to the factory or dung-yard, to earn a few pence to assist in procuring a family bread loaf. With aspirations as strong as those who claim for themselves a superiority of class, we have at length learned that we must trust to ourselves for moral elevation.

We have therefore determined that the great labour class shall put their shoulders to the wheel of improvement, calling no longer to those "in authority over us" to help them out of the mud of debasement. That the masses are moving in this direction, every day's travelling gives fresh confirmation. It is a glorious thing to know, that the fairest page of the nineteenth century's history will be the one where the whole community of mankind hailed each other as the children of one common Father.

We reverence the memories of those philanthropists who, in the dark morning of our history, laboured to establish Sunday Schools, and, on our one day of rest from labour, let in a ray of civilization upon the degraded children of toil. Feeling, now, the advantages of their self-devotion, we can appreciate their desire to make men of us, and so feeling, we in gratitude honour them.

Those Sunday School teachers were the pioneers, cutting down the cumbrous forests of degradation—

paring down the baleful weeds of ignorance, and preparing the soil of humanity for the seeds of intellectuality that were to be cast into it by a Birkbeck and a Brougham, who, in their turn, threw abroad the winged seeds of enlightenment over the wild waste. A new era was opening to us: the prejudice mists, amongst which we had been groping for ages, were gathering; and as the blessed morning broke, the rusty bolts of ignorance fell down with a powerless clank—a ray, that pierced the hearts of millions, burst from the golden sun-gates of education—and the people's schools, the mechanics' institutes, reared their fair proportions in the clear cerulean! Within those normal schools, hundreds were fitting themselves to carry the glorious mission of self-culture into the towns and villages that lay remote from the parent institutions, glancing their soul-healing beams of intelligence into every nook and cranny of our island.

Food for these growing minds simultaneously sprang up in the "Penny Entertaining Library," "Penny Magazine," "Chambers' Journal," "Penny Cyclopædia," "Knight's Store of Knowledge," the cheap reprints of the poets, "Chambers' Tracts," &c. If the villagers were too poor to purchase these books, new modes were adopted to satisfy their mental cravings, and the Book Clubs and Artisans' Libraries reared their heads in those obscure nookings, where, hitherto, the smithy, the village green, the "road ends," and the ale bench, had been the rural seats of learning; and that mighty engine, the press, aided by the steam of science, superseded the ancient traditions of those village news-rooms.

Knowledge, ever powerful, once implanted must go on. Higher schools were needed, and in 1842, the Rev. R. S. Bayley opened the first People's College, at Sheffield; to the best of my knowledge, the first that opened the whole range of science to the working man, and in January, 1846, more than one thousand pupils had passed through it. There is a peculiarity in the town of Sheffield above all others that I have noticed: in that town, all classes of labourers dare to speak out the truth that is within them, ay, and labour while they think. Has the diffusion of mind, combined with the examples of a Montgomery and Elliott, had anything to do in producing this high and manly tone in the masses of that town? In Sheffield, the People's College opened the sciences in all their soul-refining fulness to the people of that district; and preparations are making to engraft branches from this "tree of knowledge" into the large towns of the empire—a second College being established at Nottingham, in April, 1846.

Gatherings of the master-minds of the age now throng the "Athenæums," and the press re-echoes their thoughts to the remotest corners of the country, giving new life to the village libraries, and inspiring new hope on the cottage hearth-stone. This congregation of mind, too, pleads for the millions, calling for their advancement and recreation; and the people's parks are planting—the "pleasure grounds" where science joins hands with recreation—where the factory child and the hard-wrought artisan together traverse their flowery mazes, and taste a breath of the air of heaven. Honour to the memory of Strutt, who gave the Arboretum to the people of Derby, and established a precedent, the advantages of which can as yet be but faintly guessed at, which is pregnant with good for forthcoming generations.

There is another of the people's schools, the Odd Fellows' societies, destined, with moderate management, to work a great moral change amongst the poor, illiterate, self-neglected sons of men. This school is too mean to be noticed by many who can see nothing good in the things they choose to condemn before they inquire into them; and there yet remain a great many of that class—the men with innate perspicacity—who can at once approve or condemn, without giving themselves the trouble that some people are forced to take, to understand a thing. Assuredly I do not intend to champion all that passes under the name of Odd Fellows' societies; but there is at least two of them—the Nottingham Imperial Order and the Manchester Unity—whose principles are based upon truth and enlightenment. Great objections are made by many persons to the name. They do not like the words "Odd Fellows," forgetting we have every day to deal with titles equally strange. The objects of these societies are, to refine and to elevate the working classes; and, if the name be quaint, "that which we call a rose, by any other name would smell as sweet;" and we should not be over fastidious about names, if good can be done under them. These societies are capable of doing good—they have done good, and have yet much more to accomplish. If their regulations are not perfect, much of the defect must be laid to the ignorance of the working classes, who were left to perfect these institutions by experience, often dearly bought. Their advantages, and failings, I shall note hereafter. These institutions have saved thousands from the miseries of the workhouse; they have sown, broad-cast, over the country, the seeds of thought, which will bring forth a golden harvest of mind. Many a piece of rough humanity has entered these schools—some from sheer curiosity—others from a desire to have a savings' bank to fly to in sickness and adversity. The blunt, horny-handed day labourer has there thrown out his unvarnished thoughts, which have been canvassed, approved, or amended by his frankly-spoken and frank-hearted peers; and as the waves of the vexed ocean toss to and fro the rough pebble on the sea-beach, until ages of friction make it as smooth and polished as if it had passed through the hands of the lapidary, so have those rough lumps of humanity become polished and thoughtful men, by this washing and clashing of opinion.

My faith in the progress of our class is full and firm, based upon the mercy and goodness of God. We have but to expand our minds to enjoy the fulness of our redemption. If we are true to ourselves—firm and abiding in the truth—never fearing to leave ourselves to its dictates—the God of Progression will help us. That this necessary oneness of purpose will be cemented amongst us, my hope in humanity bids me be of good heart. Let us, then, at once, henceforward and for ever, declare that the poverty stain of ignorance shall no longer sit on our brows, as if it were the felons' brand; let the blessings of enlightenment and truth dwell in us—loving man for God's sake.

The want of self-dependence, without which it is in vain to expect comfort, has been the rock upon which the working classes have foundered—always trusting to Parliamentary aids, to local charities, workhouses—to anything, rather than trust to themselves. We are living in the dawning of a new epoch. Mind and science are now doing the work that, a century ago, was left to hands. Mind has yet more to do; the mental will subdue the physical. If we have suffered acute privations in the old slave state, so galling that we cannot look back upon them without pain, let us prepare ourselves for the mid-day of freedom, that even now glances her rays upon us. We can soften all the inconveniences that arise out of, and are a necessary consequence of, every change, by preparing ourselves for it.

> "The fault is not in the stars,
> But in ourselves, that we are underlings."

Arouse, then, from the slumber of apathy! It is the morning of man-making! No longer blink the fact, that it is our own fault that we are not elevated. We can demand a fair share of the rewards of labour, as soon as we prove ourselves capable of using them. Then welcome labour! and by the honour of man, let us pledge ourselves never again to sell such a glorious privilege for a mess of pottage and iron collars; but work for the right, the true, the good, and never again sacrifice freedom and duty at the shrine of mute conformity.

Brother artisans, up, then, with the banner of education! The reward is sure. God and Love are in the world, and unfelt blessings shall gladden the hearts of posterity. The mysteries of the great Book of Nature, which by our ignorance has hitherto been a sealed volume, will be revealed unto us in all their soul-healing fulness, and there shall we learn to enjoy the innumerable comforts that the Beneficent Creator hath sent to cheer the toiling sons of labour under their "blessed curse," whether engaged in the studio, the factory, or the field.

> "How blest is he whose faculties are quickened
> From the primeval fountain of all life,
> And vibrate in full unison and joy
> With the wide circle of all living things!
> When light of star, or moon, or solar orb,
> The fragant incense of the virgin earth,
> Or song of birds, or ocean's sounding roar,
> Find a responsive echo in his breast.
> Glory answering glory! ascending
> As on terraces of stars, the expanse—
> Peopled with distinct and visible forms—
> For ever widens on his kindling eye
> To farthest verge, wonder linked to wonder!
> While thrills through each pulsation of the soul
> Rapt amazement and intelligent awe!"

CHAPTER II.

EARLY DAYS.

I SHALL not fatigue the reader by tracing the branches of our genealogical tree, for the best of all reasons—we never had one. My birth was as fortunate as most of my fellows; I had a father and mother—poor, but honest. Of my father's parentage I know but little; he was, as he has often told me, a Scotchman, and born of humble parents; his "mither was a howdie;" my mother was the daughter of a poor bricklayer; she was born at Kingston-upon-Hull, in Yorkshire.

That the son of such parents should trouble himself with any other work than such as befits "poor people," will be the opinion of a class—one which we know to be a fading class. If this book should by any chance fall into the hands of such a class, it will, I have no doubt, soon be dismissed with an expression of— "What! a labouring man to think of writing books! Shocking, truly! What next? La!"

As my task is but to dot down the unvarnished facts of a working man's life, if its bluntness should be too inelegant for refined taste, I trust, as common sense has decreed that there is no aristocracy of mind, a poor man may aspire to give written embodiment to his thoughts, for the benefit of those who may choose to read them. And, once for all, allow me to say, that so far from being ashamed of the poverty of my parents, it has always been my boast that " I was not born with a silver spoon in my mouth."

In the town of Kingston-upon-Hull, at about ten o'clock in the morning of the 25th day of December, 1799, my mother is reported to have sent her nurse down the stairs of a "second story," to present her second-born to my father, who, on seeing me, exclaimed, "He'll nae do for the Highlands." I was such a diminutive baby, that he offered to cover me down in a pint pot.

The christening soon arrived, and to keep time with "the season," my "godfathers and godmothers" gave me the name of Christopher. My father was by trade a shipwright, and before I was old enough to remember the first incidents of my earliest years, he was called to serve as first carpenter in the "transport service."

My first recollection of external objects, except my dear mother's smile, was on one health-embracing May morning, in my fifth year, about four o'clock, when my mother (who was, until ill-health broke her energies, always an early riser) came thus betime to my bedside, bade me awake, and pointing to the open window, took me in her arms, and placed me upon a chair that stood near to it, directing me to the full clear song of a cuckoo that was there saluting the opening day—my mother singing to me the nursery rhyme—

> "The cuckoo is a merry bird, she sings as she flies,
> She brings us glad tidings, and tells us no lies.
>   The cuckoo sings in April,
>   The cuckoo sings in May,
>   The cuckoo sings in June,
>   And then she flies away."

This, too, was the first song I could repeat, got by rote from my mother's teaching; and a delicious lesson it was, and is. It has been the delight of many a later year. The joy of that morning was stereotyped upon my memory, and I read it anew each year, when the speckled herald proclaims her springtide mission. I become a boy again, and look back with fondness to that May morning, and hear again my mother's chaunt. I may here add, that although born in a flourishing commercial town, my first home was far enough away from the noise and bustle that necessarily belong to such towns, and might be called, as indeed it was, "out in the country," it being the parish of Sculcoates.

The parish of Sculcoates is entirely independent of the town of Kingston-upon-Hull, though forming an important portion of it; indeed it is joined to Hull in such a manner, and is of such considerable extent, that its limits cannot be distinguished by the visitor. It is therefore now named with the town, although not comprehended in its municipal jurisdiction.

"Sculcoates can boast of a higher antiquity than Hull, being mentioned in Doomsday Book as one of the lordships of Ralph de Mortimer, who was one of the fortunate adventurers that accompanied the Conqueror from Normandy, and was lord of several manors in this district. About the year 1174, Benedictus, or Bennet de Sculcoates,* appears to have been in possession of the manor. In the year 1378 it was in the possession of Michael de la Pole, the first Earl of Suffolk of that family, who then granted it to the Carthusian Priory of St. Michael, which he had founded there. After the dissolution of this monastery, the manor of Sculcoates appears to have continued annexed to the Crown till the fourth year of Philip and Mary, when it was sold to Sir Henry Gate, Knight, and Thomas Dalton, Alderman of Hull; after which it passed through various hands, and was divided and subdivided by successive sales and portions."

In my boy-days, the parish of Sculcoates was partially dotted with cottages, and a few warehouses were sprinkled along the river's banks. The river Hull, which traversed the parish in a bold sweep, emptied itself into the great estuary, the Humber, about a mile from my first home.

In the autumn of 1845, after a twenty years' absence from my native town, an irrepressible desire to visit my birth-place took me to Hull. My relations were all joy at my visit, and with swelling voices welcomed my arrival, and told me "I should scarcely know the old house again—no! nor the street,—there were such wonderful improvements!" With a heart leaping as if to burst from its fleshy confines, I hastened to the spot. They were right—indeed I did not know it.—Improvements! There were changes manifold. Years of absence—the quiet green-field enjoyments of a

* He was one of the principal benefactors to the Abbey of Meaux, near Hull; and it is probable that he acquired his name of Benedictus from his pious charity in favour of that religious house.—FROST.

country life—the glowing recollection of boy-day frolics—had been constantly tinting and re-touching their happy pictures of morn-tide bliss upon my mind, until I had at length imagined that the spot where I was born was an earthly Eden. Although a progression-man, with "Onward" for my motto, I had never dreamed of steam-engine pictures upon that spot, and hence I sought in vain for the improvements. The gloomy day, too, was against me; the sky was of a leaden grey, from the chimney tops, where the first ray of light was to be seen, to the zenith; and a drizzling rain, mingling with the volumes of smut from the crowded chimney stacks, fell densely about me—and where, thought I, are these improvements? Where is now the old hawthorn hedge-row, where the cuckoo perched and hopped from twig to twig, and awakened the spring mornings with her song?—where the green meadows in which I gathered the king-cups, and held them under my playmates' chins, to see if they "liked butter?" There, in life's morning, I wreathed regal collars with the flower-stems of the dandelion, or blew away their downy seeds to tell how many hours I had been absent from my mother. All were gone. Rugged Utility, with pick-axe and brand, had uprooted and exterminated them!

Piles of red bricks had taken the place of the green fields, and columns of smoke, vomited from stacks of chimneys, mingling with the murky sky, filled the clear blue overhead. And is this the cottage, methought, once famed for its tidyness and comfort? There was no welcome for me—no, it looked black at me! The windows were smutted over with a map-like tracery, curiously pencilled by the falling rain—a pane or two were variegated with a material less transparent than glass—one, with a tawney-coloured cap-paper glued in with yeast, the other with the grimey cover of a torn-to-pieces old book. A sickly horse-shoe-leaved geranium, that had struggled upward from out of an old tea-pot without a spout, was clinging to a ladder-like trellise—through the bars of which it was interwoven to support itself during the last stages of consumption; *it* sympathised with me, for, with a convulsive sigh, it exclaimed "Alas, stranger!—no green thing must hope for comfort here!" I was turning away from the place, when a plaint chirp bid me look up again. It was the prison-cry of a poor linnet, in a wired box about eight inches by four, which hung from a rusty nail in the window lining. The *bird*, too, was kind: " Aye," said he, " there are strange changes since you hunted after the nests of my progenitors that brooded in the green hedges that stood over here! You remember how wantonly you destroyed their moss-wrought homes, and took away their speckled eggs—yet despite of your persecution, how they sung on to make you happy! I hope you are wiser now—and now that you have heard and appreciated the fine music of our choral-race, singing through the wild woods, gladdening the luxurious hedge-rows and shady lanes of our sylvan country—that you will teach your sons and daughters to admire our architectural skill, to listen to our warbling, and not to drive us houseless from bush to bush, with as little mercy as the heartless ones across the channel are said to drive your race shelterless from their mud-and-stud hovels in green Ireland." I pondered the rebuke of the poor linnet, and promised to do all in my power to respect the liberty and comfort of those gleesome things of God's creating.

I turned slowly away, inwardly debating upon the stern necessity that had converted the garden of my boy-days into a hugh pile of brick, wherein half-starved artisans were huddled in ignorance, scarcely aware of the beauties that adorn God's world.

Pardon the digression, kind reader; the impression of my visit was too strongly made to allow of its being smothered for chronological order—besides, I cannot promise such an arrangement—for, according to the phrenologists, my bump of "29" is not so finely developed—therefore, I must be excused for rambling.

At this period (1805), all Europe was mad with the war fever. My father's return was therefore uncertain, for fresh troops had each year to be sent off, to glut the insatiable maw of the "glory demon." The ship in which my father served—"the Osbourn," so called in compliment to one of the "merchant-princes" of Hull—was re-appointed to convey more men to the seat of war; and her "touching at home" to provision, presented a favourable opportunity for my mother to join my father on ship-board. As soon as the vessel "made the Downs," my mother prepared for her departure, and the boy, Christopher, was to be transfered to the care of his grannies. As a visit to my grandmothers was always looked upon as a treat, it was no hardship to be given over to their keeping.

The morning for my mother's departure had now arrived—a fine sunshiny morning in early June. About seven o'clock, we left my grandfather's cottage—my mother, her boy, and my two grannies. We had scarcely proceeded one hundred yards, before I tore myself from them, and flew back terrified—the long-drawn shadow of the tall chimney of a linseed-oil mill was sun-painted on the ground; and the dancing smoke was capering fantastically across our path, and I could not be persuaded to step over this high *sprite*; and I cried and sobbed deeply at each coaxing to get me over it. My grandfather at length took me up in his arms, and carried me a considerable distance forward, and—to me, at least—all was pleasure again. But this incident was of deep interest to my mother; by her it was regarded as an omen of ill; and at such a time, too, what did it portend? Either that she would, on her arrival, hear of my father's death, or that she should never return, or, if she did, that I should be no more. At such a juncture, it lay heavy upon her heart.

After walking a mile, we reached the jetty; all was holiday to me, until the moment arrived when my mother was desired to seat herself in the "jolly boat," that was now to convey her on board of the cutter, then under weigh for the Downs. I cried bitterly—my grannies, mother, all wept; even the hardy coasters and boatmen, familiarized to such scenes, thought "the young piccaninney made an extra go to," and dashed a tear from their rough cheeks, as my mother, amidst tears and kisses, commended me to heaven, and hurried away into the boat. The boat put off, and was bearing away—perhaps for ever—my mother! Amidst hope and fear we stood; we saw the white sails of the vessel unfurled and flaunt the sea breeze—saw her, like a mighty sea bird, skim over the wild flood, and fade dim, and more dimly, until lost in the drizzling haze—mingled with the blue heaven and the broad waters in the far distance! Oh yes! I recollect *that* morning, it was graven upon my memory!

Often, as my silver-haired old grandfather dandled me upon his knee, and hugged me to his breast, and ran over the recital of that morning's adventure, the warm-hearted old man would dash away the big tears from his dim eyes, and promise to be a father to me, should the deadly shot or the angry waves deprive me of my parents.

My grandfather was by trade a bricklayer, and considered a good workman in his day; his intellectual acquirements were of the average character that distinguished the mass of artisans of the eighteenth century. King-worship and war were his favourite topics—the absorbing one, battles! On his return from labour, he used to tell over to me the glories of war, and the amount killed, with a gusto equal to the mad boast of bacchanals, who swagger how the table was flooded with champagne at the midnight hour. He would sing of the doings of Marlborough, Collingwood, and Nelson, and paint the day when England would hold empires in the leash, as a hunter does his hounds, ready to slip them for new conquest, wherever the game could be started. Hence the doings of war was the burden of the old man's song.

We smile derisively at the Yankees' boast "to whop the British," and forget, that a century ago, we ourselves were teaching the breadless thousands that were seeking food across the Atlantic, "that we could whop all the world."

My old grandfather had, nevertheless, a high appreciation of talents, of a superior order to fighting, and dwelt with admiration on the wonderful discoveries of Columbus and Captain Cook, and would tell me with a degree of marvellous wonderment, how "Captain Cook's cabin boy had learnt the whole art of navigation, and how astonishingly he told the circumnavigator the precise day they were sailing under London Bridge in another hemisphere, with the ships' bottom towards this side of the earth," and would hold out bright hopes for me, one day, to emulate those worthies; and, as he coaxingly danced me from his knee to his chin, used to sing over, with a deep bass chaunt, his favourite couplet,—

> "Labour for learning before you grow old,
> For learning is better than houses or gold."

My next elevation was to the day school of an old crone that "took children to learn their letters, and be out of the way." This ancient had the reputation of "keeping a good school," which goodness consisted mainly in having a large number of pupils—so large, that the "letter learning" was all she could afford time for, except drilling into the young mind a goodly array of ghost stories. Amongst them, she had a few good-natured ones,—fairies who changed the cream to butter, during the night, without churning, and likewise planted roses upon the southernwood; but her staple consisted of mischievous sprites; the foremost and fiercest was a "barguest." Whether that imp belonged particularly to Hull and the vicinity, I am not *devil*-read enough to affirm; I have not heard much about his highness in other countries; in my native town, he was (according to my dame), each night, roaring about the streets—he was a very monster, with a body like an ox, large horns, fiery eyes as large as saucers, his nostrils snorting forth brimstone—he had a long tail terminating with a fork, which he darted and lashed about tremendously—he was always in motion, the pace a brisk one, between a jog and a run—he amused himself with dragging and rattling a large chain; thus equipped, he was threading the streets and bye-lanes, seeking whom he could devour. She had also a plentiful assortment of wood-demons and river-sprites, each with their peculiar frighten-you-to-death conformation!

This mode of "shooting young ideas" is out of fashion. Our infant schools, gymnasiums, and Wilhelm have come to the rescue. The old fashion has not been to me the most comfortable; for, many a time, when a grown boy, I have cast a careful glance, or a fearful squint down a dark alley or round a corner, to see if my dame's talisman had conjured up a sprite to kidnap me. Often, in the lone woods, the sudden start of a scared bird, the rustle of the leaves, or the melancholy sigh of the autumn winds as they have stole down the russet glade, have filled me with trepidation, and my spectacled old mistress and her monster train were all present in my fear-stricken imagination.

I was never lucky enough to receive a visit from her generous goblins; being a lover of flowers, I have planted shrubs of lad's-love, but hitherto, they have not bloomed roses.

The play-grounds, the picture cards, and singing, are better companions for the tender things, than barguests and fairies.

Another step forward! Having got my fill of A, B, C, and goblin lore, the Free School of the parish of Sculcoates was opened to me, where I made tolerable progress, and after six-and-forty years of world-battling, I now humbly tender my grateful acknowledgments to my old master, Brocklesbank, for his attention to me, and also crave pardon for the many tricks I assisted in playing off upon him. Some portion of my offences were absolved at the time, through the infliction of sundry thwacks with a cane across my shoulders, and by divers elevations to the school window seat, where I stood during school hours, decorated with a tall sugar-loaf-shaped cap, made of white paper, with an inscription now of "DUNCE," sometimes of "DISORDERLY."

The clergyman of the parish, the Rev. —. P———, remarkable for his eccentricity, used to attend the school occasionally to inquire what progress the pupils had made; sometimes to examine them himself. On one of those occasions we were requested to attend the Rev. Gentleman. The first class were all ordered to stand up, and the clergyman put the question,— "Can any boy in the class spell *transubstantiation*?" An awful pause followed the question, each boy looking askant at his fellow, then on the ground, anon casting a shy look at the clergyman—the silence continued, and returned the significant answer "No!" The second class was next called up—the same question put, and there too all were silent. The master rose up, his face crimsoned with rage; pointing directly to me, he exclaimed, "Cannot you, Sir, spell that word?" And the answer was, "Yes, Sir!" The Rev. Gentleman then said, "If you can spell the word the first time, without blundering or turning back, I will reward you with this golden watch-key," holding up the key that was suspended to his watch. I began "Tran-sub-stan-ti-a-tion," and with a "Good boy," I received the promised reward, and was sent up to the first class. The watch key was always looked upon by me with pride, and, during thirteen years, frequently exhibited as a trophy; it was lost during a voyage to Greenland.

Although my old master, Mr. B——, was very anxious that the boys under his care should become scholars, and by their talents procure for him a good reputation as a teacher, he was one of the old school instructors—he had no faith in the finding of

"Books in running brooks:"

he thought the books printed with good black ink, the only ones to study from; hence he took especial care that his pupils should have plenty "to get at night," and we were always sure of having from ten to twenty words of spelling black-margined, "to say in the morning." He was always at his post, and his industry was rewarded by witnessing several of my school-mates filling good situations in the town, gained by the superiority of their penmanship, and other school acquirements.

One pleasing recollection of my school-days was occasioned by a simple occurrence. It was the custom of the school-boys of Hull, on the holidays, then made frequent by the news of victories, the death of heroes, and the varied "pomp and circumstance" so often the theme of the "Gazettes Extraordinary," for the boys who first got the holiday, to go in a body to the nearest school—or, should the nearest prove one where past experience rendered success doubtful, then they sallied off to a more favourable one: here they commenced " shouting them out," which ceremony consisted in all the boys hurrahing and clamouring as loudly as their flexible lungs and counter-pipes would allow; frequently throwing at the windows vegetable and other refuse, gathered up during the march. If the door was unlocked, a few of the most brazen-faced ventured within, annoying the boys and insulting the master. Perhaps during the in-door sally, two or three of the more mischievous and daring would throw stones through the windows of the school; thus attracting the master's attention to the expensive point of the boy-battle. While thus engaged, the sortie within would coax, or carry off by force, some of the assailed school-boys, who, like sheep breaking through the gap in a fence, if the first get fairly through, the rest of the flock scamper after him as quickly as possible; so one or two of the boys enticed, or carried off by the assailants, furnished a starting point for the others to follow. To aid the breaching party, an incessant fire of refuse and missiles was generally kept up at the windows—for broken windows were most dreaded by the masters—shivered squares must be mended and paid for. When the boys, either by leave or stratagem, got the holiday, the majority usually joined the first band, and sallied off to the next vulnerable point, until at length "all were out." The campaign finished with a congratulatory cheer; and each departed to tell their parents that "master had given them a holiday!"

On one of these shouting-out occasions, "our school" was attacked. The master held out until the bumping of roots and decayed cabbage leaves at the windows, intimated that harder materials might be used; and the question of holiday, or resistance, became a serious one with "Cockey B——." At this juncture up came the Rev. Examiner; respect for the parish clergyman caused a cessation of hostilities; nevertheless, he could not persuade the belligerents to retreat, so they bivouacked upon the causeways and stone-paving around the school. During the truce, our eccentric parson proposed to the master, that he should give the boys a holiday; but, to discountenance the shouting system, we should be advised to go direct home, and being in the forenoon, that we should return again at one o'clock, when he and the master would accompany us into the fields, where he would provide each boy with a bun. Derrycoates, about two miles from Hull, then a spacious tract of meadow and marsh-land—now covered with villas, and traversed by the Hull and Selby Railroad—was the chosen spot. The novelty of the plan was sufficient to raise our spirits, and induce the hope that master would consent. He acquiesced—with a rush to our caps, and a loud hurrah, we were quickly in the streets, despite the minister's cry of "Order, boys!"

At the appointed hour we all assembled, decked out in our holiday clothes, and at the word of command marched two-and-two for the Derrycoates. The selected place commanded a view of the river Humber, bounded on the right hand of us with the rich undulated fields of Lincolnshire, dotted with ferry-houses, and intermingled with deep grey masses of foliage; before us the various craft, with their white sails and waving red pennants, were gliding, gunwale-laden with merchandise, over the glossy bosom of the great river!*

The fields were teeming with perfume from the wild flowers—the birds were singing their earth-blessing. Amidst this music and redolence we were ordered to halt, and give ourselves up to the teachings of nature. Wild as the colts over the Arabian fields we bounded —rolled over each other, and buried ourselves chin-deep in the grass; unfettered as the winds, we gave a loose to enjoyment, until the declining sun caused our guardians to signal us together, and prepare again for home. During the afternoon I had captured a nest of young black-caps, which I intended to carry

* The Humber is the receptacle of all the eastern rivers of England, from the Swale to Trent; it is the boundary of the East Riding in Yorkshire, and Lincolnshire, and is at Hull from two to three miles in breadth—formed by the conflux of the Ouse and the Trent, and rolls its mighty waters to the German Ocean at Spurn Point.

home with me, to rear. My master objected to my doing so, descanting upon the cruelty of tearing the young ones from their parents. In this lecture the clergyman took a part, and took occasion to introduce the natural history of that bird; also, the history and uses of the wild flowers, particularly the caraway, which there grew luxuriously, and was gathered by the town's-people, then dried, and the seeds used to give a peculiar aroma to their cakes and buns.

The novelty of this holiday—the varied field blossoms—the present of buns—the lecture on birds and plants—the panoramic picture of river, woods, and cottages—the forest of masts from the harboured fleet in the docks of the port—the heaven-reaching tower of the church of Holy Trinity,* watching like some guardian spirit over the homes of the thousands that send their country's commerce over the highway of waters, stood poised in the pearly-smoke cloud that was dancing over the town—the march home, laden with nature's sweets—the moral effect of such a day's

* The earliest notice of the Holy Trinity Church of Hull, said to be the largest parochial edifice in England, occurs in a MS. in the Warburton collection in the British Museum. In the year 1285, it is stated that the "High Church, dedicated to the Holy Trinitie, was at first founded as a chapel by one James Helward;" the Mother Church, as the author of the MS. states, being Hessle, it continued a chapel of ease to Hessle until 1661. This church is two hundred and seventy-two feet long, from east to west; the breadth of the nave of the church is one hundred and seventy-two feet; the length of the transept, ninety-six feet; and the breadth of the chancel, seventy feet. The transept is of brick, said to be the oldest brick building, not Roman, in England. The revival of the art of brick-making has generally been attributed to Hull:—" In 1321, William de la Pole had, without the north gate of the town, a tilery or brick-yard."

enjoyment, contrasted with the mischievous shouting-out system, were of such an elevating character, that, although school-boy like, I was always glad to hear of enjoying the holidays, I never again took pleasure in the cabbage-leaf and window-smashing attacks of my school-mates, nor could I ever again be induced to sanction them. Indeed, our clerical superintendent was little aware, that this simple incident was to be to me the dawning of after-years of close communion and never-ending enjoyment with her who waits

> "Through all the years of this our life, to lead
> From joy to joy."

I have told you our parish clergyman was an eccentric one. There are many yet living who remember the doings of old parson P——, and his jolly clerk, B——; the meddling world thought their movements rather unprofessional—they were called the vicar and Moses of their day. They had a kind regard for each other, were constant, whether in the exercise of their ghostly duties, or the not less agreeable business of cracking a bottle.

The festivities of Easter are ending—it is Wednesday in Easter week—the vicar and his clerk visit your house; a sort of how-do-you-do tap at your door, and the pastor, with a bland smile, enters your cottage; he is followed by Moses, who, with a full round tenor voice, salutes with "Good day, Madam—just called upon you for the Easter dues." "Oh! Sir," replies the frugal housewife, "between you and the tax-gatherer, my door-stone is always occupied." "Pray, Madam," continues Moses, "don't confound the Church with the tax-gatherer: the parish officers merely pave your streets and protect your windows; we prepare for you the pleasant road to heaven—marry, christen, and bury;—eightpence, if you please, Madam—you see I've crossed it out!" The good woman tenders a shilling, and desires her change; how unfortunate that the "heavenly road" makers had to give change at the last house. The clerk must go to the neighbouring shop, and get some coppers, for it is an invariable rule with them never to leave any house without apportioning to each his proper share—sixpence to the one, the other twopence. It is a safe mode to keep the books right, and to prevent any misunderstanding between themselves.

The day wears apace—their next call is at a snug little inn. "Ah! B——, we are all right here—we are known here—and here we can stop, without having the fear of the petty scandal-mongers before our eyes; we know the landlord, the parlour's snug, the liquor's good—let us take stock, and settle down for the evening." Agreed. Now fatigue gives place to rest, the spirits rise, and they mutually affirm that it is the best thing to be happy when you can. They are all comfortable, B—— begins to sing, and the mirth grows loud; the parson applauds, and being elevated, he begs of Moses to screw up his flute—the "poetry of motion" inspires the priest, the clerk pipes, and the parson dances; and thus they merrily while away the night. The clerk is a married man, and married couples are not always agreed upon the time required for tavern mirth—too often the wife thinks that the husband might have finished the business earlier. Mrs. B—— was of that opinion—experience is a faithful teacher—she at length learned that patience was a virtue which had its bounds—it was with her severely tested, and after repeated trials, her patience broke down. She had just learned the whereabout of her lord, and she flew off to "start him." Yes, home he must come, either by coaxing, entreaty, or force. As usual, she was too soon. She must wait. Oh, patience! She bites her lip, and "nurses her wrath" until it reaches scolding point; and thus prepared, she ventures her opinion, first upon the follies of her husband, and then upon the parson's fitness for a parish beacon. These attacks, so frequent from Mrs. B——, had become intolerable, and the priest declared that some remedy should be forthwith adopted; and with solemn menace thus addressed his brother churchman: "Thy wife is the worst termagant in my parish. I will have a ducking-stool erected on the river's bank, near to the church, and thy wife shall be the first woman ducked therein!"

Whatever might be the foibles of our vicar, he was not over-proud; for if, after the exercise of his duty of marrying a young couple—however humble their lot in life—they invited him to dinner, he seldom refused their invitation. He was charitable, too: sometimes, when asked to partake of more of the dishes than was agreeable, he would answer with "No, thank you; but I will just put a wing of that fowl in my pocket, for Betsy." He had an affection for Betsy not usual between master and servant.

We were always glad of a visit from our clergyman, at the school; for despite his whims, he was really anxious that the boys should learn to write, spell, and read well. In exercising his duties as a superintendent, his efforts were at all times directed to the accomplishment of those desirable objects. Nor on catechism-days did he ever attempt to mystify us with abstruse theological questions; it was enough, in the days of "the good old King," if the boys were taught to be loyal and orthodox; there was but one State Church then. The Methodists were the only *Tractarians* in George's days; and they had not reached No. 90. We, however, had no Tractarian proselytizing in our school—boys of eight years of age were not expected to understand and tell what the Blessed Presence is. Truly, with all our wisdom, instructors expect too much, if they really imagine that boys or girls, at such a tender age, understand any presence, unless indeed it be a material one.

After an absence of three years, my mother again returned. I was sent home, and remember being taken by her to see the parade that ushered in the morning of October 25th, 1809, when George III. had reigned King fifty years. The bustle of the occasion I well remember—the procession, the banners, and military array—the bonfires, sheep-roastings, and drunken men, who, in their loyal excitement, best did honour to that saturnalia by sinking themselves several degrees below humanity. The illumination was to me the most magical, and I owe to the effects made upon me by the transparent paintings, my first desire to dabble with paints and pencils. After some days of incessant teasing, my mother purchased for me a sixpenny box of water colours, and I began to try to paint a ship, from the recollection of one that formed part of a group in a large transparency, exhibited on that occasion. In the morning of the day of parade, we hastened to the church of the Holy Trinity, and with pretty tight squeezing we forced our way in. Nothing of the service remained with me, except the recollection of the intense thrilling that pervaded my whole frame during the performance of the "Hailstone chorus." One lady in the choir particularly astonished me. I have never listened to good music since that time without flying back to the mystic witchery of that performance, and the spirit of her angelic voice hovers around me like a blessed presence.

In the year 1810 my father returned to Hull, being tired of salt water cruizing, biscuit, and junk. I thought him a strange austere being; his manners were at first terrifying to me. From the demoralization of war, and isolation from all society, except those hardened, and trained to legal murder, and to laugh at danger, his bluff form contrasted strangely with the soft smile and the fondling manner of my grandfather. I shrunk from my father's embrace, and on every occasion ran back to my granny's cottage, and felt that there was my rightful home. Use soon reconciled me to my father's seafaring lingo and blunt manners; and I began to look to him for protection, as warmly as I before had done to my foster parent.

During my father's cruize, by frugality, together with the earnings of my mother, gained from washing and sewing for the officers on shipboard, he saved about eighty pounds; this sum he was desirous of employing in such manner as should, if possible, lighten some of the toils of life, and allow him to lay up something for the winter of age. Various suggestions crowded upon him; at length, having gained, somewhat reluctantly, the consent of my mother, they engaged in a public house: the house was known by the sign of the Ship, in a good street, called Trippett, a situation near to the docks, and it was expected to be a favourable speculation. The new occupation soon proved a failure, and the business one which my mother abhorred. I can well remember the drunken revelry of those evenings. The customers were principally sailors and soldiers; and although they could generally agree to get drunk together, they seldom separated without a fight—and fiercely each party contested the fray. In their mad orgies, their conversation was of the most disgusting character. The loyalty and superior advantages of each class, to the nation, were disputed with a rancorous hatred for each other. However naval and military discipline might curb their fierce natures whilst engaged in their lawful blood-flooding, whether deluging countries or making the " green sea red," in their drunken revels they branded each other with taunts and cowardice, until words were followed by blows. Every piece of furniture, fire irons, anything that the room contained, were all called into requisition during the contest; and often the parties were seriously hurt; now " the lobsters"—the soldiers—now " the tarpaulings"—the sailors, prevailing. At last, the piquet, or the constables, were compelled to take them off to the guard-room, the watch-house, or prison.

During our stay at the public house, a poor wretch who had known my father in early life, sought refuge with us, after his desertion a third time from the naval service. Twice had this wreck of a man been "flogged through the fleet" for desertion: a cold chill runs through my frame, as even now I gaze upon his lacerated back, all cicatriced and many coloured. His description of the brutal chastisement was so vivid, that during his recital you might hear the deep oaths and low jokes of the men who tied him up—you could hear the whiz of the *cat*, as these "jolly tars of Old England" swung it over his bowed-down head—see the red blood spout in copious streams from his channeled flesh—look upon the degraded crew, summoned around "to profit by the example," but who were so hardened from the repeated floggings, and every day "startings" of coarse boatswains and pert middies, that they stood unmoved; idly gazing, until the poor wretch, from loss of blood and exhaustion, was ordered to be taken down—perhaps to receive another dozen on the morrow, while his wounds were yet green!

During his stay with us, his favourite amusement was the drawing of ships; in which he used to give me lessons, describing the masts, and the various ropes, and explaining to me their uses; he also prided himself upon a rare colour for the tinting of the ship's sails—it was a sailor-like composition—a solution of tobacco water; this, with Indian ink, gamboge, and vermilion, constituted his palette for ship painting. After secreting him for a few weeks at the Ship, in Trippett, one of our customers betrayed him to the press-gang for the sake of the blood-money;* and one morning, while taking his breakfast, the ruffians forced their way into the room, hand-cuffed him, ironed his legs, and took him to the rendezvous—and we never again heard of the poor deserter.

Our business at the inn was a series of losses, high rents, heavy taxes, unprincipled men getting into debt and never paying their bills, the constant destruction of furniture, occasioned by the drunken fights, and the accumulated losses caused by the frequent marches of the regiments from the town of Hull—all united to bring on bankruptcy and distress, and the inn was given up in despair.

It was the soldiers' boast, after they had ingratiated themselves into your favour sufficiently to procure them credit—that when "the route arrived, they would crack their fingers, tell you to come to the barrack yard on the morning of their march, and they would pay you with the roll of the drum." O'Keefe knew them:—

> "How happy the soldier who lives on his pay,
> And spends half-a-crown out of sixpence a day;—
> He cares not for justices, beadles, or bum,
> But pays all his debts with a roll of the drum."

It was so proverbial of the soldiers of the time of which I speak, particularly the "militia-men," to commit every species of debauchery and vice, that in compliment

---

* Blood money was a sum paid by the press-gang to any person who informed them of, or caused to be given up to them, any person who had deserted from the naval service; or informed them of any one who could be impressed; usually it required that the person informed of should be a sailor; but in the heat of the war they were not very particular on that point—in a "hot press" they took "landsmen" or any one they could kidnap.

to the Warwickshire militia, then stationed at Hull, and who were notorious for their vices, the slang term of the day was, "Go it, Warwick!"

The influence of those debasing times has been too severely felt to make us over anxious for the renewal of "militia-days." Humanity sickens at the bare recollection of them.

The distress occasioned by the failure of the public house threw a gloom over the whole family. Soon as the first effects of despondence had in some measure subsided, and reconcilement to present circumstances softened the pangs of disappointment, my father set about retrieving his former position by renewed industry. A small cottage was taken, and all the members of the family betook themselves to such pursuits as their past abilities or present acquirements admitted them.

In the beginning of my eleventh year, I was put out as an errand boy to a draper, a situation I always disliked; indeed there was so much artificial civility interwoven into our polished draper, that I regarded it as better adapted to men compounded of "clock-work and steam," than to those sturdy flesh-and-blood Saxon bred, as if it required a bad French bow to sell a good French shawl. I was considered too uncouth to succeed in a business requiring so much conventional polish; and want of address was thought to be rather a disadvantage than a service to my master. My playing and loitering, when sent on errands, became so frequent, that in a few months I was discharged as incorrigible.

Necessity would not allow of my remaining long at home idle, and again I was on the look out for a place. One day, while engaged in my favourite pursuit of gathering wild flowers, and bird-nesting, on the skirts of the town, I strolled into a brick-yard, and sidled up to a bench where an operator was busily engaged throwing off bricks. As I watched the process, I thought the art of brick-making so simple, that already I was master of it. Venturing this opinion to the brick-maker, adding that I wanted a place, and was sure I could soon do it, he jocosely said, "I was a sharp lad, and should have a try." The trial, however, proved me a "poor tassel," and amidst the jeers and laughter of the men and boys gathered around, I had to desist, and brook the mortification of being told "I was good for nothing." I still lingered about the ground, until about eight o'clock in the evening, when the men were preparing for home; then the person before accosted told me to go home. I again asked him if he could not give me a place, to help the other boys to carry away the bricks? He answered, he was pleased with my perseverance, and I must come on the morrow to try my hand; and if I promised well, he would employ me. I was all joy at the offer, and was wending my way home as light as the glossy swallows that were darting through the soft twilight around me, when my attention was fixed upon a stout, dark figure, hastening toward me through the red darting glow of the evening; as it approached, I observed it was my father. Although full of spirits at my success, I had some misgivings about his presence so far from home, at that hour. We met; and before I could inform him of my good fortune, he drew a clothes-line from his pocket and beat me severely. In vain I cried for him to desist, and I would explain the cause of my stopping out so late—for that was the reason why I was so unmercifully striped; he had no compassion upon me, until his rage found rest in repeated lashings; my birds' eggs were squandered, my back was smarting, and I was ordered to make all speed for home, or else I should have more. Home was soon reached; my mother scolded in turn, but mercifully allowed me to tell my tale, upon hearing which she condoled with me; on my father's arrival she explained to him why I was so late, and of my promise to have some work on the following day. My father's walk home had softened his temper; he now bade me be a good lad, and go to bed, and in the morning he would call me up to try my fortune. My sleeping hours were few; my whole thoughts were fixed upon my chance of success the next day. Scarcely had the grey of the morning welcomed the June day, before I was up and anxious to be off. Whether my first essay was anything better than that of other boys I do not remember; it was sufficient for me to be accepted. Even now, while writing, I feel the self-importance that animated me, when, after my first whole week's work, I marched into the house, and tendered to my mother half-a-crown, the amount of my wages—adding "there mother, we shall soon have another public house, if I keep at work at the brick-yard." My mother, years after, repeated my expression, and contrasted my rueful face, while describing to her the beating, with my bragging of making them rich by my two-and-sixpence per week!

The close of the summer finished my career at the brick yard, when I had again to seek for employment.

My next business was at a pottery in the vicinity of the brick-ground. My new trade was an easier one, and, what was still more important, I was to have better wages,—four shillings per week! If I had cause to boast of my earnings before, it will not be wondered that I now felt myself a man. I had, however, many a hard struggle here during the winter, particularly in the season of intense frost, being indifferently clad, and severely afflicted with chilblains. Often, when starting to my labour at five o'clock in the dark biting mornings, the big tears rolled down my cheeks, as, at every attempt to step forward, the friction of the flagged pavement made my boils bleed anew, and the cutting pain made me writhe with anguish. Youth is the season for endurance—pains are but feather-light while hope is young. The winter soon passed, and the warm rays of spring-time rendered my business at the pottery more cheering; the absence of frost, and the renewed demand for crockery ware, confined our operations to the pot-wheel. There was more variety, too, in my new occupation; and to our foreman, William ——, I am indebted for much useful information connected with the art of pot-making, as practised in 1811-12. He made it a part of his duty to instruct the younger branches of the establishment in the various chemical combinations and effects produced by glazing and annealing, as well as other processes. We carried on a brisk trade at old Mayfield's pot-house, in the various domestic utensils manufactured in "coarse-ware," from a beetle-trap to a chimney-pot; one extensive department was the making of sugar-moulds, to retain the liquid sugar during crystalization—they of course resembled an inverted sugar-loaf. There was much to delight me at the pottery, and I was desirous of being apprenticed to the trade. The kindness of William, and his repeated lectures on the antiquity and uses of clayware—his pictures of Etruria and the famous Terra Cottas—all threw a charm around my labours, that, under less favourable circumstances would have made the pot-house a mere drudgery. To that man I am in a great measure indebted for the pleasure often experienced, by endeavouring to understand the true value of the various callings I have been engaged in—not only economically, but politically and morally.

I hold to the opinion, that if our youth were instructed in the various uses and civilizing agencies resulting from our manifold trades and manufactures, they would not only become individually better workmen, but would learn to respect their labour, and instead of regarding it as an "hereditary curse," they would reverence it as the highest privilege bestowed by God on man. Lacking this usefulness, the civilian is not a whit the better man than the savage, who whittles his bows, and withes them together for his wigwam, as instinctively as the fox excavates his hole amongst the brakes of the deep-browed forests.

In 1812, when "Johnny Bull" was converting his old spade-ace guineas into cannon balls, my father's business of shipwright was in its prosperity—then was this land of oaks and jolly tars kept at its tension. Ships must be built before they could be manned, and ship-building was consequently a well-paid trade—and as war-glory threw its gold dust into the dull eyes that hereafter were to gaze mournfully upon taxed bread, tea, sugar, and daylight, every one that intended to "make a man of himself" was struggling to get into the well-paid war-flushed trades—then my father decreed that I must renounce the peace-trade of pot-making for that of shipwright; and as the custom is, I had to bow to my father's resolve, and, at the expiration of my twelfth year, I bade farewell to the pot-house.

CHAPTER III.

APPRENTICESHIP.

To be "bound 'prentice" is usually an event of no small importance in juvenile history. It is the April of life—" tears and smiles," hope and fear, alternate. The aspirant will sometimes venture to look back upon his boy-days, and with mock gravity call them foolish—an age of trifles. He now fancies himself of importance in the world—is about to become a great man—lectures his former playmates with assumed dignity—yet is the struggle great within him, as to which class, the boy or the man, he really does belong. Often, when in the hey-day of his air-castle building, some trifling incident suddenly throws him back again to the green-fields and play-grounds, and, for the moment, he sighs to join his old companions at ball, or hoop, or spinning-top; then again he struts, but mimics the man awkwardly; albeit, he may be "much older than his looks," it is all in vain, Nature steps in and asserts her rights, and whether he will or no, he must be boy, and man, by turns.

My native town, in common with others of our country, possessed many useful and benevolent institutions, amongst which, the charity schools may be numbered, and "not least" amongst them, Cogan's Charity School. Under the old freemen's rights, and perquisite times, those institutions were usually most accessible to the "free and independent burgesses," and the "independent" voters took especial care not to lose any opportunity that offered itself of securing those advantages. Immense numbers of them had always the ready coin of a promise to vote for "your man" at the next election, to offer as an equivalent for the favour conferred. It was consequently of the utmost importance that every man should try his best to have his sons "made free"—city or borough voters, if not "born free."

The various modes of conferring the franchise under the "rotten borough system," is yet green in the memory of many persons, and it was, indeed, a severe satire on freedom. I can well remember, during my apprentice days, the coarse mirth that was so plentifully dealt out, whenever an election was near, about the doings of a little borough, some twenty miles over the water, seaward from Hull. It was necessary for an out-resident voter to smoke a chimney in the borough at least once a year; *faggot voters* were there in plenty, renting a room of some old crone at so much per week, lighting a fire with a penny bundle of sticks, "making a reek," and standing in freedom's might a burgess. There the fair maidens, daughters of freemen, could give the franchise to those they chose to honour with their hand: love's flame was lit anew, as the election approached, as suddenly as the weekly smoke; there the torch of *Hymen* lighted the lucky man to the temple of freedom, and the "free and independent elector" had, at once, the right to delegate a "Knight of the Shire" to proceed to London to assist in making laws to govern us all! No wonder that, in that nest of freedom, the wedding market rose when elections were near; report said, that frequently the voter went from the altar to the hustings, in severe contests. Happy spot, where connubial love secured blankets, coal, and rum, from an honoured representative, for the favour of a vote! How enviable the marriage portion, no less than freedom for the pocket of the bridegroom. It is enough to make one wish the earth one pocket borough, and to repeal "Schedule A."

It was a doubtful point, although my father was "free and independent" of the borough of Hull, whether his eldest son was "born free;" so to make safe on that score, I was to be bound to a free master, and in January, 1813, I was articled to Messrs. Barnes, Dykes, and King, ship-builders, in Sculcoates, Hull. My father had the good fortune to get me apprenticed under the Cogan's Charity, which was founded by William Cogan, Esq., Alderman of Hull, in 1753, for clothing and instructing twenty poor girls, who are allowed to remain in the school three years each. Marriage portions of six pounds are also directed to be given to each girl, who, previous to her marriage, has been seven years in respectable servitude. This school is placed under the direction of three trustees, being Aldermen, who have the power to increase the number of scholars according to the increase of the funds. In the year 1822, the number of scholars was augmented from twenty to forty. The annual income appropriated to the support of the school, is upwards of four hundred pounds. The salary of the school mistress is fifty pounds per annum; and the annual stipend paid to the clerk of the charity is twenty pounds.

Mr. Alderman Cogan bequeathed, also, in the year 1787, a sum of money in the public funds, for the purpose of placing out poor boys as apprentices to mariners, handicraftsmen, and artisans; preference to be given to the sons of freemen of Hull. The management of this excellent institution is in twelve trustees, who, in addition to the expenses of binding each apprentice, pay to his master twenty shillings per year for clothing; and, at the expiration of the term, presents the master with two pounds, and the apprentice with four pounds towards his outfit in life.

The advantages conferred upon the poor, who were fortunate enough to partake of such an institution, were manifold. My masters did not take the money as allowed to them, but transferred the present to the apprentice. The youths in their establishment were of the class called "out-door;" our wages were low, but as an equivalent, no premium was required from the parent. My wages for the first three years were three shillings per week, the fourth year four shillings, the fifth, five shillings, six for the sixth year, and seven for the last year. We had some perquisites arising from Christmas boxes, and extra pay when engaged in repairing vessels, called "*old work.*" There was another consideration, and to the boys not a small one: on our annual assembling to receive the "twenty shillings," we each received half-a-pint of spiced ale, and a bun. The twenty shillings, ale, and buns, were dependent upon our good behaviour, and the master usually sent a written character, or attended in person to speak to it. At the expiration of our servitude, we were each rewarded with a Bible, and sometimes another book in addition. We were expected at the end of the seven years to be able to read, as a Sunday school was always open to us, and if we could not read tolerably well, the money was detained.

Most of the boys in this charity had an opportunity of attending an evening school, during the winter, which was conducted by a master paid by a benevolent individual, named Thompson. This gentleman was possessed of a small fortune, and dedicated nearly the whole of it to the educating and religious training of the boys of poor families,—it was called King's Court School, situate in High Street. There, for about four months in the winter, we were instructed in reading, writing, arithmetic, navigation, and other useful branches. Mr. Thompson's religious opinions were those held by the Methodists; and in the several chapels then belonging to that persuasion in Hull, he either took a separate pew for the use of such of his scholars as approved of his religious views, or otherwise he took one large pew, with sufficient accommodation for a few boys, in addition to his own family. The attention paid by this benevolent man to the education and morals of the youth he drew around him was unremitting: nor was it confined to the school alone—he frequently invited them to his own house, to take tea with him, and receive other little civilities. During the week, his visits to the dwellings of their parents were frequent, relieving their wants, praying with them, exhorting them to lead religious lives; so kind was his manner, and so sincere in affections, that he was ever hailed as a comforter; and I, in addition to the hundreds that were instructed by him, have cause to bless the memory of Mr. Thompson.

Under the tuition of a Christian so sincere as Mr. Thompson, it may naturally be expected that numbers of his pupils would lean toward, or adopt his principles of Methodism. From his extreme kindness to me, I became so attached to him as to follow him during the Sundays and week-day nights to the various chapels, and he ranked me amongst his proselytes. When I had been in school about twelve months, he resolved that one of the boys should read a chapter from the New Testament every Sunday evening after the opening prayer. I was the first one selected, and had to choose my chapter; I read, in a somewhat tremulous voice, the first chapter of the gospel according to St. John. The master applauded my execution of the task. On the following Sunday, two or three others were named to read, but each one demurred, and I had again to read the lesson. This circumstance, being new in the school, was sufficient to bring down upon me the ridicule of my fellow apprentices. At that time, a ship-yard was anything but a place for the exercise of morality—so in consequence of my frequent readings, and attendance at the chapels, they altered my nick-name of "Shrimp" (so called from my diminutive figure) to the one of "Parson Christopher."

Under the guidance of Mr. Thompson, and the teachers of the North Street Sunday School, I soon became an accredited Methodist—met in their classes, attended their love feasts, and became a zealous young sectarian. About this time an offer was made to me to go out with some of the missionaries into the East. One of our apprentices, Mr. David Wray, had been recently sent to Demerara, through the same interest. I was in extacies at the thought, for young as I then was, I always entertained an idea, that our first duty in this world was to exercise our talent, however humble, to educate those amongst us, where-ever our lot might be cast, who were less informed than ourselves. "Forward" has ever been my watchword, although the retrospect shows my path to have been a sinuous one. My success in the missionary labour was not so favourable as my fellow's, Mr. Wray. The ship-building business was then a flourishing one, and the price set upon my release from indenture was more than the parties thought fit to pay; whether they considered the demand an exorbitant one or not, I cannot at present remember,—whatever the cause, I was compelled to stick to the ship-yard, spinning oakum, and turning the grindstone.

The extreme views of many of my theological friends puzzled me strangely, particularly those whom I thought the over-zealous—those who, on various occasions, had to fight the devil, not in the spirit, but in proper person, in the very flesh. Such an air of the supernatural was sometimes thrown around these realities, that although I was never over-valiant, I can remember my anxiety, at that time, for a chance of doing battle with some of the fiends, on terra-firma; however, I never had an opportunity! One of my companions, a man of middle age, and zealous, even to fiery expressions, used to amuse and terrify me, by turns, with the recital of his frequent adventures with the "arch enemy," and the troop of tempters that gave battle under him. Methinks I see him now, stalking across the room in Scott's Street, where we held frequent prayer meetings—he would stride across the floor, with his head bent backwards, until his face was almost at a right angle with his body: then falling down heavily on both knees, near a corner cupboard, exclaim at the top of his gruff voice, "Bless this corner, this corner saved me!" It was so usual an entrance with him, that profane wights, out of doors, used to call him "Corner Dickey." So literal was Dickey in his prayers, that he included every thing he expected to be engaged in during the next day. His profession was that of a pig-jobber, and on one occasion, "in an agony of prayer," he did not forget his old sow, but after drawing a deep inspiration, shouted at his usual pitch, "and send, my sow may have a good litter!" And Dickey's earnestness drew forth loud and approving responses of "Aye, aye! yes, yes!" from most of the persons there assembled.

Between one and two years, I was diligent in cultivating an acquaintance with Methodism, usually rising at five o'clock on the Sunday mornings, and continuing until ten at night, scarcely allowing the proper time for refreshment. I now became anxious to read all that came in my way, and like most juveniles, felt a deep interest in the reading of Robinson Crusoe, Philip Quarll, Boyle's Travels, and such other books as our school library contained. My father was likewise very fond of reading; he now proposed to encourage my love of books, by entering me a subscriber to one of the circulating libraries. I had the pleasure of being my father's instructor in reading and writing, and this kind offer to procure me books was a high reward for so doing—previously I had a great difficulty in getting books to read, except the tracts and magazines supplied by the chapel libraries and Sunday school teachers.

On presenting ourselves at a little shop in the Market Place, a popular circulating library, the old spectacle-nosed keeper told us, that his invariable rule was, before *boys* were entrusted with his books, to have some one as a surety for the payment—he accepted my father as such, and registered my name. The old man now asked what book I would like, but being unacquainted with works of fiction, I could not tell him; he handed to us a catalogue, which only made the choice more bewildering. I at length selected one, which from its title I thought would be very mysterious—it was "Splendid Misery." This I took home; it was on a Saturday evening. With the first broad light of morning, I arose and greedily devoured several chapters of the first volume.

My absence from the usual Sunday morning meetings at the chapel was observed, and I was called to account for it; by way of defence, I pleaded my desire for, and indulgence in, reading. This appeared rather to aggravate than serve my cause. It was evidently their opinion, that all books, except such as they deemed religious ones, ought not to be read by young men. I ventured somewhat timidly to hint, that it was possible for a young man to read novels, and other works of fiction, and still keep his mind free from irreligion and vice. One of the bench of class leaders, before whom I was arraigned, spoke a few words in my favour, and said "he thought a good case was made out," and expressed a wish "that I should be acquitted." The senior, with a sternness that reminded me of some of the bigots in those famous councils written in Fox's Book of Martyrs, declared, that "if I did not at once, and unconditionally, renounce all books, except such as they should approve of, I was for ever lost!" At that sentence I paused, and wept; the iron mandate was driven to my soul, and after a long self-struggle, I renounced my connection with all bodies who would prescribe the free range of thought in matters of such vital importance. Although I lingered with them some time after, from the very moment of that unchristian sentence I belonged to myself and God.

My own case forced me to become an observer, and for a period of thirty years I have carefully noted these juvenile conversions to particular sectarian views, and find them one mass of failures. I would speak with all charity of this mode of training; hitherto I have seen no good results follow the persuading of boys and girls—they know the very moment when a regeneration takes place with them. All attempts to awe the young mind, instead of leading, will fail. Mind, whether trammelled by sectarians or politicians, will never sit easy under the chain—it will sit ever watchful, hopefully waiting its time, and will at length enfranchise itself. In my short time, I have witnessed troops of youth, boys and girls, whose ages have ranged between ten and eighteen years, parading our village streets in classes, singing aloud, and proclaiming their sudden conversion—have heard them talk of their juvenile class meetings—talk about controversial theology with all the gravity of age; aye, and I have heard older heads applaud them for it;—but alack! after a year or two, if indeed those youths hold on so long, where are their early professions? Let experience answer. Alack! where?

For three years I continued a regular subscriber to the circulating library, during which time I read various works, including Milton's, Shakspere's, Sterne's, Dr. Johnson's, and many others. It was an usual practice with me to sit up to read after the family had retired for the night. I remember it was on one of those occasions that I read Lewis's "Monk." On rising from my seat to go to bed, I was so impressed with dungeon horror, that I took the candle and stole up stairs, not daring to look either right or left, lest some Lady Angelo should plunge a dagger into me! I passed scatheless, and can yet exclaim with the rustics of Sherwood Forest, that in all my witcheries, "I never saw anything worse than myself."

The first, second, and third years of my apprenticeship passed in the capacity of errand boy and general servant—my only business with edge tools being to turn the grind-stone for the men to sharpen them. When the men were employed in the docks, I was usually dispatched an hour before the time of leaving, to "look out" if any of the press-gang were lurking about to press the men. On one occasion my vigilance was baffled, the press-gang having contrived to secrete themselves near the place of landing: as soon as the carpenters set their feet on shore for going home, one of the party was seized by "the gang"— a regular fight took place, and at length the assailed man jumped into the Humber Dock, hoping to effect his escape by swimming. Immediately two of the human blood-hounds took to the water after him; meanwhile a regular row commenced on shore, between the carpenters and the press-men. The parties continued to struggle in the water, where the strife was apparently to end in death: our man had seized one of the miscreant gangs-men by the throat, and held him with an iron grip; the other gangs-man beating his antagonist over the head with one hand, and furiously striking the water with the other. During this time, several attempts were made by that portion of the gang remaining on shore, to jump into the water, and go to the rescue of their men; this was, however, prevented by the congregated mass on shore. Fiercely was the strife contested in the water, each struggling with hate and death. A large piece of wood was thrown from a vessel lying near to them, and which struck one of the gangsmen over the shoulders, and forced him to release his grasp. The vampyres were now so much exhausted, as to be in immediate fear of drowning, when two hardy sailors from the vessel put off in a boat, and dragged the shipwright into it; he was so far exhausted as to leave it doubtful whether he could recover, and was taken into a neighbouring public house, where medical aid was called in, when after a time animation returned. He was put upon a large board, and carried to his home, escorted by a large body of the populace. While the contest had been raging in the water, those of the gang on shore had been separated and driven to their dens, some of them severely wounded by the people congregated.

For several days the press raged hot, and on every hand could be heard curses deep, poured upon the gang and the tyrannous system. On one occasion, a young sailor was impressed, a few minutes after touching the shore, and after a voyage up the Baltic. He contrived to release himself from them, and sought refuge by flight, the press-men following him. This took place about six o'clock in the evening; at that time a large body of excavators was employed in repairing the basin of one of the Docks. Through this body the sailor passed, presently followed by the gang. The "navies," however, intercepted the progress of the "harpies," and a regular fight took place, during which one of the gang had his head laid open by a blow from a spade, fiercely levelled at him by one of the "navies." This was the signal for a general riot; and being the hour when the workmen were leaving off toil for the day, the gathering soon became numerous, and arming themselves with bludgeons, or any other weapons that offered themselves, the whole body bent their way to the rendezvous, determined to liberate the poor souls that were confined within until they could be drafted on board " the tender," then lying in the Humber, and which was to convey them to the respective war-ships. By this time, the mob was congregated in a dense mass around the building where the kidnapped wretches were huddled together. The violence of the mass soon found vent in a regular volley of boulder stones, fired at the building—one part of them keeping up an incessant fire, while the others were digging up the stones from the streets, and supplying the besiegers with missiles. The windows were first demolished; then the doors forced open, and the prisoned inmates brought to light and liberty. One hardy fellow ascended the flag-staff, and tore down the ensign, which he waved triumphantly as he clung to the top of the staff from which it had been flying. The conflict was raging, and the municipal authorities arrived, and proceeded to read the riot act. The mayor ascended a chair for the purpose, but was suddenly dragged down by the gold chain that hung around his neck; the infuriated mob were still proceeding with the work of destruction, the furniture being thrown from the windows, and smashed into pieces as soon as it reached the ground, by the mass in the street. One of the naval officers now menaced the assembly, and ascended a ruined heap of furniture and bricks, with the intention of reading the act; he drew a brace of pistols from his pocket, and threatened to shoot the first person that should throw a stone at him; scarcely had he delivered the sentence, before a blow from a stone laid him senseless amongst the shattered fragments. The mob continued masters of the ground until a late hour, when the military were brought to the place, and they were dispersed. Several of the depredators were imprisoned for the riot: the man who tore down the flag, escaped from the town—he knew the consequence of remaining to be taken.

I could detail a score of such heart-harrowing scenes; but the soul sickens at the thought of such a blood-stained system. A volume of atrocities, more sanguine than are found in the "Newgate Calendar," might be written on this impressment. Impressment? Yes! in the most Christian country in the world, where Exeter Hall and missionary meetings are held, to subscribe money to send out men and means to teach blacks and red-skins HUMANITY!

The law which sanctions this kidnapping, yet remains unrepealed upon the statute book; and whenever it suits the ambition of war-spirits to light their brand, free-born Englishmen may be stolen from their homes again,—again torn from the embrace of their wives, even while

"On downy beds lying;"

entrapped for "blood-money," by vulture Judases, immediately after landing from a long voyage, as soon as they set their feet on English soil, where Cowper says,

"There are no slaves."

This is a part of our boasted "Constitution." This is the law in happy England, where "every man's house is his castle." O, land of equal rights! where peer and peasant are alike protected; where well-paid preachers tell us that "God has made of one flesh all the dwellers upon earth."

"Is that the law?"

Ponder over it, brother artisans! ask yourselves the question, "If in this land of equality you should be 'impressed,' whether you will be honoured with the *cat*, or a commission in the Admiralty? An epaulet, or a *round dozen*?"

The years of my apprenticeship were rolling along; three of them had passed, and I knew but little more of the practical business of shipwright than on my first going to the trade. It was now evident that I was a dull boy. My slow progress was a source of discontent to my father, who was a first-rate hand, and exceedingly proud of his superiority. From the first I was discontented with the business; young and unthinking as I was, there was no comfort for me with such dare-devil companions. My attention was turned to books, to drawing, to questions of political moment, to the theatres, but above all, to the flowery fields and the green country. Few of my pursuits found a response in the breasts of my every-day associates; their tastes were of the lowest grade; their conversation generally disgusting; their books, the obscene trash raked up from the pest-holes that unfortunately may be found in every town: their amusements being card-playing, tossing with halfpence, and other low modes of gambling, with drinking, smoking, and chewing tobacco. Such blighting company contrasted strangely with the educational character of my former situation. There the young mind was nurtured—here it was withered, and hope blasted. I could not share in their mad roysterings, and hence was their butt, at which they shot plentifully their coarse jokes and taunts, which they generally wound up with a satirical addenda of " parson," " lawyer," " painter," " player," anything; they considered refinement and reading as a degeneracy fit only for " lubbers and gentlemen." Our average number of apprentices was about fifteen; and wallowing daily in such an immoral miasm, they were fearfully ignorant of every thing necessary to build up the moral man, or fit themselves for a world of progression. We had also another class of apprentices, more dangerous, if possible, than the younger ones—these were up-grown men at the time of their being articled to the trade. The impulse given to our business by the lengthened continental war, induced our employers to take persons as apprentices, who had already attained their majority; for advanced age and physical ability were expected to yield good per centage for their extra wages. They were generally well paid, having eighteen and twenty shillings per week; some of them received more wages at the latter part of their service, as apprentices, than they could realise as journeymen. This class of men-apprentices was principally from remote towns and villages, and by our smoothly-spoken fraternity were called "Johnny Raws;" however unsophisticated they might be when they joined us, they soon caught the contagion from our sinks of vice. This was when the peace of 1815 was to allow Bonaparte leisure to cultivate cabbages, and plenty was to load the tables of the cottage homes of England. We had leisure afterwards to reflect upon the "national greatness" purchased by the "heaven-born" William Pitt's war taxes, when "glory" made all men drunk, under the "pious good old king!"

Does the moralist wonder at the sunken condition of our artisans? Let him consider that the fathers of the present generation were trained in such pestilential earth-hells, the round of whose recreative lives was drowned in drunkenness, lewdness, and base animality! Who, then, that thinks for one moment, can refuse to lay a helping hand to the education and moral expansion of the growing thousands that are to mould the new generation. Look to it, "Condition of England" men! Do not slumber now—look to it, every man and every woman who wishes for the happiness and permanence of our country. If home and comfort be worth anything, educate yourselves, and be Englishmen once more. If happiness and domestic joys are but dreams, why then remain in your ignorance, and, slave like, give up your heritage for self-indulgence and serfdom.

Whatever the cause, certain it was I made but little progress in my business, and now can only look back with anything approaching satisfaction, to one year of my servitude, and believe I am indebted to a simple circumstance for that pleasure. I had always experienced great difficulty in procuring paints and other materials for drawing, in consequence of my limited means; my perquisites were few, and the poverty of my parents always demanded them. One day, while indulging in my loiterings at the picture shop windows, I was intently gazing upon a fine landscape view of a Highland loch, in the shop window of one of the artists of the town, Phineas Lowther, Esq.; he had noticed my frequent calls at his window, and on this occasion he advanced leisurely to the door, and thus accosted me: "Young gentleman, it appears you are an admirer of pictures?" At which I drawled out, "Yes, Sir." "Aye," he said, "I have observed you before now, so if you will come with me, I will show you what I have got within." Overjoyed at this invitation, I followed him, and he conducted me to his studio—it was indeed a treat of no ordinary degree. He afterwards accommodated me with colours, and drawings to copy, so I was at last set up with the material; for however valuable the article I went to purchase, my pence were never refused. His motive was one of pure kindness, with a wish to encourage me—profit was not a consideration. To imagine the artist selling me a penny-worth of ultra-marine, and giving me five shillings' worth for the penny, will at once shew his account of profit and loss in my transactions. One evening, while engaged in my so-called purchases, one of my masters entered the artist's studio, on business. I was about to retire, when he asked Mr. Lowther if I had any taste for drawing? He answered in the affirmative; and added, "If I could be given up to his care, he would soon make an artist of me." This opportune meeting was of great service to me. On the following day, my master sent for me to meet him in the "mould-loft"—a large room, where the ship to be built is drawn, or technically "laid down" upon the floor, to a given scale; afterwards the moulds for the various timbers, floors, and beams, are constructed from the lines, to enable the workmen to proceed with precision and expedition. My master then told me, that in consideration of the opinion and character given of me the preceding night, he should take me into the loft, to act in the capacity of servant—to imprint the names upon the various moulds, and for such other jobs as I should be found capable of doing. This was an important step forward, and assuredly the most comfortable part of my servitude. After a year spent in agreeable labour with the pen, pencil, and line in the mould-loft, it was considered time that I was "put to my tools." This turn-a-head was by no means agreeable to me, but there was no alternative; into the yard I must go, and, if possible, learn my business. Although I had now some claim to the respect of the upper-apprentices and journeyman, nothing could induce me to turn my attention seriously to become a good workman, although I had no prospective view of a better trade. Chance was to be my future guide. The stream of time was gliding along, and I closed my apprenticeship wtih very little attainment; practice just elevated me to the niche of mediocrity, and I never reached a higher point in the art and mystery of a shipwright.

CHAPTER IV.

THINGS THAT I REMEMBER.

Although in the last chapter the company was not always of the best, my boosey companions were not the only ones; there were a few, even in such dens, who held it not unprofitable to improve themselves. One of the workmen, in particular, held in abhorrence the vulgarity of the mass. Towards that man I had a constant yearning, and could have hung upon his words for whole days together; nevertheless I had a dread of him. I had been cautioned to avoid such men. Why? Because he was an Unitarian. Yes; amongst my early lessons, there was one to avoid Schismatics, Socinians, and Infidels; and that man was included in the number. I had numberless proofs that he was a Christian, if rectitude of conduct, and pure morality, had anything to do with Christianity; he was benevolent, too—not exactly practising the benevolence of clubbing for drink, or relieving a broken-down, head-aching shipmate, who had been drunk yesterday, and had not a "shot in the locker" to purchase another noggin with, after the spree—but he was benevolent enough to spare a shilling from his wages to help a poor sick family, that was short of a bread loaf; he had a copper to spare to purchase a picture book occasionally, for a boy or girl that had done him some little civility; he was Christian enough to read in, and talk of, the Bible and Testament; and as to his character and conversation, none but those who professed to be better skilled than ordinary people are, in looking into the hearts of men—none but those "unco guid," could find out that he was not so religious as other men. He was a reading man, and, still better, he delighted to impart knowledge. In our leisure hours, before work commenced, at noon or night, whenever opportunity served, I lingered near to him, and swallowed greedily whatever he let fall. But my lesson was, to be careful of these Infidels. One day, after a severe struggle—the same question had many times risen within me before, and as often it had stuck in my throat—it now found utterance—did he believe in Jesus Christ? The answer was, "Yes!" There would have been nothing startling in that answer, had I not been taught to avoid Unitarians! With the mass of my self-sanctified and Sunday-righteous companions, religion was often a very tedious affair. After a year or two, they left me to enjoy my companion—they had told me of the danger from such men, and, of course, they were free from all blame. Aye, old friend Robert ——, we have had many a laugh at my fears; and if I could see you now, and again grasp your warm hand, we would grip each other and laugh again—a regular duetto. My friend Robert was a man, yet he had his whims. He would never give himself the trouble to cut a throat or pick a pocket to gain riches—he thought it more manly to earn a sixpence. He was not often seen reeling to and fro in the streets, or sitting upon a step drunk at midnight; for he liked his own bed better than a berth in the watch-house. As for pulling down the church—the Holy Trinity might stand aloft in her majesty, and smile at the storms of a generation, before Robert would give himself the trouble, either to pull a stone off the pinnacle, or even to cut the print of his *shoe* upon the *leads*, or inscribe thereon his simple "R. T." He pull down the church! Not he, indeed! But I had been told to be careful of Robert. I remember the first correction he gave me; it was when all tongues were turned to one of those fearful changes that was to ruin England—the one that made the late Duke of York shudder in the Lords' House— Catholic Emancipation. Boys, especially boys with just such a modicum of education as might be expected to be given to the boys of poor artisans after a six-and-twenty years' war, would be frequently catching at hard words, without stopping to get at the meaning. I had caught a *sound* instead of a *meaning;* and when I talked of Catholic Anticipation, Robert taught me the difference between *Emancipation* and *Anticipation;* and he also taught me many other useful things—yet Robert was an Unitarian, and I had to be careful of him.

In early life, I have said, my attention was turned to politics. My first impressions were for universality. "Cobbett's Register," and "Wooller's Black Dwarf," were the first works I purchased and studied on political economy. It was my custom every Saturday evening, after my work was over, to go to the Market Place, and from a stall there, to purchase the breathings of those men of mind. How, at the early age of sixteen, my attention was turned to "that side of the question," I know not; doubtless an undiscovered influence, working through those forcible common-sense writers, was directing me in spite of myself. I cannot, however, give such a reason for my political bias, as a neighbour of mine, here in Sherwood Forest, can give for his. When pressed to shew cause why he was a "Tory," he said "he had the best of all reasons for it: his *father* was a Tory before him!" My father was a Tory also; so by my friend's rule I break from the breed. It amuses me, now-a-days, to hear many of our politicians, who cannot tell to what section *they* belong, because the leaders are so slippery. Are not their reasons as good as my neighbour's? To be a Tory because Sir Somebody is, *must* be patriotic.

I have some recollection of the great Radical meetings we used to hold in Salthouse-lane, in Hull—how the world was to be thereby regenerated in a twinkling—and how, at one of those gatherings, an ambitious Thistlewood entered the room in haste, tearing from his pocket a bundle of greasy despatches—how he mounted upon a form that stood near him, his eyes flashing lines of fire, each glance a torch; then laying his pulpy finger upon the butt of a pistol that was just peeping out of his waistcoat pocket, bid us, with a voice roaring like a "sixteen pounder," "BE READY, for at that moment there were ten thousand up in the North," and he had come before to marshal us. He forgot to state to us whether he had himself been north of Stepney* that day, or not—however, we only rose to go home on that occasion. We do not dream of any more risings now; we have found out a bloodless mode of righting ourselves—we intend, in future, to do battle with our tongues and our pens; and by-and-by, we shall have our old swords beat up and put through the rolling-mills, which will prepare the laminas to make pens of.

The elections of Hull were calculated to make me anything but a Tory. There were strange doings at the elections "in the good old days" of our Thorntons, Staniforths, Mitchells, and Grahams. It was a glorious time for the apprentices—especially for those whose masters took a " deep interest" in the success of a particular candidate. Then was sport for the boys—it might be fourteen days of polling, a long previous canvass, and perhaps, afterwards, a scrutiny. Rare times then; not an eight-hours' job, as now ordered by one of the "death to old England" measures,—the Reform Act. Then we had holiday all the while, and it was something to look forward to; that was the time for youth to receive sound practical political education! The election at hand, one candidate would promise you "Ships, Colonies, and Commerce," if you would vote for him—ships to bear you to Canada; large fields of ice to skate over when you got there; and timber to fell and beaver-skins to cure, to send home as commerce to mother country. Who would stop in England and eat dear bread, when such promises were

---

* Stepney is a hamlet about one mile from Hull.

held out in the colonies? Who would not vote for "Ships, Colonies, and Commerce," and receive a "blue ribbon" and a neat half-pint black bottle of Jamaica rum, with a nice blue label upon it? Rum-commerce do you call it? Planters must encourage trade, and if they do not buy you, what is to become of slave-grown sugar? Look at the mighty pageant, when free and independent electors have emptied the rum bottles—they can be yoked like asses to Sir Sell-them's carriage, and pipe him round the town, to the tune of "See the conquering hero comes!" Once they drew him into the Humber, and it was with difficulty that the carriage was extricated—that was a *rum* mistake. Then were the days for moralising. See, the brewer's dray has hove in sight, freighted with large eighteens and six-and-thirties of nut-brown—they are set down in the broad highway, their heads knocked in, and *free*-men make a rush at their contents—virtuous maidens are running with their pots, and staid matrons limping towards the barrel, with their pancheons, to get a sup of the ale to drink the "candidate's return." Ardent youth, who always improve the present hour, dip in their shoes for lack of glasses, and they drink "the election" in a bumper. All men are equal at an election, and so the chimney-sweep thought he might as well have a "good blow-out" as the rest of them. If he cannot vote for the candidate, he can shout for him, and help to break the windows of the opposing party. Common justice will decide his right to a drink out of the barrel, and he will be pushed back no longer. Why is he to be thus jostled? his calling is a necessary one; then why is he despised? He has a friend near him that will give him a lift up; and now he is up—and in too—to the waist in the barrel, and for the want of shoes to drink out of, he tries his cap. He has scarcely time to drink "may the best man win," before the mob, who, disliking smutty ale, upset the barrel, sweep, and all; a regular fight ensues, a few heads are broken, eyes are blacked, and the major part sally off to the next barrel. One or two of the cunning ones steal away with the empty cask, which the cooper (sly dog) has promised to buy in again at a moderate price.

The greatest anxiety in my young days was evinced to have a "third man" at elections; without him the whole affair was worth nothing; it was spiritless—no beer—no blankets in winter—no coal-tickets—nay, even when all was over, and the freeman had returned to his usual half-starved condition in the winter, the soup ticket was not so secure, if there had not been a "third man" to enhance its value. Then, to secure such advantages, who would not save his vote for a "third man." The balance due for carrying flags, running with messages, suborning voters, getting your men made free, voting paupers and dead men, and other eminent services, were not worth a thought, if there was not a "third man." Who would not vote for him then? What! if he had already promised to split between "Church and State," and "Ships, Colonies, and Commerce!" what of that? What are election promises? Like "pie-crusts, made to be broken." "More rum! we will have a third man, and vote for 'Reform, and no barley bread!'" How strange that such pure old school training did not make me a

Tory, as my father was before me; and make me toss up my cap for the "Glorious Constitution!" It has failed to do so; and I have thought deeply on the subject, ever since I wore an orange lily in my buttonhole on the chairing-day of that memorable election which returned Sir James Graham for Hull. From that day, the conviction has strengthened within me, that until every man in England, who pays the *taxes*, has a vote in choosing the *tax-maker*, our boasted freedom is a sham.

> "We have found a mental raiment,
> Purer, whiter, to put on;
> Old opinions! rags and tatters!
> Get you gone! get you gone!"

At the election just noticed, the portrait of the patriot, Andrew Marvel, was paraded around the town; I know not for what purpose, unless it was to inspire us to emulate the blunt honesty of purpose which guided the "British Aristides." We now hear much of "five points," and "paying members to the house:" Andrew Marvel was the last "paid member" of my native town; and with the exception of Colonel Peyronet Thompson, the celebrated author of the "Corn Law Catechism," the only member for that town, who, as far as I know, ever thought it worth their notice to write frequently and publicly on the passing events in the "People's House." Both these senators were frequent in their correspondence with the burgesses who sent them to do their business. Andrew Marvel is reported to have corresponded with his constituents every post; and this famous correspondence still exists in the archives of Trinity House, at Hull.

Now that the people are again thinking seriously about reclaiming the Commons' house, and asserting their sovereignty, the following anecdote of the last of the paid members—the friend and companion of Milton—may not be amiss:—" His parliamentary correspondence continued for several years with little or no interruption, and affords ample proof of his indefatigable industry and unremitting attention to the most minute, as well as the most momentous, matters. In some of them he mentions six o'clock in the evening as a very protracted hour for business in the House of Commons; and at length the attendance became particularly onerous and fatiguing. The dissensions between the two houses, arising from the undefined nature of their privileges and jurisdictions, occasioned perpetual conferences and prolonged discussions, so that on one occasion, the House of Commons sat, without intermission, until *five o'clock in the morning*. Every session brought forth some new bill, or forced proclamation, against conventicles and sectarians, and also in favour of a prohibitory system of commerce."

There is scarcely one of Marvell's letters which does not afford some proof, that the house in which he sat was no friend to free trade, even between the several parts of the kingdom; and there was a manifest inclination to exclude French commodities altogether. Marvell applies the epithet "terrible" to the conventicle bill, and characterizes it as "the quintessence of arbitrary malice." During the Spring session of 1670, the king thought fit to frequent the debates in the House of Lords, and declared it was "better than going to a play." Marvell mentions the circumstance with surprise to his constituents, in his letter dated the 26th of March in that year. The prospect of affairs was deplorable: Charles had abandoned himself to the notorious cabal. Even Marvell seemed affected by despondency; and although he stated in a private communication, that "the Parliament was never so embarrassed," and, "we are all venal cowards except some few," yet the Commons proved an overmatch for the Lords and the Court. At that period, to use Andrew's words, "the court was at the highest pitch of wanton luxury, and the people full of discontent." The King had become the concealed instrument of France, yet Marvell speaks with tenderness of Charles the First, whose errors and misfortunes he attributed mainly to the rash counsels of the prelates. In his satirical works, however, he is less lenient, and the power of his ridicule rendered him obnoxious at court. He was threatened, he was flattered, he was beset with spies, courted by beauties, and, it is said, even way-laid by ruffians; but his integrity was proof alike against danger, adulation, and corruption. Respecting himself, and revering virtue, he had a spirit armed against the assiduous assaults of the tempter. It was about the year 1673 or 1674, that the Lord Treasurer Danby, an old schoolfellow, presuming on his former acquaintance and Andrew's good-natured facility, visited the patriot in his humble lodging, with a view to induce him to barter his poverty and probity for profligacy and place. This interesting incident is thus related:—"At parting, the Lord Treasurer, out of *pure affection*, slipped into his hand an order on the treasury for one thousand pounds, and then went to his chariot. Marvell looking at the paper, calls after the Treasurer, 'My Lord, I request another moment.' They both return to the garret, and the serving boy of the house is called:—'Jack, child, what had I for dinner yesterday?' 'Don't you remember, Sir, you had the little shoulder of mutton, you ordered me to bring from the woman in the market?' 'Very right, child, what have I for dinner to day?' 'Don't you know, Sir, that you bid me lay by the *blade bone to broil?*' ''Tis so, very right, child; go away.'—'My Lord, do you hear? Andrew Marvell's dinner is provided; there's your piece of paper. *I know the sort of kindness you intended: I live here to serve my constituents.* The ministry may seek men for their purpose: I AM NOT ONE!'"

To enhance the merit of Marvell's rejection of this large bribe, it is further related, that after this memorable interview, he was under the necessity of applying to his bookseller for the loan of a guinea. Perhaps the above simple and sublime fact stands best by itself; and whether the *addendum* be authentic or not, it is scarcely necessary " to add another colour to the rainbow."

Andrew Marvell died suddenly on the 29th of July, 1678, while attending a public meeting in the Town Hall of Hull; it is supposed by *poison*, as he had previously been in remarkably good health. Thus, it is supposed, was fulfilled the *Christian*-like denunciation of Dr. Samuel Parker, in his reproof of Marvell's "*Rehearsal Transposed:*"—"If thou darest to print any lie or libel against Dr. Parker, by the Eternal God I will cut thy throat!"

Marvell's heart was with the oppressed, and spurned the oppressor's gold; he battled with his pen, as well as confronted the tyrants in the senate. He has written some ironical observations on the *Invention of Printing*. No doubt those "letters" were caustic doses for the parasites in Charles' time—they are boluses now-a-days.

These seditious "meetings of letters" are wormwood to the self-appointed conservators of mind, who vainly expect to kick them back as easily as Canute was to roll back the ocean-tide. Canute knew better than to stop on the beach, all divinity-hedged as he was. Will our opposers sit wrapped in their vain glory, waving their hands, and crying out "recede," until the tide of letters gives another heave or two? Marvell says, "There have been ways found out to banish ministers, to find not only the people, but even the grounds and fields where they assembled in conventicles; but no art could prevent these seditious meetings of LETTERS. Two or three brawny fellows in a corner, with mere ink and elbow-grease, do more harm than a hundred systematical divines, with their sweaty preaching. Their ugly printing letters look but like so many rotten tooth drawers; and these rascally operators of the press, have got a trick to fasten them again in a few minutes, that they grow as firm a set, and as biting and talkative as ever. Oh, Printing! how hast thou disturbed the peace of mankind!—that lead, when moulded into bullets, is not so mortal as when formed into letters! There was a mistake, sure, in the story of Cadmus; and the serpent's teeth which he sowed were nothing else but the letters which he invented."

From childhood I was an admirer of flowers and the beautiful in Nature; though a town life was not the most favourable for cultivating such a taste, still there were opportunities for gratifying it. Amongst my visits, those to Sam W———'s Strawberry Gardens were delightful floral lessons. Sammy, be it known, was a Scotchman; he was proud of his country, and it was his boast, that his countrymen had taught the science of gardening to all Europe; he had pictured over his house door Dick Whittington and his cat, and sold refreshments to those who needed them. Sam was no churl, while he had a stoup in his cupboard, a broken-down countryman never fainted for the want of a "drap." He wished to live by his garden, and was wont to charge an admission fee to his grounds; but only let him hear that you were North o' th' Tweed, and as surely as night follows day, so certainly had you the key to open Sam's heart, and therewith his garden-gate. It was by being a fellow-countryman, that "Jock Thomson and his lad" had a standing invitation to Sam's borders, and, occasionally, to his whisky-gill.

There is something admirable in the brotherhood that unites men of one common country. Call it Scotchman-like if it so please you,—let the cynics sneer at it,—there is humanity in it. Imagine a benighted son of the world, drifting down the stream of poverty, neither hook nor tow-rope on board, and see him in his misery, perhaps in despair, hoist his plaid as a signal of distress. How great must be his joy, when this very display of his nation's colours induces some warm heart to hail him, to throw him the rope-end of fraternity, therewith haul him to, and moor him in the harbour of kindness, and make his heart rejoice. What gave the impulse? Why, the "honor of auld Scotland." Curl your noses at it as ye will, you very-sorry-for-you, pity-you-sincerely, but cannot-help-you sort of men! Again I say, there is something comfortable in such a nationality, one that sets all hearts a-kin. What if you do not think so? They simply wish you to be so good as "to stand out of the sunshine."

Yes! "Brither Scot" was the password to gay flower beds, where bloody-walls threw their perfumes into the morning breeze—where lilies hung out their snowy bells, as fair and as sweet as the lovely maidens that were there gathered to admire them—where pinks as round as a shilling, and tulips streaked as uniformly as the folds in Miss's fan—where, indeed, a countless host of the gay children of Flora were flaunting their gorgeous hues, and sprinkling their luscious fragrance in the dancing sun-beams.

Sam drove on a considerable trade by selling nosegays. Could you have seen the bustle in his kitchen on a bright Sunday morning in June, you would have supposed he was wreathing materials to festoon the Market-place with, on the anniversary of the "good king's" birth-day. There were long rows of benches covered with brown-ware pancheons, each half filled with water, to keep the polychrome bunches in perfection; within them the gay circles of various qualities and prices, from one penny to a shilling. The whole family were employed in this sweet service. It was the province of the guid wife Nannie to arrange them in their crystal beds. Madge and Jenny, two pretty daughters, as bland as a May morning, and as warm-hearted as their father, were each seated on three-legged wooden stools—or rather the roots of trees, sawn level at the top, into which three pins had been driven as substitutes for legs; though rude, they were as picturesque as their trade. Their business it was to group and bind up the posies. Sam supplied them with flowers; for although he was glad of a little help on what he called his wholesale-days, if he was at all aware that any one but himself had cut his gay blooms, he had a perpetual twitching of his body, and such an absence of speech, indeed—taken altogether, so comical a personification of doubt was never before witnessed. See him come bustling in to them, with a green serge apron full of perfume, and a bundle of sweet-briar and lilacs over his arm "to make the backs with," his dark grey eyes glancing all around, measuring both quantity and quality with a single roll of his orbs. Then his ordering of each by turn, but with such an impetuous stuttering, as if he could ill afford to wait the necessary time required to deliver his orders. Hear his torrent of splutter—"Ah! Madge ye puss, dinna ye ken ye are owre blue there—a' Canterbury-bells; they'll no ring lassie—take ye some mair o' th' sweet Willey, and put in a wee bit o' th' mignionette, just to tempt their noses. Eh Jenny, bairn, that love-lies-a-bleeding does na become ye there—take less o't, and put in a gilliflower, and a pink or twa; they will suit the counting-house cheilds—o'd there, the very devil for pinks—I really think some o' these days, i' th' absence o' cloves, they'll buy me!

Madge! Madge! ye extravagant slut, dinna ye use so much o'th' mat there, you'll ruin me—I gave tenpence and a gill for that old rush-mat 'tither day, to Andrew o'th' wharf yonder, and you'll use the full half o't this blessed day—think o' your porridge, my bairn! Here, Nannie, put thae twa dozen moss rose buds into the China bowl there, they'll a' go up at threepence the bud, for the young bucks to stick i' their button-holes, when they're walking their mams upon the pier to-day! Here, Jennie lass, make up a lot o' the cheap anes wi' lads-love backs for the sailor chaps,—the blue-jackets are the deuce for lads-love—they're arrant rogues wi' the lasses them tarry dogs I've been told, just on the sly d'ye see, that mony a slip o't from my garden has taken root in them same sow-westers."

Sam likewise accommodated the townsfolk with sweet-briars and monthly roses in pots, to stock the gardens of those whose garden-plots were laid out upon a board three feet by eleven inches, and which was usually hung out of the best chamber-window. Jack Thomson was a yearly customer in this branch of trade, for some how the plants never did well after leaving Strawberry Gardens. I observed in the newspapers a short time ago, the account of a philosopher who had been extolling the advantages that land in the vicinity of railroads would derive from the soot that fell upon it from the smoke of the engine chimneys. I fear my father was not much of a philosopher, at least he was not one of the smoke improvement school, for he always maintained that it was the smoke that killed his potted briars and roses.

Mr. W—— was a master in that exalted style of gardening that characterised the past age. In his grounds, a profusion of bright-leaved hollies and sombre-toned funeral yews were trained and clipped into the Dutch-cheese fashion. Let it be understood that Samuel had always the best models for this style at hand; he had only to walk down to the Docks, and there were opportunities innumerable for studying the balls themselves, all perfect as Mynheer's bluff-sterned dairy-maids—here were patterns for his scissors and pruning-knife; never did more symmetrical ones issue from a turner's lathe! He could find none such in the wild woods. No! Nature appeared to Sam perfectly indifferent in that branch of her art; letting long branches dangle and wave to-and-fro in the breeze, as if in very defiance of all rule. Such flirting and irregularity might suit your man who did not understand the *mystery* of gardening, but freedom of that kind found no favour at Strawberry Gardens. It would have done any-bodies' heart good to have seen Sam's privet hedge in the middle of April. Talk of the level of a garrison platform, of loop-holes, and regular masonry—they were nothing to his privet hedge! Oh! such beautiful shaped port-holes, and chamfered capping were surely never seen before—and as for ranging, why you could not find one leaf higher than another from the top to the bottom of the hedge. There was one yew-tree—Sam called it a *view*-tree, and I believe he was right. It grew near to his draw-well, and he said that was the reason it always looked so well. He said that tree was worth any man's while to come twenty miles to see it. It was for all the world like a peacock, only it was all green, and had only one leg, but then it was clipped so nicely into a body, and a tail, and a comb—to be sure there was no eyes in the tail, but that was made up by its always spreading it out whether in the snowy days of winter or the burning heat of summer—beautiful as peacocks really are, they are nothing like Sam's *view-tree* peacock.

There are many people now-a-days who try their hands at the peacock and Dutch-cheese style of trimming trees, but they might as well give over, for, let them try their best, they will never surpass the precision of Strawberry Gardens. They will stand a better chance of excelling, if they will only make up their minds to grow their trees on the wild plan—just trimming a branch here and there for the sake of convenience, or to allow of head-way over a walk or in similar situations. They can only ape the old school; the "knotted garden" belonged to a stiff age, starch in trees, as well as cravats. It is time to give it up, and instead of it, to copy Nature. Though Sam knew better than nature, it does not follow that every gardener is to be a Sammy.

Young in life, I had a love of plays, but my mother always checked it—she condemned play reading, and regarded theatres as sinks of vice, rather than temples wherein "to hold, as 'twere, the mirror up to Nature—to show Virtue her own feature, scorn her own image, and the very age and body of the time, his form and pressure." My religious friends, too, were then, as now, constantly preaching against theatrical amusements; albeit, I could never agree with their wholesale condemnation; nor has maturer years revealed to me the enormities wherewith self-sanctity has filled the theatres. Like other institutions, it has its share of good and evil. Time, who purges other abuses, will some day look into the theatres again; and again "the wise saws" of the dramatic poets will be found useful, even in the days of cheap reading, steaming, and out-door rollicking. What if the master spirits that walked the earth, wrapped in the mantle of the "legitimate drama," sleep with "the Capulets," their principles still live, and yet "shall flourish in immortal youth." The spirit that animated Euripides, Sophocles, Shakespeare, Massinger, rare Old Ben, and a host of others, whose philosophy has furnished texts for divines, and household words for all mankind,— this spirit only slumbers, it is not dead: even now it is awakening in our Talfourd, Jerrold, and Knowles; and who can say it shall not again walk over the earth, wide awake, singing aloud its soul-refining songs? Shall excrescences of rant, and melo-dramas of real water, and real horses, lions, balloons, real Thurtell's gigs, Jack Sheppards, and Tom Thumbs, extinguish the drama, any more than " unknown tongues," and Southcottonian cradles, shall destroy the power and simplicity of religion, or induce the belief of an incarnation in a maiden living up a three-pair-back?

Now that the banner of education is waving over every town, and every village, will not an intelligent people have their amusement and instruction walk hand in hand in our theatres, freed from all the false glitter and bombast that have veiled it for more than half a century, perhaps through our ignorance forced into it, to glut "the poverty-maw" rather than "the will" of those whose duty it should have been to cater for the elevation of the masses, rather than pander to their ignorance, by "out-doing Termagant," and "out-heroding Herod?" Hence, those who arrogate to themselves the right of ordering our recreations for us, have preached down the drama; they have never stirred themselves or lifted a pen in its purification, nor have they provided us with other amusements. Some would have us believe that none such are needed, but that it were holier to sit the live-long days and years gloomily brooding over our infirmities, until our studied sullenness finds vent in hypocrisy, and thus our vaunted "merrie England" has become a mockery. It is indeed true, that they tell us such things may be tolerated in London, because royalty may wish occasionally to indulge their tastes; then, titles are made to consecrate the deed, and there is no harm done; but to the million, who earn the wealth they use, have enough to do without such indulgences, and the conventional mode of telling him so, is to proclaim the indulgence immoral. Let him toil and eat, if he can get food enough for his hungry cravings, but never let him sin by indulging in purifying pleasures. Then for the degrees of vice, very few talk of it at the Opera; they can ride to it in stately carriages; they can loll in velvet-lined boxes, and the price of the tickets renders the thing respectable. If you take a cab, and a half-crown ticket, "you set a bad example;" but the mischief is enormous, if you foot it to the shilling gallery. O yes! the immorality is complete, when brown faces, and blue stockings, crowd together to listen to the mighty soul-breath of Shakespeare, divided into acts, eked out with fine painting, and accompanied with heart-moving music; then, indeed, it is vicious! and with such cant

> "We do sugar o'er
> The devil himself."

Near to the close of my seventeenth year, after incessant entreaties, my mother was prevailed upon to allow me to go to see a play; one of my fellow-apprentices took charge of me, and promised to escort me home again after the performance. The promised day arrived, and to me it appeared as long as a week, although it was a November day. I thought the twilight of evening would never return; at length night-fall proclaimed the hour of departure was come, and so intensely were my thoughts rivetted upon the coming event, that I could not take my tea with any relish, for every minute was to me an hour; I thought my companion was now more laggard than the lazy-paced day had been. The long-expected tap at the door was given, and I flew to open it, and could scarcely tolerate the needful compliments, because they appeared to consume our time. There was a fearful expression upon my mother's face, that on ordinary occasions would have troubled me; but now, nothing gave me pain, although my mother followed us to the door, and seemed wishful to recal her leave for me to go; but I could not think about it—the theatre and King John had taken deep hold of me, and absorbed every other thought. As we threaded the various streets in our journey to the place, I was

K

all wonderment as to what we should behold. We reached the house, and late as we expected to be, we found ourselves waiting the opening of the doors of the "eighteen-penny gallery," where we intended to seat ourselves. We wormed our way amongst the crowd that were waiting admittance, and by-and-by the door gave a loud groan, which was followed by a buzzing sound of "they are open," and in a few seconds we were seated on the third form from the front of the gallery in the Theatre Royal, in Humber Street, Hull. It was an event to be remembered; the mass of gorgeous decorations—the myriads of iris-tinted rays, glancing their diamond fires from the costly chandeliers—the spirit-stirring strains from the orchestra—the piles of human faces, each as comfortable as smiles and laughter could make them—the babel of noises from the "gods" overhead, their bawling for the "Downfal of Paris," "Rule Britannia," "Play up, Nosey," "The Bay of Biscay O"—their whistles, stamping, barking, and mewing, were all commingled—such a scene as I had never before witnessed; yet so absorbing as to render suspense a stranger. Hark, the bell! Slowly the dark baize curtain leaves the foot-lights—"hats off," simultaneously burst from a hundred tongues as from one, "down there in the front;" and I jumped involuntarily from my seat, as the loud "flourish of drums and trumpets" revealed the mimic John and his haughty court. So enwrapped was I in the business, that at the fall of "the drop" at the end of the first act I felt bewildered, and almost doubted my existence, I was so struck

"By the very cunning of the scene."

I had read of the chivalric daring of bold knights, and of the subduing charms of "fair ladies" with their loves; but now I was in company with them. It might be a dream, but what if it was? it was a waking one! the only fear was, would it be as

> "Baseless, as the fabric of a vision,"

and so throw me back again upon the every-day world? I had read of "Magna Charta," without knowing its importance, but still believing it to be a something worth the fighting for—now was I in sight of that very Runny-meade, and moving with

> "A braver choice of dauntless spirits"

ready to grapple with the pale heart, and wring from him anew that deathless germ of liberty. I longed to mingle with them, and

> "Rattle the welkin's ear,
> And mock the deep-mouthed thunder;"

with any one in their grim-visaged band! As the scene moved onward, I was every thing by turns; now ready to "hang a calf-skin" over the recreant Austria, or rave with Constance for her "absent child." By the time the fourth act came on, all my fear of the play ending was gone. I thought of nothing but the story—Arthur's wrongs were mine. I shuddered at the burning iron; an awful clammy sweat over-ran my frame. It seemed to me that Arthur's life was hung upon each sentence. When the iron cooled, I saw the blood-seeking King foiled—

> "The breath of heaven hath blown his spirit out,
> And strewn repentant ashes on his head."

Now the climax of joy was felt;

> "I will not touch thine eyes,
> For all the treasure that thy uncle owes."

My joy was but a span, but half enjoyed, before I had to see him climb the parapet, and topple from the frowning battlements, and hear his

> "O me! my uncle's spirit is in those stones,"

outebbing with his life's-blood. Despite the fine acting of Fitzgerald in King John, I could not tolerate him. He was no actor to me. No! He was indeed

> "A cold-hearted blood-gorged villain."

The knight was kind when he exclaimed,

> "All Kent hath yielded."

Nor was there any crime in the monk's chalice, he had done well—

> "Poison'd, ill-fare; dead, forsook, cast off."

Oh! there was pleasure in those writhings; I enjoyed those tortures, both of soul and body; it was a just retribution. I would not, if I had held the snow-blast in my grip, have answered his prayer to

> "Bid the winter come,
> To thrust his icy fingers in my maw,
> Nor let my kingdom's rivers take their course
> Through my burn'd bosom; nor entreat the North
> To make his bleak winds kiss my parched lips,
> And comfort me with cold."

It was a truly solemn moment, when in that twilight of lamps, the green curtain was slowly let fall, fold after fold, its sombre pall over the bier of the "poor player;" it had a serious effect upon me, as I sat absorbed in that new mode of visiting the inner-soul by such strange realities. Let those, who swim upon the surface stream of life, echo the purist's cry of the irreligious play-house if they choose; it would be sheer hypocrisy were I to join the puritanic shout.

Many a time have I felt my soul light up with pure and holy fire at the altar of our Shakespeare, but the first offering was cast upon the shrine when first I witnessed the tragedy of King John.

So intensely was my mind rivetted to that play, that as soon afterwards as I could raise a sixpence I purchased a copy of it, and soon I could repeat all the most striking passages by rote. I was now often lingering about the theatre in the evenings, and thought it no small honour to follow in the wake of the actors, as they were walking the streets, or returning from, or going to the theatre.

I soon became acquainted with Mr. Nevill, who was a good actor, a kind-hearted man, and occasionally a boon companion; about six months after I had first visited the play, I was introduced by Mr. Nevill to a select company of comedians and Thespians, who were enjoying themselves over a glass at Sam's Coffee-house; there was I to recite some passages from King John to them. This being the first time I had been in such close company with those "dare-devil" looking fellows, who were all so grim in their gilt-leather chain mail and their corked beards, I made several attempts at speaking before I could succeed, having the fear of those once savage men before my eyes; I was very tremulous; however, after some cheering words from them, a beginning was effected; but instead of select passages as intended, in my confusion, I went through the whole of the first act, running each part into the other; this appeared to amuse them. I was now going on with the second act, when Mr. Baker, the low comedian, interrupted me with "stop my man; as we are to have the whole of the *five acts*, we had better send for old H——, the prompter." This sarcasm was delivered with all the mock gravity for which Mr. B. was so famous, and it at once set all the room in a roar of laughter, which so discomfited me, that I ran straight out of the room, leaving my hat behind me. When I had been out in the street some few minutes, I felt the want of my hat, but durst not return for it, and at last prevailed upon a boy that was playing near me, to fetch it for me, giving him twopence as a reward for his trouble. The wags, however, refused to give it up to the boy, as they were determined, if possible, to have me back again; but neither coaxing, or the fear of losing my hat, could induce me to return. After a delay of half an hour, I prevailed upon the landlord to fetch it out of the room for me, and as soon as I got possession of it, I decamped at a pretty round pace.

The fear occasioned by my "first appearance" before the players was soon dispelled—more intimate acquaintance was the best antidote to fright; and the actors were soon found to be good fellows, and jolly companions. My hankering after the performers led to an introduction to the stage-keeper, Mr. G——, by whom I was engaged, occasionally, as a supernumerary. This body was more or less numerous, according to the pieces; generally the most were required in tragedies and melo-dramas; amongst other duties, they administer liberally to the laughter and jibes of "the gods" in the galleries, by their awkward gait, and their inelegant treading of the stage. We had, on great occasions, when any popular actor was going to "star it," to attend at rehearsals, at such times, I have to confess, that my "dinner-hour" was often extended to two hours. It was a somewhat amusing scene, to witness the drilling we had to go through, under the direction of the facetious Mr. G——, on the *grand days;* also to observe the temper displayed by the great men, which, as may be expected, was various; but there was the most remarkable contrast between two popular and eminent tragedians; they were, in this respect, the very antipodes to each other. Kean usually took the unready movements of the supernumeraries in perfect good humour—sometimes laughing uproariously, and addressing us ironically, as "my brother stupids"—"my brave associates"—"partners of my toil," &c.;—but in his dying scene in Alexander the Great, where his by-play was that of an accomplished artist—in this scene he always expressed more than usual concern to have "old hands;" and he was in the habit of rehearsing "the fall" several times with them, requesting them to pay the strictest attention to the business of the whole scene. Our terror was a Shakesperian, who, since that time, has made a great noise in the world, and was as irritable as Kean was affable. The poor supernumeraries were in fear and trembling when he was near, and at these times they stood peeping round the wings like scarred rabbits peeping from their lair, over the tips of grass and brushwood. With "the Colossus" we had never any ironical compliments— we were never brave fellows with him, but more frequently "fools, bores, and d——d stupids." There was no forgetting that a *star* was present; whenever he made his appearance he took especial care to impress us with his constellating power and magnitude; by his snarling, he might have passed for a *dog*-star; but such twinkling was too dull for him—nothing less than a Mars, or perhaps Saturn, was blaze enough for the mighty one! nor were the poor supers the only ones who had to

"Walk under his huge legs and peep about,"

in the very fear of his importance. The "walking gentlemen," and the "messengers," had often hard work of it. On one occasion, when the Colossus was rehearsing the part of King Richard III., the poor fellow who had to deliver the message of—

"My Lord, the Duke of Buckingham is taken,"

had to go through the rehearsal of this simple line an unnecessary number of times: on each occasion, he either came too far down the stage, or stood too near the wings, in short, he was any where but in a place to suit the great man; hence, at each re-entrance, the answer was not

"Off with his head,"

but "Too far, Sir,"—"There—here—just there, Sir!" suiting "the action to the word," by giving an Herculean stamp with his foot on the stage; and, at last, he called to the stage keeper to bring him a piece of chalk, with which he drew a line on the stage to mark the precise boundary, where the "messenger," entering in haste according to the stage book, was to deliver his message! This school-boy mode of drilling so insulted the humble "messenger," that after the rehearsal he gave up his part in dudgeon; and the *star* had to hear his message delivered by another person with one rehearsal, regardless of the *chalk line!*

Doubtless, the old adage of "Birds of a feather always flock together," holds good in every thing; it did so with the supernumeraries, and the amateur theatricals, in my juvenile days; so much so, that some dozen or more of us formed ourselves into an amateur company, and at the renowned Sam's Coffeehouse, we undertook to present such of our friends, and the public in general, as were *fortunate* enough in procuring tickets for the occasion, with the representation of the tragedy of "*Mahomet*," and the interlude of the "*Intrigue*." Properties for the occasion we had none, still we had assurance enough to imagine, that by the time our play would be brought out, we should be enabled to give our friends a treat; so without delay, one of our company, Mr. Samuel H———, by profession a coach herald painter, was commissioned to paint us a scene, an interior, which we, forsooth, dubbed a palace. As we could only afford one scene, our painter had to show his skill in design, by contriving a picture,

"Which served us for parlour, and kitchen, and all."

Our stage manager was a carpenter, a Mr. W———, now a celebrated teetotal lecturer. Whether, in consequence, he is ashamed to look back upon our juvenile freaks, where at the Coffee-house we recited our parts and took our "swats" together, I do not know; however, Mr. William showed judgment in his managerial department, and accommodated our wants to our means; he selected the tragedy of "*Mahomet*," because there was but one female part in it, and that our "generally useful" scene might decently serve the purpose. The interlude was happily chosen to accommodate itself to our necessities—there was but one scene required, " a room in an inn near Bath," and but one lady performer, Helen, the bar keeper. In the tragedy I was cast to play *Alcanor*, the priest; in the farce I was left out, being considered too vinegar-faced to play low comedy. To furnish dresses was the most important thing—silk, velvet, and spangles, being costly articles; our stage manager soon got us out of the dilemma, by making friends with the wardrobe-keeper of the Theatre Royal, to lend us as many eastern dresses as would dress the piece; and thus far the work went bravely on! After several rehearsals, the eventful night arrived; our theatre was set out with the one scene, and a large curtain, the latter we borrowed of an auctioneer. We dressed, we rouged, arnotted, and corked, and for the first three acts all " went as merry as a marriage bell!" We had just drawn aside the baize to commence the fourth act, when we were surprised by the appearance of the manager of the Theatre Royal, Mr. M——, in company with a constable. The manager, in a desperate rage, had come to demand the dresses, which had been lent without his permission, at the same time threatening to send every soul of us to prison. There was soon a regular confusion—the audience left their seats—some took the first opportunity of stealing away, to avoid unpleasant circumstances—others crowded upon our little stage. In vain we pleaded our innocence, and our ignorance of not knowing we had been guilty of an error in taking the dresses, and we begged to be allowed to finish the play with them; but no, the manager was inexorable; after a parley, we had to give up the dresses to the constable, and to beg pardon of the manager, to avoid the risk of a prison. The manager, and the knight of hand-cuffs, now left us; after several entreaties with those remaining to take their seats, and we would finish the play, order was at length restored; and after a brief council with *our* manager, we agreed to go on, and in lieu of dresses to play out the piece in our shirt sleeves, which, in our opinions, would be a good substitute for Turkish costume! We then resumed—the costume, white trowsers, and whitey-brown shirt sleeves! In the interlude which followed, we were not so much at a loss for dresses, the cast being light, only three men and one lady; and the costume a modern one. Our Sunday's best made excellent substitutes for the swallow-tails and the surtouts of the ton worn on the Bath Road. Thus, dressed up at little expense, we finished our evening's business; and, but for the untoward event, every thing gave perfect satisfaction to our audience.

If the foibles of youth were sometimes objectionable, it must be remembered that, at the commencement of the present century, our young men in the large towns were, generally speaking, more familiar with vice than virtue. The dawning of mind which is now, happily, so fast spreading its influence into the artisans' class, was then but glimmering over an age of mental gloom, occasioned by the depopulating continental war, which spread its blight over Europe. In that era of rapine and aggrandisement, as the money-class grew rich, they grew tyrannous therewith. The want of education amongst the masses, left them, as it ever will leave the uneducated, a prey to those whose inhumanity prompts them to trade in the sinews of all that they can attenuate. A brief period of high wages, the consequence of a demand for men to be crushed beneath the juggernaut of "glory" abroad; the necessity for the few remaining at home to work hard at the dock-yards; to make swords and bayonets, to cast cannon and balls; to fill up the militia; and drill themselves by the hundred, to make one huge human-automaton-red-coated-battering-ram; all tended to increase the wages of the few that remained at the handicrafts. This flush of wages was of little or no value to the workmen; it was for the most part spent in dram-drinking and vicious indulgence; and it was much to the interest of the traders in human vitals, that it should be so spent; for the men who were content to work like machines one week, to riot and give loose to mere animality the next one, were just the tools the tyrants wanted; hence, the lower the mass were sunk in animality, the better the money-gorged could suck the means of wealth from their dull carcases.

However politicians and moralists may differ as to the causes, such things have undeniably existed! Hope, however, lay at the bottom of our social box of ills. There is a retributive Providence, which will not allow such pestilential visitings to darken this earth for ever. Will they not have an end in countries called CHRISTIAN, even as they were outworn in the plague-land of the Pharaohs, and the empires of the Cæsars? It is indeed strange, how men professing to be the disciples of the "meek and lowly" Jesus of Nazareth, the man "in whom there was no guile," should, on the slightest pretext, clamour for war—that the lords of a territory "on which the sun never sets" should be unceasingly exclaiming for more. We have yet to learn practically, that of whatever colour or faith—

"A man's a man for a' that;"

that while we are vociferating for self, we must learn to respect the RIGHTS OF ALL.

The follies of my juvenile companions were such as might be expected to belong to the age. In 1818-19, they passed muster as the mere "tricks of youth." Sometimes with those aspirants to the "sock and buskin" they were of a witty character; at others, satirising the prejudices of the age. One of those wags, now, poor fellow, gathered to his fathers, took the advantage of having "a lark" at the expense of the jealousies that existed between the captain of the first packet that sailed from Hull, called the "Caledonia," and the skipper of one of the old sailing packets. At that time, a steam packet at Hull was considered an innovation, and the old coasters took especial pleasure in annoying them. Meantime, the old skippers never lost a chance of informing the public of their increasing desire to do every thing for their accommodation; that fares should be reduced. and that the lives of the public should not be sacrificed by the "tall chimneys!" The skipper of one of the sailing boats sent the bellman round the town, crying "O yez! O yez! O yez! this is to give noatice, that John Jacklin, maister of the Thorn Packet, will sail from here to-morrow mornin for Thorn, near Doncaster; fares reduced; *if wind and weather permit.*" My companion, who was a go-a-head man in packets as well as in plays, got a sketch of the " Caledonia" steamer drawn upon a piece of paper, and put in the front of his hat; he then borrowed a pestle and mortar to serve as a bell, and followed the crier. As soon as he had finished his "wind and weather permit," Jack B—— began to ring his mortar, and to cry "O yez! Take notice, the 'Caledonia' steam packet will take passengers to Selby, every morning next week, and land them there the same day;* they will sail two hours before high water, take the passengers for nothing, and proceed *in spite of wind and weather!*" Jack's waggery so offended the bellman, that it led to a case of assault, and he had to pay five shillings, with a promise not to offend again.

On another occasion, an elderly lady had been guilty of an indiscretion, and was anxious to ascertain the

---

* Sometimes the sailing packets were prevented by stress of weather from proceeding with their passengers, having to return, or put in to some of the creeks along the river until another day.

probable consequences of the act. Some of her neighbours advised her to consult a "wise man," and he would tell her how the affair would end. Jack heard of the report, and immediately set on a person to cause the woman to be brought to him, and *he* would assume the office of "wise man." The plot succeeded; Jack had his garret cleared of his store of old trunks, hats, and musty shoes, and to give effect to his divination, he had the walls coloured black, and the floor whitewashed. I was commissioned to paint upon the floor a large magic circle; this I managed to perform by copying the Chinese figures and squat dragons, that were emblazoned on the canisters of a grocer, who was one of our party. We had also four lanterns of transparent paper, each one decorated with a skull and bones. Our conjurer dressed himself in one of our stage costumes, and added a long beard of horse-hair, arming himself with a brush shaft for a magic wand. Three of our party, wrapped in sheets, bearded with horse-hair, and holding the lanterns, were placed around the circle. One of our female acquaintances, who was fully acquainted with the woman's situation, and her desire to know the worst, was secreted in a closet, to answer the demands of the magician. Thus equipped, the woman was conducted to the garret; on entering, she was evidently alarmed, but bore it with tolerable firmness. We now threw the light of our lanterns upon the face of our "wise man," which gave him a wild, and coupled with his dress, a very mysterious appearance. The seer now asked the woman her business. She hesitated. He then consulted our "weird sister" in the closet, who made a full statement of the woman's faults, and her further desire to know the worst. Jack, in a voice gruff enough to make the very purlins tremble, desired the woman to confess if what she had heard was true. Again the woman hesitated. Jack spared her the trouble of confession, by telling her that his spirit knew her every thought, and that she was to stand in the centre of the magic circle, taking especial care, that not even the hem of her gown touched the ring, or she would be taken away. She was now to listen attentively, and his spirit would inform her whether she would be the mother of a boy, or a girl. The affair now became serious; the old woman fainted, we were speedily undressed of our horse-hair and sheets, and had her carried to a bed-room below, where *sal volatile* and smelling bottles were in active use, and fortunately the poor woman was brought round. She had a firm belief in the truth of this sham oracle, and was so deeply impressed with the power and fore-knowledge of the "wise man," that she applied to the parish authorities for additional support, on the ground of her soon having another in family to keep. The alarm occasioned by the woman's fainting, however, had such an effect upon all the party, that I am of opinion not one of us has again attempted to play at "wise man."

The belief in conjurers, magic circles, the turning of the key in the Bible, the nailing up of horse-shoes, the dressing the house with the berries of mountain ash, or wigan tree, to keep out the witches, with other similar charms and antidotes, are, thanks to the march of thought, nearly exploded. But there are hundreds who still believe in the power of divination in these "wise men." There is now (1846) resident at Wellow, a village in Nottinghamshire, a shrewd, but simple-looking old man, who has made it his business to seek out and confute these "wise men," and on every occasion he has succeeded. I will give one case as an illustration of his mode of proceeding:—After hearing there was resident at Newark one of these "wise men," whom report stated to be no quack, but had of a verity told the truth on many occasions—had the power of "ruling the planets," and at his nod could

"Call spirits from the vasty deep"—

old Ned, taking with him a companion to bear witness to the proceeding, started to Newark, and soon found the domicile of the "wise man." After he was admitted, he thus accosted him: "I say, they say that you can tell things?" "I believe I can," was the answer. "Tell where things are what has been lost, like?" said Ned. "Yes, I can," was the answer, "have you lost anything?" "Yes," continued Ned, "I have lost a valuable pit-saw; can you get it me back again?" "O yes!" said the man of fate, "I will soon get it; have you suspicion of any one?" "Ay," said Ned, "I have, and I believe he is a great rogue." Should you know him, if you saw him?" asked the planet ruler. The answer was, "Yes!" The magician handed to him a magic mirror, and asked "if the man he saw in the glass was not like the one he suspected?" "The very morale of him," said Ned. "Yes!" said the soothsayer, "I knew the moment you entered the house what you had lost, and I also knew the thief; I will make him return it within fourteen days, and the thief shall have no rest either night or day, until he return it." Edward now put on an expression of joy, and asked the man what he had to pay him? He said, as Ned's garb did not bespeak him rich, he should "only charge ten shillings, half his usual fee." Ned pleaded poverty, and after an entreaty, he prevailed upon the "wise man" to take seven shillings and sixpence, which he paid, and departed. In about an hour afterwards, Ned again made his appearance, taking with him his companion, who had been in the meantime waiting at a public house. He was again civilly invited in, the fellow doubtless expecting he had got another "seven and sixpenny" customer in the companion; but judge of his surprise, when he was accosted by old Ned, with "Why, you must be a d—— rogue, I say!" "What do you mean, Sir?" was the reply. "Why, that you are a d—— rogue! for I never lost a saw in my life, and if you don't give me my money back, I will fetch a warrant for you, and have you taken up for a swindler." After some parleying and explanations, the "wise man" gave up the money, and begged that he might not be exposed, as it was the only means he had of getting *an honest livelihood!* He said, if people would be such fools as to come to consult him, he must tell them something. He confessed to having numerous applications, and said that he enjoyed a notoriety for often telling the parties something that led to detection.

How pitiful it is that we should thus cheat ourselves, and put money into the purses of tricksters, who laugh at our ignorance. If the artisans will become "wise men," they must exercise their judgment, maturing it by reading, and the science of the class-rooms, and then, as they become mind-enfranchised, will the jugglery of impostors be exploded, and a death-blow given to the trade of the WISE MAN.

CHAPTER V.

A VOYAGE TO GREENLAND.

I HAD now entered upon my twenty-first year, and so far as trade was concerned, was unable to earn a living; and what was still worse, I did not feel the responsibility of my situation. Time has proved that my being articled to the craft of shipbuilding, was at least a mistake. Doubtless hundreds of men have been led into the same error, by the custom of parents apprenticing boys to any thing that promises to pay well, without ever bestowing a thought upon their fitness for the profession selected.

If phrenology, or any other branch of science, can reveal to us the way to avoid such failures for the future, we ought to listen thoughtfully to her counsels, rather than, as it is too much the fashion to do, to scoff at and revile every thing that our conventionally-hooded prejudices will not allow us to search after. It is no just argument to maintain, that because we lack the demonstration, all things new are visionary. We would not believe Fulton—we had no faith in Wheatstone, yet he has proved to us that he is the best messenger, and the most efficient thief-detector that has yet connected himself with our great highways of civilization—the railroads! The "myriad-minded" prophet, while living in an age of mental gloom, could translate for us, from the scroll of time, the profound truth, that

> "There are more things in heaven and earth,
> Than are dreamt of in our philosophy."

One thing was imperative, that I must try, amidst the great human scramble for food, if I could not get at a bread-loaf. As ship-building was now at a low ebb, I secured a chance to serve as carpenter's mate to Greenland. My father had occasionally done well in seafaring, hence I saw no reason why the son should not try also. So, in the early part of the month of February (1820), I got promise of a berth, and in the following March, articled for the venture, at the general muster.

Although at this period the trade to Greenland was rather on the decline, it was still one of great consideration to the town of Hull. In this year there were only sixty vessels sailed from that port to those frigid climes; in 1818, there had been sixty-three, the largest number that ever sailed from thence on the fishing business. The merchants of my native town were the first in England who fitted out ships for the whale fishery, about the year 1598. This trade was prosecuted with more or less success until the year 1765, when it declined, and was afterwards entirely monopolized by the Dutch.

In about 1766, "the active and enterprizing spirit of Mr. Standidge, a merchant of Hull, induced him to equip and send out to the Greenland seas, a ship on his own account—an adventure which was thought extremely hazardous, and of which individual speculation did not at that time afford an example in all Europe. This ship returned with one whale and four hundred seals. Stimulated by his success, he twice after visited Greenland, and prosecuted his commercial concerns with distinguished spirit, both at home and abroad."

In my seafaring days, the Greenland sailors were notorious for their daring, and for their disrespect of speech; prefacing or ending every sentence with an oath, or some other indelicate expression. Even in those days of uncouth language, a "Greenlandman's galley" was proverbially the lowest in the scale of vulgarity. Greenland sailors were generally illiterate, and very superstitious; they would exercise any artifice to get "shipped" with a *lucky* captain: indeed every officer in the trade, from the line-coiler to the captain, was obeyed according to his *luck* in procuring fish. If a captain was successful during a series of years, he was venerated by the sailors, and was by them supposed to

"Wear a charmed life."

The late Captain S——, who for many years commanded a vessel called "The A——," was a fine sample of the lucky class. So uniform was his success in whale fishing, that I have heard the sailors say, in their superstitious veneration for the man, "that even when the vessel could hold no more, the fish would still follow him to be killed;" and they would relate anecdotes to prove the truth of their assertions. One of these stories will suffice. One year, after the ship was full, and she was bearing homeward from the ice, and they had got out into clear water, a large "greyrumper" was observed to keep in their wake for a day and a night, when "old But-but" (so called by the sailors, in consequence of an impediment in his speech), came on deck the next morning, and again observing the fish playing and tacking about astern of the vessel, the veteran whale charmer ordered the boats to be unlashed, and the men to prepare for the chase; after which, he walked coolly up to the taffrail, and looking towards the monster,

"Which God of all his works
Created hugest that swim the ocean stream,"

exclaimed, "But-but, you ——, I'll give you a passage to England! but I will! but I will!" The boats were lowered, the fish was easily captured and taken in, and as the casks were already all filled, a great part of the dead fish lay in the boats, for the want of more appropriate accommodation. This piece of seeming good fortune was attributed by the sailors to a mysterious power with which he was gifted, and that skill in fishing, or knowledge of the country, and such other requirements, had no part, or the least to do with Captain S——'s success.

On the morning of the 20th of March, 1820, the "Duncombe," the vessel in which I was entered, sailed down into the Humber, where we anchored until the next tide. Although my previous trade might be expected to have initiated me into much that would form part of a sailor's life, I soon found that out at sea I was out of my element. I had nothing at command that appeared to be useful there. For several days I was prostrated by sea sickness; when I recovered, and began to look with mingled pleasure and dismay upon that new world of sky and water, I was asked if I trembled because I could not see the smoke of my mother's chimney! I was told, that to look with delight upon the wide waters would not assist in working the vessel; to be gazing upon the limitless world of blue, was the business of land-lubbers and fellows let out from Bedlam! To be charmed with the phosphorescent crest of the billows as they danced to the star-lit glory of the spangled heavens—or to give vent to the soul-fulness, inspired by the majestic roll of the silver-edged waves, as, sun burnished, they were chasing each other into illimitable space, until the present was lost in contemplating the untold magnificence of the world of waters, and of the Omnipotent Power and Goodness of God, in arranging every thing in inimitable beauty! Or, to shrink within one's-self at the wild lashing of the foam-crested ocean, as, dashed by the strange wind's sport, we were sunk deep in the green sea's trough, while above us, far above the mastheads, the mad waves were rending each other with deafening roar, and before we could ejaculate "God bless us!" to be again upheaved upon the crown of some fantastic surge, and peering our "sky-rakers" into the cloudless arch of deep azure, that spanned the immensity!

All this might do for a fellow to talk about, provided he could keep his feet upon his mother's hearth-stone, and hold himself by her apron strings—but of what use, they would ask, was such a "chaw-bacon" on board of a Greenlander! With those amphibious creatures, they were moon-struck ravings. Jolly tars! It was tarryism indeed; but whatever might be their business acquirements, in every thing else they were lamentably sunk below man, and seemed to partake of the animal. To talk of books and of reading was high treason against the blubber-kings. Two or three of our crew had Bibles with them, and sometimes made use of them; but those men were exceptions, they being Dissenters—I believe Methodists, and their piety was the butt of our boasted tars. The general conversation was, how soon they should be able to spend the money gained by the voyage, and how long it would find grog for the support of a fiddler, and a company of lewd women. Four-and-twenty hours of the stern reality was sufficient time to prove that there was more poetry in Dibdin's songs, than was likely to be found with those jolly tars, even in ploughing the German Ocean. We were but a few hours out at sea before I imagined the sentiment of the old song,—

"Peaceful, slumbering on the ocean,"

had more of comfort in it, than appeared to belong to the sailors with whom I was to voyage. I had scarcely closed my eyes in my berth, before I was again awakened by the creaking of masts, which was followed by a noise like the bursting of a thunder cloud; in a moment it was knocking at my cabin door, and at my heart too. It was evident that a gale was springing. The loud shocks were occasioned by the grind-stone, that had got loose, and with every heave of the vessel was rolling from larboard to starboard, staving in the bulk-heads and cabins. Next the temporary lashings of the blubber knives and lances gave way, and speedily the whole of the half-deck was strewn with these dangerous weapons. As the wind got up, so my fears increased, and by the note given by the watch on deck, there was a necessity for all to be in readiness. As the watch below left their berths one by one, the question was repeated, "Where the d—— is that lubber of a carpenter's mate? The grind-stone adrift—the knives unlashed—the casks loose:" added to which, about half a dozen of them assembled at once around my cabin door, and dragged me out of bed, although I was torn to pieces with severe sea-sickness. My pain of body was increased by the forlorn hope of enjoying any thing like comfort with such degraded companions; altogether made me sigh for the land and home. All hands were now aloft, the breeze continued to stiffen, the sails were close-reefed, and all made snug; and although it blew "great guns" all the night, as day-light came on, the wind ceased, and all went smoothly on.

We were again running before the wind, and in a few days we made the Shetland Isles. Before we could get safely harboured, a stiff gale again sprung up, and rendered this dangerous entrance still more fearful. We sprung our fore top-mast in the squall, but with a little tacking and trouble, we succeeded in getting safe anchorage in Lerwick harbour. We were riding here for a week, repairing the effects of the storm, and mustering our extra hands, which were usually supplied from the Shetland and Orkney Islands. Those hardy northmen were considered useful auxiliaries in the whale trade; for, inured to the inclemencies common to their sea-girt home, bred to the water, and particularly to the management of boats—as they have to fish for their living as soon as they are old enough to put off in a boat—they were consequently very useful to man the boats in the ice-bound seas of Greenland.

As usual on making a port, the anxiety was as to who would first be allowed to go on shore. The captain and his crew soon went ashore, and as many as could get leave followed. Meantime the harbour was peopled with small boats, with one or two of the islanders in each of them, pulling towards the vessels at anchor, all anxious to sell them fresh fish, eggs, and chickens, or to exchange them for salt beef, pork, or biscuit, cotton handkerchiefs, or other articles of wearing apparel; and although but a short time dieted on junk, the apprehension that we were to subsist six months on salt provisions, made their merchandise courted as a luxury.

To so young a traveller the town of Lerwick appeared extremely inviting, as viewed from the harbour. The houses on the water side were built principally of stone, and its sober grey colour seemed to repose quietly amidst the dark purple hills around it, while the whole mass was encircled by the dense grey sky, and the dark rolling waters of the bay.

The next day I had leave to go ashore, and was too near that grey and mysterious looking town, which, when contrasted with the piles of red brick I had been accustomed to look upon at home, appeared to be a large arsenal, or the outwork of some ancient city. Five minutes after landing was sufficient time to dispel this dream of castles, and to substitute the poverty-stricken reality of miserable cabins and ill-fashioned shops. The streets were narrow, and strewed with refuse. Companies of sailors, the greater part of them reeling drunk, were parading about, as if the island belonged to them. At the time when the Greenland sailors call here, particularly on the passage out, these islands are kept in a state of fermentation. The retailers of whiskey, the shop-keepers, fortune-tellers, and the loose females, which even here are found in numbers, keeping a sharp look-out upon the cash and whiskey of the sailors—all were intent upon making the most of "the southern boys" during their short stay; and to a considerable extent they succeeded; for with nine-tenths of the Greenlanders, if they can command plenty of grog, and a fresh sweetheart, it is the sum of their enjoyment.

One of my shipmates, who was to initiate me into the revelries of the island, took me to a whiskey shop. On my entering it, I was really afraid; never before had I seen such a stew, into which were huddled such a number of human beings. The place was one dense pit of smoke. In these cabins there were no chimneys: the fire, which is usually made of peat, smoulders away upon the mud floor in the ingle; the smoke pervades the whole area, and then lazily makes its escape from the door. The roof and walls of these "smithies" are as black as a moonless midnight in December. As I stood a few paces within this pitchy den, I trembled; my eyes were smarting with the effects of the turfy fire. Around the glimmer, in the ingle, were seated a troop of crones, attired in coarse grey woolsey petticoats; over their heads were thrown a dark plaid, just shewing their brown profiles; some of them were knitting; each had a short black pipe, blowing away their " 'bacca," and chattering in broad Gaelic. This shop was literally stowed with both sexes, the greater part of them sailors, some singing, others swearing coarse oaths. In the centre of the den, two of the tars were reeling with a dark-eyed island girl, to the drone of a bagpipe, driven by an old and lank-jawed piper, attired in a grey serge jacket, and leaning against the smutty wall. Here was such a commingling of the low and the ridiculous as I had never before witnessed—a strange-looking lot, dimly visible through the veil of peat-smoke, singing, roaring, yelling, dancing, and snapping their fingers, and stamping their feet to the mysterious " naw-a-aw-a" of the piper. I knew of no parallel to it. It was like to the entrance to the fabled pit of Acheron, and here were the infernals assembled, to yell over their hellish mysteries; yet the sailors called it fine pastime, and drained their pockets, and mortgaged the voyage to prolong it! There it was that I first tasted whiskey, and their liquid fire was not the best antidote to my fears. I swallowed the noggin, as I was ordered to do, at one draught; but as soon as I was able to caw, I cursed their " hell-broth," and then they accommodated the " southern" with a bottle of ale. I soon had an offer from an old wrinkle-faced witch, in figure as broad as she was long, to tell me my fortune, and to shew me, in mystic numbers chalked upon the wooden bench, the whole course of our voyage—whether we should be wrecked or not—how many fish we should have—and also to answer any question I might put to her. This was all to be done for the low charge of " saxpence and a noggin," which, considering the information to be imparted, was dog-cheap. No; I had not nerve to listen to the weird one, and really dreaded her devilries.

Lerwick, although sterile at first sight, has a wild grandeur about it, despite its want of trees and other verdure. The women were famous for knitting, and were untiring in seeking to make exchanges for their merchandise for articles from England, particularly cotton handkerchiefs and Staffordshire pots. So fine was the texture of some of their knitted stockings, that they boasted of being able to draw them through a wedding-ring.

After a short stay here, repairing our top-mast, taking our additional force, and other necessaries, we were again under weigh, and skimming along for our destination. After leaving the Shetland Isles, we were relieved from taking the regular watches. We became eight-bell men, and so enjoyed our bed through the night. Our duties were to have the harpoons, blubber knives, and lances all sharpened, re-handled, and in all respects made ready for " blubber-hunting." We had also to have all right for the boats, such as oars repaired, the stretchers to give elasticity to the men whilst pulling, all fitted in their places, and to overlook everything that pertained to the carpenters, previous to commencing the fishing. Our situation conferred other privileges on us: while the " men before the mast," line-coilers, and boat-steerers, were limited to the galley, as their place of recreation, we were admitted to the "half-deck." This place was the "sanctorum" of the second mate, the spikeoneer, or officer having the command of the harpoon chest, and next in command to the second mate, also of the harpooners, carpenters, coopers, boatswains, and all the secondary officers; and frequent were the petty jealousies, gibes, and sarcasms engendered by this division of parties. The half-deck men were indulged with their sea-pie on the Friday evenings, at eight o'clock. This savoury dish was made in layers, or decks: the first one of bones, to keep the paste from burning to the bottom of the pan; then followed strata of fresh beef, paste, and seasonings, deck after deck, until the great kettle was full; sufficient water was added to enable the mess to be cooked; and so much was this fresh mess courted, that the oldest sailor in the ship would turn out of bed to take his share of the pie. We had also the luxury of boiled flour puddings on the Sundays and Thursdays, with half a pint of ale on each occasion; and about once a month, we had an indulgence of about half a pound of cheese. These revellings were the exclusive privileges of a half-deck man.

Never was the insolence of caste more overbearing than in the half-deck bashaws of a Greenlander; and their pride of place, imperious as it was, was the best thing they had to boast of. True they were fishermen, many of them "lucky" ones; but beyond the mechanical, the sensual made up the rest. Their leisure hours were frittered away in low conversations; card-playing and a song were their higher qualifications. A book was a rare thing among them; one or two of the more serious would occasionally take a book on the Sunday, but they were exceptions. Little, indeed, in the way of seriousness, was to be expected from men whose ribald boast was the doggrel creed of—

> "Six days shalt thou work, and do all thou art able;
> On the seventh day wash the decks and scrub the cable."

To the commander's honour, this creed was but a Jack tar's boast. And who can "throw the hatchet" better than an old Greenlander? Although we often washed the decks on Sundays, we never had the toil of cable-scrubbing on the seventh day.

If the half-deck was not remarkable for its morality, the "galley" was sunk below the zero of coarseness; and in 1820 it might be said, that in a Greenland-man's galley, licentiousness sat enthroned! It was proverbial of those whose disregard of all decency called forth the animadversion of persons of more refined feelings, "Such an one was too low for a Greenlander's galley." It may be easily conceived what filth was continually flowing from such a polluted source.

One indulgence the whole ship's company held in common—that was, receiving our mess-pots, or drams, on Saturday night; then, every man was expected to drink to "Sweethearts and wives!" It was not unusual with many of the crew to save their drams until they had a bottle full, to enable them to treat with more liberality any friend that might board them during the voyage.

About the end of April we neared the fishing ground, or, to be more technical, "made the ice." At various times, the whale fish have been observed to change their locality, on each occasion going further northward, finding greater security against their common enemy amongst the large fields of never-thawing ice that accumulate around the pole. Thus the fishery has been rendered more and more dangerous, and the chances of reward proportionally less. With these disadvantages, the merchants of Hull clung to the whale trade, and despite of Government bounties, and all other appliances, the trade could not be kept up. Science has, however, stepped in between them, in this, as in hundreds of other instances; and gas-lighting has in a great measure superseded the uses of whale oil.

We kept up a cruize on the southern, or sea side of the ice, proceeding with caution up the country, waiting until the ice was more open, and filling up our time with seal-fishing.

Seal-killing is an uncomfortable business; those engaged in it having often to jump from one " hummock" of ice to another, in quest of their prey. These hummocks, or large fields of ice, detached from the main flaw, or land ice, are often very deceptive; when to appearance they are firm and dry, they are often covered two or three feet deep with loose ice, snow, and water: and in those freezing latitudes, jumping up to the middle in such a cold bath is not the most pleasant thing imaginable. It is said that necessity has no law; so it is here. Very few voyage to those seas for mere pleasure, and those who have done so, have found it of a roughish staple. In seal-fishing, the whole of the boats often leave the ship, taking the entire company, and leaving the vessel to the keeping of the doctor, the cook, and the cabin-boy. On reaching the ice, the crew divide themselves, each man taking a seal-club, an instrument prepared for their destruction. Thus armed, they plod their way over fields of snow after their game. To prevent the seals making their way to the water, the whole assembly keep up a regular yell, singing or shouting; for any noise, however terrific, is tolerated, that tends to amaze the animal. If the vessel be near enough to assist in the alarm, the bell is rung, or drums beat, or horns blown—anything to increase the din, and stupefy the sea-calf, which else would propel itself with all speed towards the water. If the seal once succeed in getting before his enemy ere he is "amazed," he throws such a trail of snow behind him with his fins and tail, as to render it impossible to follow him, thus insuring his escape to the edge of the flaw; he then throws himself into the sea, and defies capture. Hence the necessity of the "amaze;" and it is wonderful how the poor creature gazes with a vacant stare upon his butcher, and the louder the noise, the more the animal seems riveted to the spot; the fell blow is dealt upon his forehead, and if well aimed, seldom needs repeating. There is, however, one species very difficult to kill; this is called by the sealer the "bottle-nose," from the animal having the power to throw at will an inflated shield over his forehead, resisting the stroke of the seal-club in much the same way as a bladder when struck with a cane. This species are somewhat dangerous to encounter, and are not much sought after. The labour of seal-killing is very fatiguing; we had to capture one thousand of them, to make the reward equal to the taking of one "payable whale fish;" so to that part of the crew who were not paid by the ton, the toil was excessive. To the merchants, a great number, or fall, of seals, was of importance, seal oil being more valuable than that of the whale.

Since the time of our voyaging, I believe all who now venture in this hazardous enterprise are paid by the tonnage—a more equitable mode than by the fish; as all the small fish did not render the required length of bone, yet contained a certain portion of oil. The harpooners—the "arctic blubber kings"—were always paid by the liquid quantity, but all below them in grade were paid by the fish. To determine a payable fish, it was necessary that the largest blade of bone in the whale's mouth should measure twelve feet and one inch. The contention was often fierce between the payer and receiver, when, perhaps, a quarter of an inch would put a guinea into the fisher's pocket, or keep it out. The justice of the tonnage will be apparent; for if the capture were under size—albeit the toil of the fall was the same—the reward was wanting; nor had the sailors any pecuniary advantage in the vast quantity of whalebone procured, except in the oil that drained from it, and then only when paid by the ton. This bone, from its quantity, was of vast importance to the owners. Supposing the head of the whale to be one-third of the leviathan's length, and each side of his cavern-like head to contain three hundred bones, the weight of bone from each fish was commercially of great value; particularly so when it entered so largely into the various manufactures, as at one period it did—even to the ladies' bonnets, shoe bows, head dresses, and that tantalizing barrier, Pope's "seven-fold fence," the hoops of the last century belles! The bone in this monster mouth is a striking proof of the never-failing adaptation, and wonderful care of the Universal Parent; every blade of bone is fringed with a deep curtain of hair, and as the huge creature is not armed with teeth to masticate food, this curtain acts as a net-work, alike necessary to catch and rectify the mucid food that here studs the sea for its support. The head of an average sized whale is from fifteen to sixteen feet, as may be perceived by the jaw bones, that formerly were of such repute for ornamental gate-posts; in height it would be about twelve feet, the lips opening about six or eight feet; yet to such a mouth there is scarcely any throat, not sufficiently large to allow a herring to pass down it. This little scaly fellow, averaging not more than fourteen inches in length, is said to be able to choke the monster whale, which has been known to attain the length of sixty feet—hence the herring has been called " the king of the seas." Yet both these inhabitants of the briny deep have their uses, and each his sphere in his ocean home. Truly was it sung,

"In wisdom hast Thou made them all!"

May-day morning was made a rejoicing with the English ships in this land of eternal hoar and ice, and called the "Greenland fair!" As soon as midnight is turned, and blithe May begins her reign, the Greenlanders hoist the garland. This garland is a contribution of ribbons from every man and boy on board; a Greenland sailor would as soon think of going to sea without his pea-jacket, as to go without his garland ribbon! Before leaving home, the sweethearts of the single men usually present their beaus with a garland ribbon, and generally they present it at their farewell meeting, so that they are love-tokens. Upon each ribbon, the charmer ties as many knots as she wishes her lover's ship to bring home fish. Anciently, the lover was not permitted to count these knots until May-eve; if he told them before that hallowed night, the spell was broken, and the knots were of no avail. The married men often procure their garland ribbons from persons who are considered fortunate in this world of chances—as the blind god, "Fortune," it is expected will kindly extend his assistance to this knotty matter of the garland!

May morning is the time when the young voyager is to be admitted to the full honors of a true Jack tar; his probationary duties are to cease at the express command of Neptune himself, who directs him to be *shaven* according to his own heart. The novice has to make certain oblations of rum, coffee, sugar, or such agreeables as he can best spare! These Neptune generously gives up for the good of the crew. Upon the liberality of the probationist in the giving department depends, in a great measure, his comfort during the shave. This May-day shaving in the North, is twin-brother to the ceremony of shaving practised upon those who "cross the line" in warmer latitudes. The approach of Neptune is made known by a loud stamping of the crew upon the deck. Some old weather-beaten tar is dressed for the part, and amongst other requisites, he takes care to put on a tremendous long beard, made of horse-hair; he is also decorated with a mimic trident, and mounted upon a gun carriage. The made-up sea-god is now mounted on the forecastle, and the novices are there summoned to his presence! The hero expresses his joy at seeing them, and assures them of his great condescension in personally welcoming them to the seas of Greenland. He is then drawn around the deck, laying first the captain under contribution, then descending to the secondaries. During the triumphal progress of the tobacco-mouthed ocean-king, the garland is hoisted, and it usually remains until the vessel reaches home. When his godship is enthroned below deck, his myrmidons commence the ceremony of shaving. A large tub is provided, filled with water, across it a plank is placed (the barber's chair), upon which the luckless wight is seated to be shaved. Around his neck is twisted a wet swab—this swab is made of a great number of small yarns, tied together, and about four feet long; it is used for drying the decks after washing. This appendage is kindly ordered by the king to keep the lather out of your neck. Then follows the lathering with a compound of tar and other offensive ingredients. During this part of the ceremony, the prime operator is flourishing about for his razor, a large piece of iron hoop, set in a coarse wooden handle, and notched on the edge like a saw. When the shaving is about to commence, the noviciate is asked "what he is going to present to Neptune, as a remembrancer of his visit?" If the present be considered sufficient, then you "could not be sooner shaved in a barber's shop"—but, if it be a stingy one, then, poor fellow, he may expect the lather to be profusely applied—the plank drawn off the tub, and a cold duck into it to wash off the lather; and to be used rather roughly into the bargain.

My propitiation was a bottle of contraband whiskey, bought at Lerwick for that purpose, according to my father's direction, whom experience had well schooled in these matters.

We had an old man-of-war's-man on board, and this was his first voyage to the northern seas; being an old sailor, he would not pay tribute to our holiday-king of the "liquid empire;" the poor fellow was consequently severely shaven and ducked; he was held down by brute force, his strength and protestations being alike unheeded and powerless. When the shaving ceremony was over, our revel was continued with grog, tea, coffee—with any thing refreshing that our situation placed at disposal. One of our Shetlanders played the fiddle, while some were dancing to it; others amused themselves with singing, and telling stories of by-gone May-morn revels enjoyed in that sterile country of eternal ice. Jollification prevailed until about eight o'clock A.M. when a voice from the "crow's nest" proclaimed that there was "fish blowing to windward." All hands were now on the look-out; up to that time we had not seen a fish, and we were extremely anxious to be amongst them. The vessel was worked into the direction from whence the noise proceeded. The blowing of the whale-fish can be heard to a considerable distance, particularly when the wind is down; it can then be heard for several miles. About ten o'clock we saw some fish lying at two or three miles distance. The parties that were interested were anxious to be off after them, but it was thought advisable to work the ship nearer to them; at last, a young man, who had come out as harpooner for the first time, and who was impatient to try his hand, put off with a boat's crew. The old whalers saw little prospect of a strike, and they proved themselves good judges on that occasion, for the fish took to flight before he could approach them. This excitement renewed our hope, and the watch in the "crow's nest" was kept up with vigilance. This crow's nest is a small room constructed of staves, something like an empty cask, fitted up with seats and other conveniences, to allow the person on watch to look out, and be partially protected from the frost. The watch is often continued for two hours, and in extreme cases for a longer time.

We soon had the pleasure of being actively and successfully engaged in the chase. For some time the weather became calm, and not so advantageous, for the stroke of the oars was heard in the water, before the boat could be got near enough for the steersman to scull upon the fish; however, we were in "the ground," for we could hear them blowing from every point of the compass—we tried the gun-harpoon, but with no better success.

Nothing can exceed the magical effect of those seas when the weather is clear, calm, and sunshiny. There are seasons of the purely beautiful, as well as the sublimely grand, on the waters of Greenland: these "clock-calms" belong to the former. It is a never-to-be-forgotten sight, to observe the sun running his diurnal course, yet never setting, a season of continued daylight—the glittering ocean stretching as far as the eye can reach, lying as placid as a polished mirror, not a ripple to stir the broad expanse, save the skimming of the gulls, and the sports of thousands of sea-birds—the water spangled with innumerable stellated rays from the "pancake ice," that even in the blazing sun is ever freezing. These jets are reflected and refracted over the whole bosom of the ocean, which lies bathed in glory like the resplendence of the solemn heaven, when it is over-gemmed with its myriads of stars. On one hand of us, a cluster of "unicorns" at play;—the sailors attach the name of "unicorn" to these fish, from the long twisted horns that protrude from the head of the males, often eight feet long. These many-coloured creatures, partaking of all conceivable hues, from deep sea-green to the most intense lake-colour, lie frolicking in groups in perfect security, laughing at every attempt we made to approach them. The calm weather was their defence also, for long before we could get within shot of them the sound of our pulling was heard, and with the speed of lightning they buried themselves in the deep, but soon appeared again at a distance, mocking our toil. There too, the long "flaws of ice," and detached frozen islands, so cold and cheerless in stormy weather, were now floating, all white, and light with the sun, and dotted about with seals, whose hoarse bark was answered by the ill-natured growl of the bears, that were pacing along the edge of the flaws—sometimes putting off, as if determined to feast upon the savoury food they could scent on board the vessel—then returning again, and giving vent to their disappointment by a loud roar. The refulgence of such a sun-lit scene may be conceived, but I have no power for its expression. To the contemplative mind it presents an overwhelming grandeur, that imperceptibly steals over the whole frame, until the senses are lost in wonder and delight! In this calm we lay drifting with the current a day or two—often towing the vessel for some hours together, to keep her clear off the hummocks of ice that were floating about. We were next gratified with the springing up of the breeze, as we expected soon to have a stroke at some of the black shining whales that were lying like islands of jet in the green ocean.

All but the watch on deck were snug in bed, when, for the first time, I was alarmed with the strange cry of "A fall! a fall!" accompanied by loud knocking upon the deck with handspikes, and at the same time stamping with their feet, which singular noise reverberates from cabin to cabin like distant thunder. I had, in some measure, prepared myself for this tumult, by listening to the conversation of the men about the modes of fishing, but I found it more wild than I had conceived it to be, especially when, for the first time, you are awakened by it out of a sound sleep.

The Greenland sailors always sleep in their drawers and stockings, and have their remaining clothes tied together with a "gasket," and hung up conveniently, near to their bed-cabin door, to allow of them being caught hold of in an instant. As soon as the strange shout of "A fall" is heard, every man is expected to jump up, seize his bundle of clothes, and rush on deck, and into the boats, which are immediately "lowered away," and pulled, with all the energy the men can summon, towards the boat which has already "got fast," or, in other words, the one which has first harpooned the fish. As soon as the boats are got under weigh, the crew put on their clothes by turns—putting on one article of dress, and then pulling until your mate has put on one also, and so on whilst all are dressed; the crew have often to go for several miles before that is completed. This is one of the exposures to cold and frost that cannot be well provided against; inasmuch, as the labour at the oars must go on, as well as the clothing. It is considered contemptible to be amongst the last boat's crew "let down;" to be the last man, two or three times in succession, at a fall, is quite enough to stamp the fellow "a lubber," so the rush to the boats, and the consequent oaths and cuffing may be imagined.

Well, this is our first fish! The harpoon is buried deeply within, and holds on firmly; the union-jack is hoisted in the boat as a signal that they have struck a whale. The signal is answered by hoisting another flag at the mizen-mast head of the ship. The fall is called—the men are up, the boats are lowered away—only two or three hands are left on board to manage the vessel—and those who are left, are of the least account in the fishing business. The surgeon is one of them that is left; he is more used to pills than oars; true he knows the use of a lance, but it is one that he has folded in a neat velvet case, and put into his coat-pocket—he cannot be expected to wield a large steel one, with a handle of coarse fir-wood, and six feet long. No! the operation is too rough for the doctor, so he may stop on board, and get the grog ready for the hands on their return; he can manage to serve out drachms, although some professionals have their scruples! The cook may stop,—he is old, and fat, and podgey; up to the elbows in grease and tit-bits. The cook is in favour with all hands, for he can accommodate them with a spoon-full of fat to fry their pan-mince with. Yes! every one gives the cook a good word, and yet, they know not why, they have always a sneer at hand to give to the "slushy devil." However, he is best on board—more useful at the coppers than in the boats; let him stop to keep the doctor company! One or two others stop with them, the rest are off with the boats.

Hilloa! the fish they have struck is off at a terrible speed by the waste of line; she is going at from eight to ten miles per hour! "Pull, lads! pull for your lives, or we shall lose her. See! they put up an oar—it is a signal that their lines are running fast—one is already gone. Again they signal! a second oar is up! Pull, my brave fellows, or they will lose her! Lay-to, my hearties! another oar!—a third line is gone—a fourth! Pull, my good fellows, pull!" Old Ben is pulling for the second harpoon. See! how keenly he glances from under his large grey-arched brow, and how he measures every boat's length as he flies through the water. See! the ice dashes over his prow, and how it flies at every stroke of the oar as they rend the icy-veil of the deep. "We are as near to her as he is; pull, my boys! lay on right sadly, and we will contest the second throw with him." The "fast boat" is flying through the lipping wave, the fish is going too quick to allow the boat to rise over the surge, for the wounded monster is impelled by rage, and will not allow the boat to ride over the billow, so she must even go through it. The distress increases; a few minutes and every line is gone out from the boat! The fish will be lost, and with her seven hundred fathoms of line, for if they hold on longer, they will be dragged down by the mighty force of the animal. Bravo, Old Ben! he has beat us, he is up in time to rescue them; he is "spliced on." The fish is mad with pain, yet she lacks not of her speed! Ben's lines are out, and a third spliced on. "Ha! ha! my lads, she winds, she has taken to the flaw! We must dodge her until she comes out, she cannot long remain under the ice without coming out to breathe—she must either find a blow-hole in the flaw, or else come out again. How now?" A rare, but not an isolated occurrence, she has died on one harpoon, and without rising again. The old spikesman says, "she has killed herself by her furious diving under the flaw." He knows more of the philosophy of whaling than a greenhorn, and I must believe him, whether I will or no. The old blubber hunters are adepts at teaching a "you must" system of philosophy. The fish is dead, but the toil is greater than it would have been had she died by the lance. As it is, we need the power of windlasses to haul her to the surface. Cold and freezing as it is now, every inch of line we draw up is converted into a cable of ice. Tug on, brave hearts, the harpoon holds in, the withers have cleft her tendons, and it is firmly lashed within her—time and stout hearts will soon have her up, and tow her alongside "The Duncombe."

A day or two intervened before our second fall. We are again on the look out. A fish is blowing ahead of us—hark! how the thin ice crackles as they cleave it with their firm stroke! She blows again! The water flies from the animal's nostrils full twenty feet high, mingling with the foggy air, then falling to the sea again, like the silvery mist of a fountain. "Lay to, my hearties!" There is a slight breeze, and a swell upon the water; if we can get near her, the swell is in our favour, for the whale was not fashioned for quick hearing. See how she looms like an island of sea-coal, piled up in the ocean! "Now, boys, steady! Hush! not a word. Keep the lines clear—not a breath! rest on your oars. Now, boat-steerer, scull gently upon her—another moment, and I'll bury these steel withers deep in her 'kreng.' Cease sculling, we shall be upon her. Now, now for a stroke! It is gone, firm, firm into her vitals! Back water, boys, we are fast! a fall! a fall! up with the jack!" They answer us from the ship, and already the boats are down. "Keep clear of the line. See! what a cloud of white smoke issues from the bollard, as the line runs round it. More water on it, lads, or it will fire. Keep clear of the lines, for if they entangle you, you are dead men in a minute!" The fish, smarting with the stroke of the harpoon, has made a furious dive; the boat skims after her, and is enveloped in a shower of spray, her velocity is so great. The boats' men are plying every nerve, and straining each sinew, to get in another harpoon. There is always great danger that one may give way, or that the fish may exhaust the whale-lines from one boat, before a second can get up. So, right onward, boys! we are near to her; don't you observe her oily track through the water? the sea gulls perceive it—see how they follow in her wake, and are ready to pull the skin from her back, as soon as she rises again. See, she is up! now for another harpoon. Confusion! we have over-pulled her. She has risen under the boat, and the great blubber-mountain has upset it; all are thrown out, and into the water. Each man grasps his oar, if possible, to buoy him up in the sea. They are swimming and struggling with the waves, and for a moment the chase is forgotten in the wrestle for life. They are whirled round in the funnel-shaped sea-trough that the animal has made in her second dive in the ocean. A boat is pulling to the rescue of the stranded men— they are saved! They are drenched with water, and the frost is intense, but there is no time to admit of returning. The boat is righted, and the men must take part again in the whale-hunt. Some of the boats, in the meantime, have held straight onward. The cunning whale-fish has taken to the ice; never-failing instinct has directed her to her only hope of safety; she may there disengage herself from the harpoon, or the sharp ice-crags may strand the line, and let her escape. The ice-field is a large one—she has found a breathing place; far over its surface there is an ocean-lake, all ice-begirt. "Hark! she blows again; the breath of her nostrils sounds like the bursting of a water-spout. We must pursue her, although the track is over hills of ice and hummocks of frozen ice-rock." The boats are hauled upon the flaw, and the crews are untiringly launching them over the rugged face of the snow-field. They have to drag for miles over the surly field. Are they tired? What if they are? they must not even think of it, much more complain—for to name it would be rank mutiny against the blubber lords! So tug on, brave hearts! plash, plash, through knee-deep lakes of half-thawed ice; it freezes keenly, and soon your trousers will make shields of icicle. "We shall kill her yet, and then my brave fellows, if she measures well, you shall have twenty shillings and a mess-pot of rum; if she is not full-size-bone, you must hope for better luck next time; and be content to know, that whether she measures or not, the merchant will get his scores of pounds—tug on, brave hearts, we shall kill her yet!" High ho! for full six hours have we been dragging the boats over the snow to gain yonder lake in the heart of the flaw, and now we find that all the while the current has been working silently against us, and after all our labour, we are as far from it as when we started. Look at yon "dreadnought" harpooner, tracking his way through slush and ice, harpoon in hand, determined to have a throw at her; and the crew are following him as resolutely with the boat—the old harpooner has been heard to say, that "a chance blow might kill the devil," so he is resolved not to throw a chance away. A great toil it is to take this leviathan in his ocean home; hour after hour of fatigue he has given us; but courage! there must be no laggards here—if you but dare to wink, the boatswain has sworn to administer props to keep your eyes open. A poor Shetlander, hardy as he was, born in the gale, and cradled in the biting North, has sunk beneath the task; he laid him down upon a bank of snow; sleep, that had long been a stranger to his eyes, at length overcame him. He was not missed for a short season, but when his mess-mate saw him coiled up upon the drift, he hastened to awake him; he knew the danger of sleeping in such a situation; he shook him by the collar, and bade him arouse up. Alas! life had spent its last effort—fatigue had wrestled with him, sleep had come to his rescue—but it was the long sleep of death!

The ice, which during our pursuit had been continually shifting, now opened, and admitted the vessel up to us, and grog was served out to each man. The wounded whale-fish was uneasy, and writhing under the pain of the harpoon, which, fortunately for us, held firmly in her sinews, and now she began to shift her ground.

The boats' crews are all on the alert. The fish is out again, and the chase is renewed. She is surrounded by her enemies—two or three harpoons are quickly driven into her flesh! She pauses, and she is well watched, for all the sailors are animated with the prospect of taking the creature. The lances are thrust into her every time she visits the surface—exhaustion is doing its work for she rises frequently. "Now, boys, she weakens, this is the time—another home thrust. Ply her well with your lances, we shall prevail—see she blows up blood and water mingled together. Follow up your success; again she blows; it is nearly all blood this time." The men are drenched, and the sea is stained with her gore. "Keep a sharp look out with your boats, lest in her agony she strike them with her fins or tail, and swamp you with the stroke." She quivers again. Mark how she lashes the sea with her fins in her rage! Again a shower, all blood; her efforts are vain; her foes are inexorable. She gives a last furious death struggle, and with mad fury she lashes the sea with her tail, and writhes in her torture until she makes a whirlpool around her. Caution, or she will have us under her! In her desperation she has struck a boat on the gunwale, and cut it in two with a convulsive stroke of her tail. It is a perilous situation for the crew, for the boat is instantly filled with water; the men are taken out, and put into the other boats, and all are saved. Now this ponderous ocean-ranger yields to the iron goad of the pursuers—she turns on her side—and dies. A loud hurrah closes the chase, and a signal is made to the ship that she is captured.

When the whale is dead, she is suspended between the boats, and towed along to the ship, where the dead animal is moored, until the business of cutting-up, or "flensing" can be accomplished.

The white bears, which are found in great numbers in those seas, generally scent a dying fish, and approach as near as their courage will permit. As we were towing the whale we had just killed towards the vessel, one of these prowling rascals made signs, by following the boat, putting off from the ice, and other indications, that he should like to have a mouthful of the dead fish. He followed us for a considerable distance, sniffing the air, and growling and roaring with all his might. At last he swam to a large field of ice, that was stretching up in the direction we were rowing; along this field bruin ran with all speed to the farthest verge of it. There he turned his face to us again, and kept up a continued growl, now and then swelled into a loud roar. As we neared the spot where *ursus* was stationed, he increased his bellowing, and gave evident signs of discontent. He soon plunged into the sea, and made towards us with a menacing look, growling more loudly as he approached us. He then made a furious attack upon one of the boats, laying his paws upon the prow, and raising his head considerably above the water; then, as if he had some misgiving, he let go his hold, and turned a short distance from us. Again he advanced with redoubled anger, and again he laid his paws upon the boat's gunwale. At that instant one of the crew made a firm stroke at his paws with a line-axe, and dissevered one of them, which fell into the boat; simultaneously with the stroke of the axe, another of the men gave bruin a desperate blow upon the head. The bear made a rush at the man who struck last, but the pain from the blow of the axe appeared to annoy him, for he paused to lick his wound, and then sank into the sea. He soon rose again, and turned his back upon us, making for the ice, but not without several times turning round to look at us, and on each occasion giving a fierce growl, as if to curse us for depriving him of a meal, and lopping off his paw at the same time.

Many singular anecdotes are related of the capture of the white bears of Greenland, and of the narrow escapes of the sailors from their fury. I remember one that for a long time afforded merriment to the sailors of Hull. Although it may be no joke to be hugged by an infuriated polar bear, we often regard things as a joke to others, which applied to ourselves would be death. Like the boys in the fable of the frogs, if we have but the fun of pelting the stones of derision at an unfortunate wight who is plunged in the slough of difficulty, we seldom care about the pain we cause him.

One of the fishing captains who had sailed many years from Hull, had been so generally successful in his adventures as to be ranked amongst the *lucky ones*; but in addition to his success in fishing, he possessed his full share of tyranny; for these Greenland chiefs were mostly austere. If things ran smooth for a few seasons together, their vanity made them imagine they were something more than mortal. Captain M—— was a fine specimen of these absolute arctic sea-kings; and one year, when at Davis' Straits, and out in a boat, a large bear attacked them. He seized the captain by the jacket, and dragged him out of the boat, immediately descending with him into the sea; however, he soon rose again near to the place, with the captain still firmly clasped to his head. On rising a second time, one of the sailors had the presence of mind to seize hold of a "piggin," and strike the bear over the head; the animal immediately released his hold of the captain, and made a rush at the sailor who struck him. This circumstance gave them an opportunity of pulling the master into the boat; the rest of the crew kept on their guard, and thus they escaped the fury of bruin.

The superstitious sailors did not scruple to assert that the attack of the bear upon Captain M—— was an especial warning of Providence, and that Ursus was a type of the arch-enemy, who was sent to give the tyrant a glimpse of his fiery possessions, and then to bring him back again, and allow him time to repent of his arbitrary conduct. How far the captain coincided with their opinions was never understood; one thing is certain, that the captain had a narrow escape; and it is said that he never put himself within the grasp of the dreaded one again; but ever after his landing, he kept himself snug on *terra firma*, where, as the sailors say, "There is always a back door to escape through."

When a Greenland sailor is in full dress, he has generally as many folds of woollen round his body as a mummy has swathes of sere-cloth: he has two or three shirts, flannel and striped cotton, two pairs of stockings, worsted or flannel drawers, two pairs of trousers, two waistcoats, an under jacket and pea-jacket, two or three pairs of mittens, and a wig of lambs-wool, which fits so closely around the head, that little more than the face is exposed, and the tar peeps through his bale of clothing like an owl from the scooped orifice in a five-century grown oak. Such a load in any other clime would be very cumbrous; but there it is absolutely called for, by the high latitude and eternal frost. During our voyage, we had a painful instance of inattention to the regulations enjoined as to the severity of the climate, or rather it was the contempt of it. The old man-o'-war's man before named, was, in common with the rest of the watch, ordered aloft to close-reef the main top-sail; a nipping "sou'-wester" was blowing briskly, accompanied by sleet and hailstones; he had just stepped upon the ratlines, when he discovered he had left his mittens, which he had just taken off, and laid upon the main-hatches. He was advised to return for his gloves, but he would not, and took an opportunity of sneering at those lubberly "north-men;" and with more than his usual braggadocio, was amongst the first to reach the yard. Before the sail was half stowed, he felt the frost had seized his hands so severely, that before he could get down again, the pain was so acute as to force tears from him. He was immediately sent down to the surgeon, but he was so seriously "frost-bitten," as to render his hands useless for a great part of the voyage; and it required the constant care of the surgeon to effect a cure, as, for several days after the accident, mortification was feared.

The operation of "flensing" consists in cutting the fish into junks of a convenient size, to be hoisted up by the capstan into the vessel. This, as well as killing the fish, is a dirty business; and for that part of their duty the sailors put on an old dress, usually so patched, that it would be difficult to find a "ragman" in the home market that would speculate threepence upon it. This dress is mostly thrown overboard when the season is over. When all is prepared for taking in the fish, the harpooners go down upon it, and to aid their footing, they affix an iron instrument, armed with long points, into their boots; these they call spurs. Assisted by their spurs, they commence cutting with their long blubber-knives, and the fat is sent up in large junks, which is again cut into smaller pieces by another set of men, called "kings," and then thrown into the vessel's waist, where it waits for a further opportunity of final stowing. Often, in good fishing years, particularly if the weather be stormy, "the waist" is so full of blubber as to prevent a passage between decks, unless one chooses to scramble his way over the top of the lumps of fat.

As soon as convenient, the blubber is again taken on deck, and cut into pieces small enough to allow of its passing through the bung-holes of the casks. For this process fine weather is chosen, for in a swell, the danger from the knives is very great, and a great deal of time is required, as all the casks have to be taken on deck, to begin with the bottom tier, and so on upwards. If there are two or three fish to be cut up at the same time, the men have to follow on the business, as no sleep can be allowed until all is stowed in and the decks cleaned up. The whale ships are not so unpleasant with respect to smell, as might be expected from their wholesale trade in blubber. It is not before the ships get into "warm weather" that they begin to smell. Great caution is necessary during the flensing, that no part of the "kreng" gets into the casks, for when that is the case, and the vessel arrives where the sun has power, the casks burst. We experienced disagreeable smells with the fermentation of the "kreng" that had unavoidably got into the casks, and burst them. After the fat is cut from the carcass, the "kreng" becomes the prey of the bears and sharks, who are waiting, often in great numbers, anticipating the feast. The flocks of gulls are so numerous, that during the "flensing," they are often knocked down with the oars and boat-hooks. Flights of kittywakes, parrots, and boatswain birds hover around, all waiting to take their share of the booty.

Amongst other amusements, the sailors are anxious to possess, as relics of the voyage, preserved specimens of bears' paws, seals, fins, sharks' teeth, and also of making stay bones for their " wives and sweethearts;" the whalebone they purloined from the blades that had been taken during the voyage. As my estimate of the rights of property had not been corrected, though, perhaps, I was not temptation proof, I was often employed in what the sailors dignified by the title of " bone carving," which art consisted in cutting on the bone, with a penknife, divers cyphers of the initials of their sweethearts, with borders of diamonds, squares, and vandykes, or " tooth ornaments;" the interstices were filled up with chalk and oil, which brought out the pattern; as, in addition to the given round of ornaments, I could add panels of whales, ships, birds, and the Prince of Wales' feathers—the latter was a stock ornament at that period; besides, if it had not been so, what tar, in 1820, could be so disloyal as to forget the Prince Regent, afterwards George the Fourth, of "*pious memory*?" For these ornate decorations I received sundry mess-pots of grog.

When we found the fish were fled, or if now and then we could see them, they were so wild that we could not get near to them; our skipper decided that we should penetrate further up into the country. There the ice set in all around us, and for several days we were completely blocked up with it. From the vessel's deck and the mast head, as far as the glass could carry the eye, all was one grey dreary waste of ice and snow: the only living thing to be seen, except those on board the vessel, was a prowling bear, or an occasional visit from a sea-gull. We soon became uneasy in our ice-bound bed, and the vane was closely watched; every veer of it was a messenger of hope in this haggard and solitary place—for we had not drunk so deeply of the spirit of enterprize as to render all thought of home, and life a secondary consideration, We were now locked up at the mercy of the wind and the ice-rocks. Patience and reliance upon the All-wise were our comforters; at last a report from the mast-head spoke of water to be seen far to the southward; and in earnest we began to try to improve our chance of escape, by sawing the ice around the vessel. We had been driven to this expedient many times during our stationary position in this ice field, lest by the extreme pressure the flaw should be forced through the sides of the vessel. It was a weary toil to work the ice-saws, although we had not to quarrel about rank, for we were all " top-sawyers;" two or three saws were at work at once, with four, and sometimes eight men at each saw. When the ice was rent by the wind, and we had enlarged our dock by sawing, we found an outlet, which we had to improve by towing in the boats, and next box-hauling, until we were again favoured with room to work the vessel; but we did not get away without our "ice-knees" being severely rent, and shattered by repeated shocks from the floating masses of ice. Towards the end of July the weather was severe; dense fogs lasted for hours together, so humid that we could not see from stem to stern-post; such an atmosphere rendered our situation dangerous; if any vessels were near, we could not discern them. To mitigate this evil, we kept up a regular tolling of the bell, and firing of muskets: but our greatest danger was the apprehension that some of the shocks from the drifting ice-bergs might stave our barque. Frequently those concussions were so sudden, as to throw us flat upon the deck with the shock. Then the rain would drench down in torrents, steeping the watch with the flood, the ropes all frozen, and hung with icicles like the dome of a stalactite cavern; and every time we handled them to work the vessel, the ice fell upon us, cutting our cheeks with the frozen points, and almost blinding us with hoar frost. In such weather it is impossible to imagine anything more dreary than that country of never-ceasing ice and snow, with a dense grey sky so humid, that the vessel's top-gallants were lost in it. The sea and ice commingled grimly, threatening destruction with every heave of the vessel—a crew, with all their assumed hardiness, vacantly gazing upon each other every time those eternized ice-fields threatened to engulph us in a cold sea-grave, was indeed a picture of cheerless, and well nigh hopeless endurance. The mists and rain gave place to clear blue sky, so clear, that not even a white speck of cloud could be seen to dapple the immense arch—and the wind was " blowing great guns." This change for a while seemed pregnant with danger; for although we could now see to " tack the vessel," and thus endeavour to avoid the ice-bergs that were drifting with the wind, which was blowing dead in upon the " land-ice," it was evident that every time we put the ship " about," that we were nearer to the " pack." We knew that a Dutch vessel, which was no longer able to stand out, had taken to the " ice-pack," and was well nigh split to pieces; the crew were saved by rushing to the flaw; but with the exception of life, all else were lost; we were not sure of such a reception, were we at once to follow their example, and run for the " pack."

I have often thought of the impiety of our galley heroes in that storm, creatures who, on ordinary occasions, affect to despise all sentimental feelings as lubberly and effeminate—who dealt out oaths and blasphemous epithets, as spontaneously as rain-clouds give forth showers—whose foolhardiness would fain induce the belief that they were danger-proof; but, whenever hope was failing, their vain boasting evaporated, and they longed for a place of safety. We had on board a Methodist, who, during this storm, resigned himself to continual prayer, audibly invoking Divine protection, as he was employed in his marine duties. In their extremity of fear, these very fellows now poured their commissions as thick as the storm upon this placid Methodist, each imploring him to pray for them. He, who controls the winds and the waters, shielded us in the hour of peril; the winds were hushed, and our vessel was still floating safely over the deep; and those very fear-stricken creatures, that but twenty-four hours previously had intreated the prayers of a ship-mate, were again loading him with irreligious epithets.

The season was now over; we had taken seven fish. The long black night of a Greenland winter began to throw its dark pall over the sea. We "bore up," and as precipitately we "bore away" from that cheerless country, which lies veiled in everlasting frost around the pole, with hearts beating high with the hope of again meeting our friends and loved ones in our native country, where the copse-wood sings to the breeze, and the golden corn-fields shout "plenty" from their luxuriant gardens, all glad with laughing sun-light.

In the year in which we visited the Arctic Seas (1820) an attempt was made by Captain Scoresby, of Whitby, to introduce a new mode of taking the whale-fish, by driving congreve rockets into them; as far as killing them was concerned, this plan answered well, for the explosion of the rocket blew them to pieces. The invention had one great defect,—after the fish was killed, there was nothing whereby she could be secured for those who had killed her,—hence, the dead fish became fair game for anybody that might hereafter pick her up.

I was a bad sailor, for up to the time of our making Lerwick, on our return, I was never wholly free from sea-sickness. While new sailors are generally cured of this painful ocean companion after they have been out a few days, and renewed vigour enables them to mount their "sea-legs" for the rest of the voyage, I had to battle with its distressing effects to the last. Many a time in the hour of suffering, while prostrated with the pain, I resolved that, if ever my feet were allowed to again clasp the flagged path-ways of the streets of Hull, I would "swallow the hand-spike," and leave the green sea to those who were so fond of singing—while in a tavern,—

"I love the sea, I love the sea!
I am where I would ever be!"

to enjoy themselves to their hearts' content, in their watery choice.

The Greenland trade may be considered one of pure adventure, too uncertain to be relied on as a source of national wealth. It might enrich a company of speculators, especially when that could be done at the expense of the many. The lottery seekers in the whale trade were as clamorous for their "protection" as the redoubtable corn-lords; and it has been calculated, that the "government bounty" to the Greenland trade, cost this country from 1750, to its extinction in 1824, no less a sum than two-and-a-half millions of money! Another illustration of taxed commerce: and we may question whether the country was ever benefited to that amount, by being compelled to contribute to the wealth of a particular class of lamp-oil merchants. If we had trimmed the lamp of science with some of the money, our dark ways might have been enlightened much sooner than they were; and it would not have remained for Lord Byron to have said (as reported), when told that a project was on foot for lighting London with gas, "That of all the Utopian schemes he had ever heard, that of lighting a large city with smoke was the most ridiculous." There is no question, that with all the government appliances of bounty, my native town has not flourished as a large sea-port, in proportion to some others, notwithstanding its advantages and its antiquity. Various mercantile pursuits that have enriched other ports, have there been neglected. Nothing was thought to be so advantageous as blubber. The trade to the Mediterranean was scarcely tolerated. Trials were made of the East and West India trade, but never prosecuted with half the vigour bestowed on blubber.

P

The American trade, which alone would make Liverpool a great port, was of secondary import where blubber prevailed.

All the capital that could be raised was sunk in a precarious venture to catch whales, and the specious bounty of the government. The government grew tired, and the whales grew careful, and at last they shielded themselves in with danger, presenting peril as the best reward to any body that was reckless enough to follow them; and the speculators were left to find out, that gas-houses could generate brilliant illuminations, and the people could dispense with the especial paternal care of government for lamp-oil and whale-bone.

CHAPTER VI.

BEGINNING THE WORLD.

On my return to Hull in September, 1820, I found employment in my business of shipwright to be very slack. For nearly three months I had to live upon the remnant of my voyage, and eventually, upon my parents, although they could scarcely keep themselves. I saw no chance of present labour, except by taking to the sea again. My former vow to stick by the land was given up, as a rash one, which circumstances could afford to break. Indeed, like the sailors themselves, I became very valiant on land, and could discourse of the briny deep with a considerable share of self-importance, particularly when I was seated with a pipe of tobacco and two or three old neighbours about me, who, at every strange assertion, gave it as their decided opinion that that very sea voyage had made a man of me! I now determined, if the waves were to be braved again, that I would try a change of climate, instead of mingling with obscene blubber-hunters, in a country where vegetation was a stranger—where no human being was to be seen, except the semi-naturalized crew who annually sought that savage clime, until their manners became as rugged as the haggard snow cliffs that crusted its face. After anxious inquiry, and pacing round the docks day after day, for weeks together, I got an engagement for Calcutta, as carpenter's mate. The promise of employment filled both my parents and myself with new life, for my mother's health was daily declining. Incessant toil at the wash-tub, for a meagre pittance, and the prospect of increasing poverty, from the lack of employment for my father, were making sad inroads upon a constitution, which, under more favourable circumstances, might have battled bravely with fatigue. Misfortune stuck closely by her, day by day, for nine or ten years—disease and famine were tugging at her heart-strings; during that period she had patiently to pine, and silently to watch gaunt hunger scooping out her grave. The hope that one of the family would be provided for a few months longer, was a temporary relief, and threw a gleam of joy into our two-roomed cottage.

Strange things happen in this chequered life. Important as it appeared to be that I should take another voyage, both inclination and necessity agreed that I *must* go. I had articled, and made all safe, yet I could not get off. It was not that my former dislike to the sea had thrown its sickly spell over me, and frightened me. No! hope was strong enough to lay that demon. There was a cause—one that, whether hunger said "You must," or future prosperity said, "Now, or never," was alike regardless of consequences, and was incessantly whispering to my heart, "Christopher, my boy, you shall not go to Calcutta." A fig for whisperings! I was not going to lose such a chance, for a something, I knew not what. There would be no icebergs at Calcutta. All the romance which my former trip awakened, and which vanished with a glimpse of the picturesque in our rugged fishing island, Lerwick, would in the Indies be realized. In the East, there was every-thing to feed the imagination. There, sun-climbing groves of palm were towering in unconceived majesty—gorgeous mimosa-plumes were nodding in Oriental grandeur—temples and minarets were watching over incense-breathing bowers of myrtle and acacia—glowing costumes, cast in graceful contour, were teaching lessons of beauty to all who chose to learn them—deep-flowing, majestic rivers were hymning the anthem that the Eternal One sang in the morning of creation, "Let there be light"—strange animals, beneath whose ponderous tread the interlaced jungles groan—magnificent birds, whose glories mock the iris, and flies whose meteor train makes for themselves an everlasting day—with myriads of untold wonders—were all there, to feed the youthful fancy, and amply reward the toil of journeying to them! What, then, had the power to prevent me going to Calcutta? Why, a little, bright-eyed, rosy-cheeked, black-haired girl, who, despite of interest—aye, or poverty—had promised herself to be Mrs. Christopher in January next. And was it to be done so easily? "Oh!" said Mr. Caution, "surely you will not stop at home in this season of scarcity, when you have such a prospect before you, and lose it, merely to get married?—at a time, too, when you have neither a home, nor the means to purchase one?" I put the question gravely to myself;

and, whether it was sympathy towards the charmer, that said "I should not go," or whatever else, may be guessed; but the answer my heart gave to it was "Yes!" Mrs. Prudence asked, "in all sincerity," if I thought that a boy of twenty ought to throw himself into the fangs of poverty, and clog all his future prospects, merely to indulge an unchecked passion? That was a grave question, and as gravely I put it; and my heart answered, "that it had no room for such crabbed considerations." My grandfather shook his silver curls, and wondered what was the matter with the lad! He "was afeard his head was turned." My grandmother held up both her hands, took off her spectacles, and laid them upon the large open Prayer Book, and ejaculated, "I could not be right—I knew not what ailed me." I was not well, but it occurred to me that they did not understand my complaint; so, having no faith in their prescriptions, I refused to take their medicinal advice. As it appeared to the crones of our neighbourhood that self-will was the prompter in this matter, and that wilful people were always their own enemies, as a last resource Mrs. Save-all proposed that I should get married, and then take the voyage. "Oh!" said she, "there would be a nice handful of money to set up housekeeping with!" So, obediently, I asked myself how I should like to get married one day, and take a twelve-months' voyage the next? I had nearly offended myself by asking that question. "What!" said my heart: "leave a young wife for twelve months, after experiencing twelve hours of matrimony! What must the creature be made of, that could do it?" The answer was, "Brass and granite!" Love and poverty were the last to try the issue; the contest was brief, and—love prevailed!

The wedding was fixed, but my resources were not improved. Entreaty with my parents was in vain; they had drained the lees of poverty's cup, and felt it their duty to warn their son of its miserable effects. There might be truth in the adage, that when "Poverty enters the cottage door, love flies out at the window;" and they believed it to be good counsel to bid me wait until matured years should bring discretion, and better times would help the pot to boil.

Time never tires. We were regularly asked "three times" in the Holy Trinity, and I took especial care to be there in proper person, to hear if any one "had just cause or impediment" to offer. In that particular we passed undisturbed. There is an advantage for youth in our large towns, particularly to those who want to be "asked" slyly, as the number is usually large, and the custom being generally a bore to the congregation, it becomes a difficult matter to pick one out of the ruck. The morning of our wedding-day arrived, and I had not yet the means wherewith to pay the priest; and no matter how poor you may be, if you require the "holy rite," you must pay for it in carnal coin. It is not the fashion of priests to marry "for love." I had no hope of gaining credit, even if I had had sufficient courage to ask the Rev. J. Bromby to transact the business on trust. They keep but one set of books, and there is no column for surplice fees to be put in black letter; and as there is risk in credit, the clerk would not like to be continually writing "bad"—"very bad"—under the head of "matrimony." There was no chance left then, but to pay for it, if the business was to go on. Agreed. But how? What an extremity for a poor mortal! No money—no wife. The affair became serious; and at the eleventh hour, I had to borrow eight shillings and sixpence for the ceremony, besides three-pence for the dog-whipper. I had to ask this loan from one whom I supposed to be the best friend I had in the world—my expected bride. The request was cheerfully granted. That business arranged. we. walked to the church, with hearts as free from care as if we had seen our future world-way track mapped out, and strewn with never-fading roses. One hour of such bliss is worth three score and ten years of golden match-making. It was not the least gratifying thing to the young couple to meet my father at the altar; although we had travelled by different paths towards it, he desired the pleasure of "giving the bride away." The father of my future life partner was there also, and took part in the ceremony. As soon as "we two" were "made one," we had a jubilate of tears; and never was a quartetto from streaming eyes more harmoniously tuned by happy hearts!

We trudged from the church right merrily; there was not a blank corner in either of our hearts; we had no thought of anything but joy! We reached our home. Our home? Yes; we reached our home. There are some kind hearts to be found in this twenty-shilling world;—if we could not command a home, we at least had one lent until we could obtain another. This home was lent to us by Mrs. F——, a benevolent lady, with just pride enough to allow of her being humane; with a purse limited enough, but to allow her to do good without ostentation; and Christian enough to believe, that generous conduct will ever be its own reward. With this lady, Miss Leaf, my two-hours' wife, had lived for some years as servant, cook, chambermaid, and deputy housekeeper, indeed everything, except on wash-days, when an old woman attended to help to get the things out of the way. In the house of this good Samaritan we took up our abode for a few months, until we could provide a domicile for ourselves.

My father-in-law was by trade a sawyer, and a good workman; in fact, Thomas Leaf had the reputation of being the best veneer-sawyer in that part of the country. I, being destitute of employment, and no prospect of obtaining any, except by leaving England, which I was unwilling to do, Mr. Leaf undertook to teach me the art of mahogany and veneer sawing. From the commencement of that business I gave promise of success, and it was not the least consoling to know, that at length I had found a trade wherein I could become respectable, and at least, something more than mediocre. It was soon my father's boast, that with his "big lad"—for I was too boy-like to pass for a man—with his lad "he could turn more veneers out of an inch plank than any other pair of craftsmen in the town." Thomas was an original in his way; he had superior qualities as a workman, and seldom forgot to talk about them. He was generally upon good terms with himself; he had an unflinching independence of action, and a deep sense of honour and integrity regulated all his dealings. In a pecuniary point of view, my new trade was not so remunerative as it had been before the invention of the circular saw. Our wages now averaged about two pounds each per week, and in some "good jobs," amongst which the sawing of deep logs of Honduras wood into planks for coach panels may be particularized,—we sometimes earned as much as five pounds each per week; unfortunately we did not always use it wisely. Drinking was the curse of our trade, and nearly all who embarked in it spent one-half of their wages in that debasing practice. It was often the boast of some of the sots, that the last Saturday night's "shot" had taken the greater part of their week's money. It is deeply to be lamented, that men will so lay waste their powers, and plunge themselves into misery—for it is a satire to call loss of health and substance, enjoyment They were strangers to pleasure, and could not distinguish between enjoyment and sensuality. Often, when we refused to take a part in their reckless follies, they had recourse to the most dangerous expedients to force us, by damaging our tools, driving old files into the pieces we had to cut through, and similar destructive practices.

There is but little hope for the confirmed drunkard; however bountifully he may be remunerated for his labour, he is never in a position to resist the encroachments that competition and individual grasping are always making upon him. The drunkard is rarely a thinking man. It was once a foolish opinion, that you never knew a good workman, but he was also a "hard drinker." That opinion is, fortunately for mankind, now exploded; and where is the virtue of the boast? Can the drunkard think more deeply upon the intricacies of mechanics, science, and the arts, than the man whose head is clear of the fumes of intoxication? Are not his means thrown away upon a foolish, nay, pernicious indulgence? How often are his hopes of reward sacrifised to the avaricious dealer, who knows that half a man will, by necessity, be compelled to take half a loaf rather than starve; he knows the market value of an independence that will sell itself to an idol; such a one is ever on the downward road to famine and disease.

The meridian of veneer sawing was passed when I commenced the business; the mills were gradually superseding hand labour, and loud and deep were the curses our craft was daily venting against the new invention. They rejoiced at every accident that befel the machinery, and did not scruple, whenever an opportunity offered, to play off any diabolical scheme, that might injure or destroy their works. I have known the ends of files industriously driven into valuable logs of mahogany; and I have heard with pain their rejoicings, when report has proclaimed the consequent destruction of the machinery. Has such wanton devastation been of any advantage to the perpetrators? Has it prevented the growth and the perfection of saw-mills? Are not they themselves now convinced of the superiority of machine over handsawn veneers, aud that no cabinet-maker would now submit to work the latter?

Is the fact of hundreds being thrown out of employment by the introduction of machinery, a sufficient argument against its use? I would answer no! I believe that great, important as are its results already, that it is yet in its infancy, and that the most comprehensive mind can but dimly shadow forth its benevolent mission. I regard it as one of the great blessings of the Creator, who has destined the inanimate to conquer labour, by its iron bone and muscle—that man, the inventor and director, "infinite in faculties," "in apprehension like a god!" shall some day work by his mental might. Is machinery, then, to go on reducing labour, and our population to starve? No! Then how long is the present system of the labourers working, and the machinery reducing their rewards, to continue? Just so long as the artisans will allow it, but no longer! They are the machine makers—they are its workers; they may be its owners, and be themselves benefitted by its vast productive powers—and this they will be, as soon as they are determined to be MEN. Sheridan has said, that "All are not men who bear the human form;" and, until those "who bear the human form" will make themselves *men* by education and thought, they will remain poverty-stricken serfs, instead of comfortable mechanics and independent citizens. The thinking man knows, that although he may lack a bread-loaf, he shall not procure one by burning a farmer's corn-stacks. Though the thinking man writhes beneath the curse of indirect taxation, he does not expect to cheapen his bread and wine by pulling down a grocer's shop, or breaking into a warehouse. The thinking man knows there is enough for all, and some to spare, even were his labour restricted to eight hours per day, if the claims of labour were respected;

but he cannot expect to better his condition by servilely cringeing to an aristocratical domination, which can see nothing more in the artisan than a mere animal, sent into the world for no higher purpose than to spin, and delve, and hew—to take a scanty morsel of bread for his existence, and so drive on again, until it shall suit the money-maker to substitute a younger and a stronger man, " with more steel in him," to manufacture wealth for the already overgrown capitalist, who regards as treason against his money-bags every such expression as an " equal distribution of the proceeds of labour." Until education shall teach a majority of the toiling artisans of England to become calm, sober, thinking, and self-dependent men, uniting themselves into a deliberative league for the emancipation of labour, they will continue to be at the mercy of the mammon-lovers, who thrive by their ignorance and division. All the clap-trap cries of " charters," votes, or sects yet raised, will be useless—will be rent in twain by the machinations of political partisans and well-paid demagogues, unless the workmen themselves concrete their independence with universal brotherhood—make their elevation a deep spirituality, instead of merely canting about wrongs which they never raise a serious voice to remove. When the religion of doing " unto other men as we would that other men should do unto us" is understood—is felt, instead of being merely talked about on Sundays—then will the capital which has too long been a task-master, become an universal help-mate. Then will the wealth that has been creating all the pleasures and luxuries which pride could devise, and indulgence revel in, become the messenger of plenty, the herald of comfort, and the precursor of virtue and peace. Then will capital take its share in the school-room, throwing the soul-creating wings of education over the artisans' children, nurturing and preparing them for the discharge of the important duties of Christian, world-adorner, and citizen. Then, instead of hastening the squalid half-reared child to the black night-day of a coal pit, or the body-warping toil of the factory, or to the mind-stultifying drudgery of the farm-stead, because the degraded parents cannot spare out of their ill-requited labour a sum sufficient for its food and schooling, until it shall be matured in mind and muscle—then, instead of these blighting miseries, the mission of machinery will be understood—they will, in their declining years, joy over the manliness of their offspring, instead of looking down, as thousands now look down upon their half-humanized children, seeking bread by crime, or by what is equally dreaded, the insulting mockery of a workhouse! When unity has taught the artisans, that machinery, with its Herculean sinews, and myriad-multiplying fingers, can produce and re-produce enough for all the nations of the earth, with *man's* aid only—and that the more beauteous portion of Creation's work, *woman*, can well be spared from such ignoble toil, Nature having designed her for a more important sphere in the cottage, where the nurselings call for careful tending, and where those domestic comforts which woman's chastening presence can so well adorn, calls for her refined direction—for the direction of one whom by a sacred vow at God's altar he swore to protect and cherish—not to enslave: when education has taught, as it will teach, all this, and more—then will the artisans learn that this slave-subduing power was destined at once to feed and to civilize the world, and that by an honest distribution of the produce of this mighty iron-heart of commerce, shall all mankind be made happy!

As the trade of veneer-sawing fell off in Hull by the multiplication of engine power, our occupation was confined to sawing the logs into boards. An opportunity now offered itself of transferring our business to the city of York. A merchant of that city, Mr. W——, being over at Hull, and making extensive purchases of Messrs. Barkworth and Spalding, our employers, Mr. W. engaged us to go over and work for him, with an understanding that we were to be constantly employed on mahogany, and other rich woods. We reasonably expected, that where there was a demand for such a class of workmen, we should find remunerative employment; so, in the late Autumn of 1822, we packed ourselves on board the Selby steam-packet, for York.

There was much to interest a young and ardent mind in a first visit to York, especially after leaving a modern-built and stirring sea-port. To a spirit brim full of romance, this old city was still alive with the past: shadowy forms were yet gliding through the old gable-hooded streets, wrapped in dark sublimity, with scarcely a link to bind them to the present. If, in the "Eternal City" (as travellers assert), every thing reminds you of the palmy church days, here also every thing breathes of High Church times.

At every turn, the fancy meets with mitred priests, whose ghostly power once bound all, from the sovereign to the serf—raising whom they would to the honour point by their imperious "Aye," or immuring the schismatic in a Peter's prison, there to linger until the living flesh no longer held communion with its fellow bone. The dust of antiquity was scattered over every gate and every altar.

We have heard how, in by-gone days, the devil looked sulkily over Lincoln, because of its numerous churches; at York they were now not less plentiful, almost one for every red name in the calendar. It might be supposed, where the deep-toned bell was bomeing from many a tower, that such a place ought to be a blessed one; but, alas! for the churches! "Old Harry" had little occasion to fret himself about them at York, however they might alarm him at Lincoln. At old Ebor, in 1822, despite the guardianship of lantern towers, he could afford an occasional

> "grin,
> For his favorite sin."

There was much more of pride than piety in that dry-as-dust city. Their compressed lips and expanded brows told you, before a word was spoken, that Saxon kings had there held court—that "roses, white and red," had flaunted proudly from their walls—and Archbishops had nodded to them, from Paulinus to Harcourt!

York may justly be proud of possessing one out of the many monuments that grace our land, wherein Science and Religion have joined hands to build a temple to the Most High. This cathedral is said to stand unrivalled for beauty, symmetry, and magnificence, amongst the solemn fanes of Europe. The grandeur of its pillared aisles subdues the spectator— the pomps of earth become things of naught, as the mind bows overawed before an altar that has burnt with the incense of Christianity for twelve hundred years. Beneath these vaulted roofs, the past becomes a moment's space: what thoughts crowd upon us, as silently we pace the clustered aisles, and at each step are reminded that below us the deathless dead are silently sleeping!—those martyrs and heroes, who, in the dim twilight of Christianity, unfurled the banner of the Cross in our country, and their mission over, one by one, with crosier and sword, laid them down to sleep side by side!—They are not dead; for as we gaze upon their effigies, as all stone-pillowed and out-stretched they lie beneath their marble shroud, an inner spirit speaks—the place is full of them—and mysteriously do they tell us of our country's progress, how they quenched the Druidical flames, and how they sung of an "Unknown God" to painted boar and wolf-hunters,—when plumed and Cross-plighted warriors bore a red cross and an ensanguined sword in so-called holy wars—and thence, through missal influences, and the dim cloistered light of convent cells, to the Act of Toleration: they tell us, that however men might err in their application of principles, Christianity has been, and will be, the world's great civilizer!

If, as a trade, the sawyers we had left behind us were generally a drunken class, they were not more circumspect at York. Here, any subterfuge that would give a pretext for "St. Monday's" clubbing for drink, was eagerly sought after; and regulations, which in themselves appeared to be useful and necessary, were merely used as ready ways to indulgence. Hence, fines for a disregard of cleanliness at work, were in plenty. To go to work on Monday morning with a dirty shirt on, or unshaven, called for the penalty of a shilling for each offence; to the forfeit, each man in the company was expected to contribute sixpence—the whole to be spent in drink. This "fuddling" once begun, it usually lasted two or three days. One of our "mates" made it a rule to begin the week with a dirty shirt on, and a black beard, whenever he wanted an extra indulgence; and in his case, the exception was the rule. The misery and desolation that haunted that man's home may be well conceived: his wife haggard in countenance, lacking necessary food, half naked and desponding—his children, immoral and ragged.

Individually, I had rather see the masses brought to a sense of temperance and sobriety, by a just estimate of their own rank in society, as men to reason, rather than be compelled, as it were, by the extremes of pledges and total abstinence; notwithstanding, I regard these extremes as inestimable blessings, when contrasted with the brutal and sunken condition of hundreds of confirmed drunkards, whom I, in my time, have had to mourn over. I am still a warm advocate of temperance, acknowledging as I do, the power of example over society; and on these grounds I have often been invited to join the ranks of total abstainers, and would readily do so, if I could convince myself of the right to do it. I have tried to convince myself that total abstinence is just in principle, but I have hitherto failed to do so. I have no need to shelter myself under the drunkard's excuse. I can proclaim my sobriety without the fear of being accused of a misstatement, and declare it fearlessly, as circumstances frequently call me within the vortex of indulgence; and I am well assured, by the conduct of some of my every-day acquaintance, that let but the people feel their own importance as men, and I shall not despair of their sobriety, even should they occasionally " find much virtue in good wine." I know that many will conscientiously object to my views. I can " agree to differ" with them. The temperance advocate will doubtless say, it were better not to record an opinion at all, rather than by so doing to hang up a doubt upon its principle. Again I differ, and believe it better to be mistaken, than to cant about a virtue without its possession. Heartily do I wish them " God speed" in their glorious work of reformation. I regard their means as useful to an end, and shall be anxious, aye, and willing, to help them, on such an understanding, until I believe "total abstinence" to be imperatively necessary.— I now regard it as an extreme means to reclaim the besotted by a vow, which, once taken, a sense of moral obligation obliges him to keep; and happily, while thus pledged, reflection steps in and convinces him of the folly and the danger of an uncontrolled indulgence.

In a few months, the hope we had cherished of constant employment here, at superior work, was blighted. The demand was not equal to the supply; the machine-cut work was at our heels, and was soon imported into our newly-adopted place, and we were consequently driven to seek work on coarser materials. This, to my father-in-law, was a source of continual annoyance, and he could not refrain from venting his disapprobation of our employers' breach of promise. For my part, consideration has shewn cause for extenuation. There was not much skill required in our latter work, which, to me, was more grievous than the inconvenience of lower wages.

The want of some employment, where the mind could be in constant exercise as well as the hands, began to haunt me, and I was anxious for change. For a time I sought relaxation by the culture of flowers, and engaged a small plot of ground for the purpose. At that period, York was famous for amateur cultivators of tulips, carnations, pinks, ranunculuses, and such others as were then known by the title of "show-flowers." This, however, was but a summer exercise, and the long dark nights hung heavily upon me. There was no Mechanics' Institution, or Library, where reading and science might be cultivated. There was a Subscription Library in the city, with an entrance fee of ten guineas, and an annual contribution of twenty-six shillings; but for all practical purposes, it might as well have been ten times the amount— indeed, in those days, gentlemen in "white kids" did not court the company of "the unwashed."

With all our yearnings after the past, we have brighter hopes for the future. It is cheering to glance over the progress of twenty-four years. How changed our social aspect. Fierce politicians are sobered down to the opinion, that "measures, not men," must win their way,

"In the good time coming."

People now admit that religion is a thing of God, and not of parchment—aye, they think that even Jews may have souls, and we no longer teach our children to "spit upon their gaberdines," or bait a fork with hog's flesh as they walk our streets. The judges of the land preach prevention, rather than prisons, and doubt the potency of capital punishments—and the People's Colleges open their portals to the men with labour-furrowed hands, at a trifling cost: even ministers of state now point with evident satisfaction to the gleams of sunshine that dash the world's new spring. And who will deny, that with every step forward the carnal has not fallen away, and the god-like prevailed? Each year has been a mile-post marking our heaven-ward haste to that millenium of mind, "when righteousness shall cover the earth, as the waters cover the great deep."

I again sought excitement in the theatre, and soon made acquaintance with a few kindred spirits, and we determined upon trying our histrionic talents at a play. Living at that time in a tolerably large room, I appropriated some part of it to that purpose. The wall I painted as an interior, fitting up side wings, and adding a curtain. The old play of "*Mahomet*" was again selected, for the reasons that had recommended it before,—it containing but one female part. The heroine was to be represented by my wife, and at the appointed time a few friends were invited to witness our performance; and considering their modest expectations, all things went off to their satisfaction. Another performance or two followed, and my amateur friends increased, and I determined to come out with increased attractions. My next step was to engage an empty loft, and fit it up with moveable scenes, and raise the price of admission. There, in our wooden loft, we were toiling night after night, contriving, hacking, and nailing at boxes, pit, and gallery—now fitting up a bench, with a halfpenny tallow-dip in one hand and a hammer in the other, driving, and mouthing, with mock dignity,

> "Now is the winter of our discontent
> Made glorious summer"—

or again decorating a pasteboard altar, and trying the potency of an incense, compounded of tow and spirits of wine, and as the pale flame curled and streamed aloft, exclaimed with self-satisfaction,

> "Now, by Saint Paul, the work goes bravely on!"

Our performance at the new theatre had a run, and night after night we bored our friends with the tragedy of "*Mahomet.*" "*Douglas*" was our next grand effort, but then there were two ladies in it: that was surmounted by the most effeminate-looking young man in "the company" being "modestly attired," to fret his hour in the part of Anna. I tried the patience of my hearers in Old Norval, and my wife with the grief-worn Lady Randolph, and such "melancholy gloom" as we displayed was never anticipated by the author. It soon became necessary that we should get up a new farce, as our stock one, the "*Intrigue*," was now "worn out at the elbows." "*Bombastes Furioso*" was the next one selected, for here again the "playwright" had furnished us with a "light cast" and one lady! As the manager of this *petit corps dramatique*, I began to assert a right that older heads and practised hands have not steered clear of, when invested with managerial command, the right to take the best part out of the piece, whether possessing the peculiar ability to fill it or not, always imagining that a good part must make a good actor. So with true managerial domination, I cast to myself the part of the hero, Bombastes. In this case, as the sequel proved,

> "it was a grievous fault,
> And grievously"

I had to answer it. During the rehearsal of this burlesque, an unfortunate accident befel me. And here I may state, it is not usual with amateurs, as with your every-day actors, to have their foils buttoned, or to wear obtuse fencing swords; the play-book did not recommend it; so we were armed with keen-pointed weapons, likely to do good service when needed, and it was our wont to be right earnest in the business. Like the charmed King of Scotland, we would be "damned" before we cried "Hold, enough!" In the last scene, while I was practising the combat with Fusbos, my antagonist was animated with something beyond mimic "dumb show," and was intent upon "suiting the action to the word," so he ran his sharp-pointed sword right through my leg! I felt an unusual sensation, such an one as generally accompanies a slight blow on the side of the leg when struck by a cane, and I exclaimed, "Gently, my boy, you hit me hard!" Immediately on his withdrawing the sword, a gush of blood followed it, and I fainted from the continued discharge; my leg was then bound up, and I was conveyed home, when a surgeon was sent for. The wound proved a serious one; for several days mortification was dreaded, and I was compelled to keep my bed many weeks, and was afterwards forced to amble upon crutches.

When I fancied myself sufficiently recovered, I once more sought the saw-tail, and determined never again to invite such an "unkindly cut;" but, alack! I found I could not now bear the fatigue necessary for the discharge of my duty; my pain of body, and the swollen condition of my wounded leg, forced me to give up, and to seek some other way of supporting myself, my wife, and child. In vain I sought for a profession where the physical would not be the most important part of the business. A favourable opportunity was apparently at hand. Mr. Lysander Thompson was then performing at Pocklington, a town fourteen miles distant, and he was anxious to pass the winter in York. He tried to engage the theatre, but the proprietors were inexorable; they could not so far forget their dignity, as to allow a lot of strollers, however great their talents, to desecrate the licensed boards of a Theatre Royal!

As Mr. Thompson could not get the theatre, he was advised to hire a large room, in Little Blake Street, and fit it up for the purpose. There I got temporary employment as a scene painter, and to be otherwise useful. Mr. T. already enjoyed a celebrity in the North, in "low comedy" and the "country boys," and he expected to gain as great *eclât* in the city as he had done in many of the towns in the country, where he was respected and known by the familiar cognomen of "Yorkshire Thompson."

A five-act comedy, and the farce of the "*Review*," was chosen for Mr. T.'s opening in York; all the necessary arrangements being completed, and the city somewhat excited in consequence. Up to the day of opening, every thing appeared to run as smooth and merry "as a marriage bell." A few hours before the stated time of performance, a messenger from the lessee of the Theatre Royal waited upon Mr. Thompson, to inform him, that he must not play the "legitimate drama" in York, on pain of the visitation of the law. This was at once a damper upon the manager's hopes—added to which, the great expenses he had incurred, in fitting up his place for a Theatre, forced Mr. Thompson to try the effect of a little contraband "legitimate" play-acting.

There cannot be any species of amusement in "free" and "merry England"—much less our food and daylight—allowed to escape the money fangs of the law; nor by any ingenuity could the speculators elude its avaricious grasp.

Although our congenial soil had upreared an immortal Shakspeare, there must needs be a protective duty put upon him, for the home market of cities, else he might be imported amongst the foreign boors in the villages, and the illiterates be tempted to eat of the heart-whole bread of poetry, and the growth of cock-fighting, bull-running, and legerdemain be stopped; or in case of a war of opinion, the importation of abortions, or learned pigs, might be endangered, and the peasantry driven to clamour for a free trade in plays, and the revenue be bilked out of the price of a "patent." In every way has the people been sacrificed to the moloch of monopoly. Even in plays, "the oppressor's wrong" bound them to the curse of ignorance; for if they were offered the purity of the drama, they were not allowed "to buy it in the cheapest market;" such free-trading in genius would never do where a people were only allowed to speak by Acts of Parliament.

Nor could Mr. Thompson be allowed to glut the market of York with his talents, although the Theatre Royal had itself shut up the port. "Time works wonders:" the anti-dramatic-patent-league-men have helped us in this matter, and Macready now plays Shakspeare in "the minors," where attentive and delighted audiences listen to the soul-stirring bard in their own locality, and now they wonder why they were so very patient under the "patents" and blue fire!

The manager could not act plays, so he was thrown back upon farces, interludes, and olio entertainments; nay, he was forced to try how he could "draw the people" by the phantasmagoria, and other optical illusions. As might be expected under such circumstances, the business was a failure; and a large company, who had been looking up to the manager for the means of support, were now thrown upon their own resources.

A few of the company who were starved out, determined to try the Malton Theatre for a few nights, and myself and my wife were to be of the party. On the appointed day, we started for the town, famous for its bacon flitches. I was all animation at this start, so completely absorbed in this new profession, that nothing was before me but the stage; I would be an actor at all hazards. My partner was not so much taken with our proposed new trade; she could see no finger-post inscribed "Fame, three miles!" neither could she observe any notice of "this way to the cupboard!"

On our arrival in the town, things did not wear a very promising aspect; our money stocks were low; strange to the business, we were unused to the modes of self-introduction to any body, that players generally have at their command. We were hedged in by uncertainty, and to render our situation still more uncomfortable, we were drenched to the skin by the heavy rain which fell during our journey. We took possession of one of the dressing-rooms in the Theatre; we quickly blew up a fire, purchased some bread and tea, borrowed a tea-kettle and two or three tea-cups, boiled the tea in the kettle with the water, and wanting the other accessories, we were compelled to make a stage-dagger serve at once for a knife and a tea-spoon.

Here we took our first rough meal, after taking to the buskin; and although it was scantily furnished, it had great advantages over many of the meal-times that were to follow—for now the eatables were in plenty, but the garniture scarce. Hereafter, we were to be favoured with platters and tea-cups, but the substantials were to be absent.

We opened the Theatre with the play of "*Romeo and Juliet*," in which I enacted, as best I could, the part of Capulet. We were at Malton a fortnight, but our endeavours were not seconded by the town; whether they thought our company too mean for them, or they were too deeply busied in curing hogs and training horses, to trouble themselves with vulgar amusement, we did not learn, for, certes, our attempt was a failure; we took but little more money than was necessary to pay the incidental expenses. Our company was soon stranded, each marching on the forlorn hope of gaining a bread-loaf.

We returned again to York, somewhat dispirited and with lighter pockets, limited as they were, of the English man-maker, when we commenced our journey.

We had now to think again. In the most salubrious places, air, although an useful ingredient, has been found but insubstantial food to live upon, and but little nourishment was to be found in the gloomy projecting-storied streets of old Ebor—they might give a yellow tinge to a melancholic temperament, but little was there to add roses to the withering cheek, or to make a sad man leap to new life! We had to muse over our situation, and plan operations for the future.

CHAPTER VII.

THE STROLLING PLAYER.

The constant pain that accompanied every attempt to renew my physical labours, rendered it impossible for me to continue tugging at the saw-tail; some other trade was necessary. I had already tried the stage, and its first effect was to starve me: what, then, was to be my next adventure? As often as I asked myself this question, the ever-ready answer was at hand,

"The play's the thing."

So completely was I enwrapped in my desire for the stage, that I could not for a moment think of any thing else. It was a strange infatuation—one that shrouded all reasoning upon capability, short commons, or whether any one would engage me. Determination said, try the latter, and risk the former, and go off in search of some company—a very Quixotic errand!

With my wife and child—a strange feeling of hope and fear alternating—almost penniless, with Chance for a guide, I wandered over the fertile wolds of Yorkshire, until I reached my native town of Hull. I had not seen my parents for a comparatively long time. My mother's joy at seeing me once again was great, yet she felt sorrow at finding me so shabbily dressed; to her it was an evidence of distress. She was anxious to learn my business, and how I intended to employ myself. I dare not tell her my resolve; the recollection of my first visit to the play-house, her after-regret at having given me leave to go there, were all fresh in my memory; besides she was now ill, hastening to a premature grave, and mercy prompted me to evade her questions. To have bluntly told her my determination, might have added another pang to an already canker-worn heart, and therefore I carefully concealed my intentions. Was it right to do so?

"Thus conscience doth make cowards of us all."

To wring a mother's heart is dire cruelty. Suspense was bliss compared with the avowal that I was about to turn player.

My parent cannot be thought singular in her dislike to the stage; her education was nowise above the average that was doled out to the artisans' daughters of the eighteenth century. Then it was boldly proclaimed that the workers had no need of education! Oh, no! ignorant men could be easily prepared to receive the *cat* or the bullet; besides, to teach the needy to write, might even " lead merchants' clerks to become forgers." Pope knew we could not spare time to become gentlemen scholars, and so any thing short of that was "dangerous." Again, the drama was preached down from the pulpit, decried in the Sunday school, all (so-called) religious people declared the playhouse to be a very immoral place. Who then can wonder, living in such an age, my mother should be pained by the thought that her son was going to be engaged in such a wicked trade? Was it not charity to conceal my intentions from her?

During our short stay at Hull, I sought out some of my former "spouting" acquaintance, thinking them to be the most likely persons to give me information if any strolling companies of players had been heard of in that part of the country. While following out my inquiries, chance threw me into the company of one of my old playmates, the General J——. This General was a well known character in Hull, very eccentric—to-day you might see him dressed in the extreme of fashion, and a month afterwards he would be seen with scarcely decent covering. His want of dress never appeared to influence his somewhat forward address. The General thought himself "cut out for a gentleman," and he took every opportunity to tell those who thought themselves his superiors, "that the impress of the gentleman was bred in him." One morning, while walking up George's Street, I came up with the General; he was in one of his shabby modes; there were sundry longitudinal slits in his trousers, that showed the "flesh-tints" beneath; his boots were minus the toes, and his "sleepless hat" fitted him too much,—he was a very Guy! J—— accosted me with all the air and twang of a first-water swell, "Ah,

Thomson my dear boy, how d'ye do, how d'ye do?—ah, what, twigging my toggery, ha! ha!—never mind, my boy, the Doctor has promised to give me a new rig shortly!" We had not walked many yards before we met the Doctor; the General addressed him with all the familiarity of an equal. The subject of their discourse was, of course, unknown to me, as a sense of duty led me onward. On another occasion, when J—— was about hungered out of his garret, the presents of his friends had been slack; in this unhappy mood he was strolling up Bond Street, where some bricklayers were employed digging out the foundations of a building; J—— stopped to chat with them, and hinted at his needy situation. The bricklayers at once offered him employment, if he would condescend to take to their trade; the proffer was immediately accepted, and he prepared for the work. Being in the summer season, he took off his coat—instantly the labourers set up a loud laugh, for on removing his coat, it was evident the General had no shirt on, and his bare arms contrasted strangely with his high stiffened paper collar that was round his neck, and stuck up to his nose! Perceiving that the laugh was directed against him, he coolly took hold of the tip of the paper collar, and drew it off, exclaiming, "Ah, gentlemen, I presume you are laughing at the delicacy of my linen," and without more ceremony, he took up the barrow, and commenced his labours. The gossips of Sculcoates, who professed to know more of the General's history than the residents of the other parishes, always said, that J—— was bred a gentleman, for "it was well known, that a certain

General was his father." Who, even in our day, would dare to question a gossip's declaration, when it is authenticated by a "well known?" J—— was a singular fellow, full of ready wit, a little pompous in his address, but whenever Dame Fortune had been kind to him, and he possessed wherewith to exercise his benevolence, he was warm-hearted and generous, and distress never appealed to him in vain. If, indeed, a real General was his father, who will dispute that the son was a real gentleman?

My meeting with the General on the present occasion was a favourable one; he was the very man to give me the information now so much needed; he took an especial interest in the movements of the players; he had no objection to make one of their party over a social glass, if they asked him so to do. The question was soon put to him, and my determination to turn player stated, and that I was then in search of a company. "Ah, my boy," said he, "give me your hand; I give you joy!—a most apropos meeting!—I can procure you an engagement immediately. A part of the company, where I am now engaged as a *star*, has separated from Clarke, at Kirton-in-Lindsey, and they have opened at Barrow, just across the Humber here, under Templeton's management. I will give you a line to him, my boy;—it's a done thing, Sir—you are engaged!" This display of the top ropes was rather new to me; the lapse of time had blurred over the recollections of J——'s rhapsodies, and I doubted the truth of his statement; still his singular appearance seemed to give a colour to his assertion. His external appearance seemed to indicate, that he had lately been in comp[any] with the players, for he was half-dressed for some pa[rt] even now. He had on a pair of russet boots, [of] mediocre quality, a "shabby genteel" snuff-colour[ed] coat, white waistcoat, embroidered with red crewel[s,] a long tinsel chain hung round his neck, which te[r]minated with a toy, which he occasionally put to h[is] eye, as if to assist his vision; the other part of h[is] dress was equally quizzical. "You see, Sir," said h[e,] apologizing for his dress, "I left Kirton last evenin[g] very hastily,—came off, Sir, in the very dress I ha[d] been playing Goldfinch in;—just going to say 'ho[w] d'ye do' to my old friend Mrs. Burns, then I'm o[ff] again by the packet;—play Richard to-night, Si[r—] must return—the announcement has made quite [a] sensation in the place, Sir. As time is important t[o] me, upon reconsideration you have no need of a letter[;] give my compliments—General J——'s compliment[s] to Templeton—and say I have sent you;—don't los[e] a tide, Sir—he is in want of people—I know it, Sir;— good morning—you'll suit him to a hair!" With [a] series of bows, and right and left scrapings, and rubbing his hands, he bowed, nodded, and twisted himsel[f] a few turns astern, then took his way to (perhaps) hi[s] lady friend.

I knew not what to think of his strange story. I[n] our youthful days we did not consider that all [the] General said was the truth, nor did he consider it o[f] much importance that it should be gospel; careles[s] and light-hearted, he talked to make himself agreeable[.] Was he speaking truth now? was so much of his stor[y] as related to the company true? His dress, his apparent sincerity, coupled with the possibility of its being a verity, considerably excited me, and my resolve was to follow his advice, and "lose not a tide." I had just time sufficient to impart the subject of our conversation to my wife, and then cross the Humber in the Barton-hoy, and to walk from the quay to the village of Barrow.

I found Mr. Templeton's company just about to depart for a village called Laceby. I enquired out the manager, and told him my business. He eyed me over with a look of suspicion, and well he might; for if he judged of my histrionic powers by my outward appearance, he would think me more likely to seek an engagement as a dock-side lumper—(a person engaged in delivering and loading ships' cargoes)—than in a profession where a knowledge of literature, and of men and manners, was an essential requisite. After relating to him my spouting experience, and chatting together over a glass of grog, an engagement was made. If possible, I was to be with them in time for the opening in the next place. I found out it was as desirable on the part of the manager, as on my own, that I should form a part of this company,—they were in want of actresses—Mrs. Templeton being the only lady with them at present. My being married, and having a wife who was willing to try her head and hands in stage business, was considered an acquisition to them. I hastened back to the water side, and returned to Hull with the news, that an opportunity was at hand to try our adopted mode of living.

Fame and fortune now appeared before me. Imagination was busily painting prospective pictures of

Pleasure and Plenty on my fancy. There was not a single drawback to my future career; there were my stage properties, neat library, good salary, snug parlour, and easy chair, and lots of superfluities—all in the perspective. Nevertheless, I was sanguine enough to believe they would come some day or other, so it would be better not to show any impatience about it, but wait the issue; an engagement was procured, and surely that was the "beginning of the end!" Alas, for the retrospect! But why complain? Misfortune has its uses: to me there is a pleasure, it may be a mournful one, but pleasure it is, to contrast my dark and hungry days with the many pleasant ones that have mingled with them.

Who, if they might choose their weather, would have life one long July day, to lie basking in the bright dancing sun-beams, until their very blaze became oppressive, and sluggishly induced a day-dream of hot blood and fevers; then to awake panting for a cool November breeze to fan their parched lips, and purge away the surfeit of pleasure? I have hitherto found but one road to enjoyment,—to be always looking towards the good, never to be discouraged by disappointment, nor afraid to venture on a journey because the morning looked gloomy; for as the sun gathers up and dispels the blue mists of Autumn, making the mid-day more golden by the contrast, so the struggle-clouds of life's dappled morn break up, but to give new glory to the dashes of sunshine that cheer us on from the cradle to the tomb.

We now embarked in the Grimsby packet-ship to join with Mr. Templeton; the voyage was a short one, but the rising of a sudden and fierce squall soon after leaving Hull, made ample diversity. The dark clouds gathered over our heads, and sent us reeling to and fro like drunkards filled with wine. The rain spit all its fury in our faces, and the mad waves, all drunk with joy, romped wildly around our little sea-boat; yet it was but for a season; the storm-spirit was frolicking from the South to the North; he rode upon the blast with the winds in his leash; on he went, careering away, and left the green meadows of Lincolnshire, to greet our feet on landing, as fresh as the daisy-flowered kirtle of green Spring!

The elements were singing a fitful prologue to the wild and wayward interlude of "*Real Life*" that we were now engaged to enact. It was but one act out of life's seven, a chequered one of pleasure and pain,—plenty and hunger; but such is the drama of life,

"And all the men and women merely players."

The road from Grimsby to Laceby was new to us; it had "books" upon it, laid open on the right hand and on the left; it is a continuation of water springs; and the brooks and gurgling runlets, all dressed in silver, gush forth, and sing and shout to heaven their hymns of freedom. They beguiled the way, and made us for a while to forget the state of our pockets. It was nature's solace, bidding us to be of good cheer. Even the winds, as they *soughed* mournfully after the storm, sang to us a sympathetic song of, "It will be time enongh to grieve when you cannot help it."

About nightfall we reached Laceby, and found our new manager had begun his "season." After taking some refreshment, we had to go at once into the business. The play was "*Pizarro.*" I was required to be generally useful on this occasion, and to "wing," from the book, the messengers and soldiers that the limited numbers of this company could not afford separately to supply. My young son was just old enough for our Rolla to bear aloft; and my wife, despite of fatigue and doubt, had to personate one of the "Virgins of the Sun." The farce was "*Fortune's Frolic,*" in which Mrs. T. was at home, as Old Margery: indeed she afterwards acquired a celebrity in the old crones, from Juliet's Nurse to Mrs. Brulgruddery. This company was on the plan called by the punctilious ones a commonwealth, but more generally denominated a "sharing company." The mode of remuneration was, after first paying the incidental expenses of the night, to divide the remainder equally amongst the number of people, including the "dead shares." The managers usually took two dead shares for furnishing the scenery and dresses, and also for the wear and tear of their property; sometimes a musician or other important personage received a dead share for his accomplishments; and occasionally, actors of extra merit have received a share and a half, in consideration of their great abilities. In a company whose locale was generally in the south of England, the system was carried to such an extent, that the dead shares, even to the bits of candle-ends left after the performance, were demanded, so that any actors, except the dead share men, had no chance of living with the company. The scenery and dresses in this company were of excellent quality; and their contrast with the shares left was so great, that in the profession, they were known by the title of "The splendid Misery!" We were now to receive our first share, and we were put into ready money at once. On this occasion, the share was one shilling and sixpence each, and one shilling for my son's services in the play. Here was wealth to begin with! Four shillings sterling to buy bread and butter, tea, eggs, and beef! No! strolling actors seldom buy beef. It was, notwithstanding, a good bank to draw upon; but as it was customary to play only three nights in the week, I found out that two shillings per day would, after all, not be over fat when the proceeds were divided in my family. This village, or, to be a little professional, this town (for the strolling companies seldom condescend to talk of villages)—this town was considered a good one, as far as the monetary business was concerned. It was indeed affluent, when compared with many others. Our shares were often above one shilling each; sometimes we shared two and three shillings per night. Twice our share reached four shillings each! The notorious "*Tom and Jerry*" was the piece that brought such an overflow of wealth to our Theatre Rural! It was fine fun for the Lincolnshire boys to see us "mill the Charleys," and to listen to the low satires, and "back slum patter" of that thing of the time; they tendered their shillings right cheerfully—nay, some of the audience came from Grimsby, a distance of four miles, to hear the "slang."

It is very questionable, whether more of evil than of good has not attended the "brilliant success," as the bills of the day had it, of "*Tom and Jerry.*"

It has furnished one of the many excuses that the over-righteous have had for their unceasing persecution of the stage; and although such productions may, to a reflecting mind, "point a moral," still the mode is far below the dignity of the stage. It was almost impossible, in such an age of conventional gentility as the one which we hope we are now leaving behind us, that the horse-racing, prize-fighting, and card-playing education of the day, and without which a young man was considered a very noodle, could pass away without leaving its blighting taint upon the rising generation— it was but natural that the youth of such a school should find food more palateable in their own "form and pressure," than in sitting down to the mind-addressing viands of our neglected Shakspeare. We are now following the bard's advice, and are determined to "reform it altogether."

If the "patents" of the day, "with all their appliances," so pandered to the follies of their time, it may be some excuse to the poor stroller, who seldom knew whether he should dine at home, or, to keep up appearances, should be forced out to count the flowers for his next Sunday's dinner;—for such a hunger-haunted class some excuse may be made, when they were assured that such a method was the only one left to secure a dinner.

We passed away our time at Laceby as long as we could get customers. Stopping too long in a place is indeed a fault with such companies; and here we stayed too long. When a place answers well, their poverty tempts them to make the best of it; if, on the contrary, it does not pay, hope has an ever-ready excuse, and they wait on, and on, until it will mend; at last the flatterer leaves them, frequently without the means of purchasing their release.

There was a mine of instruction in our world-despised trade. Variety of scene and of character were ever present, whether on our mud barn-floor, or on the boards of the inn's large room—in the village alehouse, or in the cottage ingle, there was perpetual change. We had an average sample of the talent of village actors in this little scheme; and, quiz our village heroes as you may, many of the stars of that glowing galaxy of legitimates that are gone to their rest, have in their life-morning bustled their way through the village theatre. If we had an average of theatrical talent, we had also our quantum of stage jealousies: and who can imagine himself more clever than his brother, in reading and playing, than your actor? Who looks through his green glass more peevishly, when his brother brings down "thunders of applause?" Yet who so soon forgets his brain fever? Why, he wears his petty whims upon his sleeve, and the first wind that blows puffs them away, it may be to make room for others. It is something in our favour that an author* has recently given us assurance, from a great authority, that however gangrened the jealousies of the players may be, they are feather-light when compared with those of the lawyers.

The General J—— has already told us, that our manager, Mr. Templeton, had left Clarke at Kirton, and that he (the General) was starring it with Clarke. During the interval of my meeting with the star at

---

* A Suffolk Rector's " Leaves from a Freemason's Note Book."

Hull, and our leaving Laceby, misfortune paid her melancholy visit to Mr. Clarke's family: his wife was taken ill, his business had fallen off, and, one by one, his friends (?) had left him. Clarke had got into difficulties, and the strollers in the surrounding places were solicited to play one night gratuitously, to relieve his wants. To those inured to hard fare, an appeal from distress always finds sympathy and prompt assistance. Some of our company took a part in that night's business; others went over to witness the play. "*Richard the Third*" was the one chosen for the occasion, and, "by particular desire," the General was to enact the destroyer of "alabaster innocence." The General was seldom or never perfect in his parts; but on this occasion, Richard being his pet part, report spoke of him as letter perfect. All things being ready, the General stuffed, humped, and calf-padded, the "crooked back" commenced his mouthing,

> "Now is the winter of our discontent
> Made glorious summer,"

and pompously continued till he reached the lines,

> "Why I, in this weak, piping time of peace,
> Have no delight to pass away my time,
> Unless to—————"

Here he came to a full stop—then turned back to "have no delight"—then another stop—another trial, and a stop. Again,

> "Unless to—————"

Then the General came to the front: "Unless to—" "Ladies and Gentlemen, I am sorry to apologise, but a pressure of other business has prevented me from studying this part. I will, with your permission, endeavour to read it." The mimic hero then made his exit, and re-entered with a play-book and a tallow dip. He was greeted with cheers and hisses; however, the recollection of the manager's pressing necessities, and the *King's* eccentricities, had a soothing effect upon the audience; good humour was restored, and the piece allowed to go on. The tragedy talents of a Cruikshank, or a Leech, deep although they are, could not draw a more touchingly ludicrous picture than was that one of the King and Lady Anne, taken at the precise moment when Glo'ster exclaims,

"Lo! here I lend you this sharp-pointed sword."

There was a peculiar expression in the group: Glo'ster offering, with comical resignation, himself, the play-book besmeared with grease, the half-wasted tallow-dip, and the sharp-pointed sword, to his (on this occasion in particular) arch-haughty lady-love! As far as the money object of that night's performance was concerned, it did some good. The house was well filled, and some of the trouble would thereby be taken off Mr. C——'s shoulders. The relief came too late for his wife to enjoy it; disease had sunk deeply into her debilitated frame; awhile she lingered; she listened placidly to the solemn messenger that called her to leave the troubles of earth, and take a long death-sleep in the silent grave; and calmly she obeyed him.

From Laceby our corps marched to Binbrook, a neat little town at the foot of the billowy ridge that runs through Lincolnshire. Our business here was generally bad, and it was with hard squeezing that we supplied ourselves with one meal per day on the average. Mr. Templeton had frequent quarrels with Mr. Lamb, our leading tragedian. Our "leader" possessed a fair proportion of stage abilities; but, as a man, anything but an agreeable one. He was a tippler, was always coloured a murrey-brown, from the superfluous dust of the snuff he took, and was most happy when plotting mischief,—boasted of his being "an old actor," and was full of the "blood of the grograms." He was always plotting against the manager, no doubt expecting, if he were out of the way, Mr. L. would get all the "bits of fat," instead of having to divide them with Mr. T. Mr. Lamb succeeded in his schemes; Mr. Templeton left us, and Mr. Douglass Campbell was induced to take upon himself the cares of management. Mr. Campbell was a warm-hearted young man, intelligent and talented. The greater part of the scenery we had been using was his property, and he had a good display of dresses. We went to a neighbouring town, and resumed our acting; our success was equal to our expectations, and all things appeared to be going on with comfort. Market Rasen was our next place; there, night after night, we proclaimed our desire to play, but not a customer darkened our doors. But although our stocks were *nil*, our snuffy tragedian was drunk every day; his conduct so disgusted our new manager, that they quarrelled, and Mr. L. was forced to beat a retreat. We felt quite satisfied in this town, if we could get one meal per diem; and for the little we had, we were indebted to the manager. The stay at Rasen, and the want of the needful supplies, forced our manager to take a journey into Yorkshire, to endeavour to dispose of his musical manufactures, the harmonicons. Mr. Campbell was an excellent musician, and an ingenious man; and it was his custom to fill up his leisure hours with making musical instruments. He was likewise an artist, a good temperer, a painter, and to him I was indebted for many useful lessons in scene painting. To reimburse his exhausted pockets, he took a quantity of the harmonicons to Leeds, where he found a ready market for them. From distress, and similar disasters, our little affair was now reduced to one man and one woman, excepting myself and wife. The gentleman, a Mr. Manuel, was not an actor; he could not *study;* nevertheless, in a *full* company he was very useful. The lady, Mrs. Campbell, mother to the manager, could not study, so we were now in an uncomfortable situation. Necessity forced us to make up a mixed entertainment, with the phantasmagoria, the fantoccina, songs, recitations, &c. With such an olio entertainment, we visited several villages, including Tealby, North and South Kelsy, and Caistor, until our manager could recruit his store, and fix upon some town likely to answer for a theatrical season. In the late Summer of 1825, Mr. F. D. Campbell brought together his replenished company, at Tickhill, Yorkshire. We had great expectations from the place, for various reasons. It had been a long time without a company, and so was not "run out." It was near to Sandbeck House, the residence of the Earl of Scarbrough, and his Lordship was known to be a patron and supporter of the drama in his own locality. The town was also surrounded by a number of villages. Our corps, though small, were expected to be useful. We had our old snuffy tragedian (a reconciliation with the manager having been effected) and a Mr. Young, famous from John o' Groat's to Land's end, in low comedy and the old men; he was an actor of merit, and a thoughtful serio-funny care-for-nobody, love-every-body sort of a man—occasionally fond of his cups: he had fitful seasons of long drinking and a long penance, and was generally the favourite of the town. There was Mr. Crawshaw, another tragedian, with lungs louder than stentorian. How he supported such a burly corporation amongst strolling players was a perfect enigma; but there he was, stomach and all. It was whispered that he was deeply in love with one of the actresses (Mrs. Gyles), and it was also supposed that he had an "Irish way" of showing it, by annoying and sometimes ill-treating the object of his affection; and it was said that his lady-love did like him, despite of all his tricks!

We procured a barn, and had it fitted up very respectably. Our average shares were about twelve shillings each per week, and a small surplus at the "benefits." This was a rare town for visiting with the inhabitants; many of them tried to rival each other in making the actors merry. On the non-play-nights, we sometimes made visits to the "old hall" of Sandbeck; and on each occasion,

> " 'Twas merry in the hall,
> Where beards wagg'd all."

Pleasure must have its alloy; and whether our mischief-maker set the company to loggerheads, or it is a part of the actor's every-day business to be fidgetty, and fall out with somebody, I cannot say; but assuredly divisions were made amongst us, and our manager did not give himself much care about going on with the concern. His mother was now ill with the rheumatic gout, and was for weeks together confined to her bed; this had a dispiriting effect upon him, and at the close of the season he determined to remain at Tickhill with his mother. My wife was also very ill; she received a fearful hurt in her side by an accident, and being far advanced in pregnancy, the matter demanded our stopping there for a time. I tried various ways to raise the means of living, by painting transparent window-blinds, making painted-glass work-boxes, chimney-ornaments, and such other nick-nackeries; but, after all my exertions, I could find a market but for a part only of my merchandise. For five or six weeks after the playing was over, we managed to live in comparative plenty; but day by day our means were narrowed, and we began to look with serious apprehension on our situation.

In this hopeless condition, in the month of November, my wife gave birth to a daughter, and the few friends we had found during our acting season, were kind to her now. We had also presents from Sandbeck House, to meet the exigencies of our somewhat isolated situation. Meantime, I walked to town and village, trying to dispose of my ornaments; now and then I found a customer; but foot-sore and hungry as I was, it was almost impossible to save a sixpence, even though I was well content to live upon bread and water. I began to despair of keeping my family alive, by hawking my wares; and amongst other modes of providing a bread-loaf, I wandered amongst the woods, abounding in the neighbourhood, and gathered acorns, and sold them by the bushel, to feed the towns-folk's pigs. We likewise roasted some of the acorns, and used them as a substitute for coffee; but I cannot recommend the substitute to those who can purchase the real coffee berry. If they choose, they can just try it for amusement. Hunt's roasted bread crusts made a mean beverage, but the acorns made a worse!

Mr. Campbell stuck untiringly to his harmonicon manufacture; he had made up a stock, and again sought the large manufacturing towns of the North for a market, and found a good one. On one of his visits to Tickhill, it was agreed between us, that my daughter should be christened during his stay, and he proffered his aid in the purchase of such requisites as should furnish "a dish of tea" to the "god-fathers and god-mothers," and other friends, who had assisted us. Now, Mr. Frederick was very anxious to give his advice in this perplexing business of name-choosing, and I was very agreeable to his indulging his taste in that labyrinthine necessity. We were both of us up to the neck in romance; occasional hard fare had no corrective power to soften us down to your drowsy do-nothing bread and cheese conventionalisms! No: imagination, wild and unfettered, served up a meal in those days more gorgeously than could your brass-pan kitchen stews of beef and mutton. It is true at times we were *unimaginative* enough not to turn our backs upon a dish of potatoes and a mutton chop—when we could *get* one. Mr. C. did not like the vulgar fashion of having diminutives for names. It was always annoying to him to hear a lot of rough fellows bawl out "Fred!" What impudence! After it had pleased his "god-fathers and god-mothers" to name him Fredrick, two plain unmistakeable syllables, was it not really shocking to hear a man, without fear either of priest or prayer-book, steal one-half of what had been consecrated by holy rite? Yet the sacrilegious rascals hallooed out "Fred!" We had now a name to choose, and we were determined, if it took us a week to search for a precedent, that we would have one that even vulgar lips must pronounce; and if there was not a name ready made, we would have a new one. We invented a few, but we found monosyllables were neither pretty when written, nor feminine when pronounced. After running the initials from A to Z, we adopted a very pleasant one, which we were of opinion could not, by any possibility, be divested of beauty; and we decided that the young Miss should be christened Rosina. Before the priest had dashed the Christian-making liquid from his fingers, our name was shorn of its fair proportions, by an old crone declaring we had done well, "for Miss Rose was a verry pratty name." We were reconciled to the shortening, inasmuch as we were of opinion, that lisp it, or unite it as you may, Rosina, Rosey, or Rose, every way it was a lady-like name.

The christening was over, and we were still at Tickhill, battling with circumstances: my wife ill and enfeebled, and without any prospect of immediate

T

relief. In vain I offered my ornaments in the neighbouring villages: all I received was a cold inquisitorial "Where do ye come from?" "Tickhill," was the reply. "Tickhill! God help you!"* generally finished the business. Mr. Campbell left the place, and we did not hear of him again for a long time. A vacancy occurred in the National School in that place, by the death of the master. A few friends promised me their support, if I would put myself in nomination for the situation. I did so; but no! the poor despised strolling player was not to be looked upon out of his cold ashlar-walled barn! Was he not poor? and was not that reason sufficient with the Orthodox few who could sway the suffrages for the successor to the situation? Besides, a teacher of Christian charity, one who wore black superfine, and was pious, at least on Sundays, had insulted a poor tailor in the town by upbraidings about his visits to the tailor's wife, when she lay upon her death-bed. Now, some fellow, who will doubtless prove a second Milton, or a great Unknown, had written a doggrel song, satirizing the doings of this said Christian teacher; the rhymes pleased the rabble, and they had them printed, and freely circulated; to give them a due publicity, they posted them upon the pillars of the Market Cross, self-evidence that somebody had written them. Nobody knew who the poet was; O no! he despised fame. No such thing as "Lines written by ——" were to be found on them. But they were written;

---

* This singular expression falls wildly upon the ear of the visitor.— I could not learn its origin; they tell the inquirer it is an "old saying." It is a very usual one; for several miles around, if you mention Tickhill, the usual response is, "God help you!"

and who could do such a nasty trick? Why every body (almost) said it must be that player-fellow. However, they thought so, and that was enough to forbid all serious people from helping him to the school-mastership of Tickhill. "God help all such folk!" said the player-fellow.

As I could not get a school with a name, and rations "to match," I set up on my own account. I took a room in an old projecting-storied building, called St. Leonard's Hospital; yes, and also put a paper in my window, expressive of my business, with "N.B. No connection," appended thereto. In the "old hospital" I opened a school for boys and girls to learn plain work. There can be no surprise excited at my "keeping a school," anybody could make a school-master. People must live; and as well to keep a school as do anything else; every sixpence will buy a loaf; and to be a school-master is one of the few comfortable trades which require no previous training. It has pleased the guardian spirit of England's mind and morals to furnish her with ready-made "maisters and dames," fitted for schools; and I was one of them. O privileged nation!

I was not quite so easy in my new stool as are many of the rulers of the birch; I had scarcely time to "Ahem!" and measure the distance from wall to wall, and tuck my hands under my coat tails, before I began to count over my qualifications for a teacher. *Imprimis*: I could read a little, write a decent hand, and figure simples and a few compounds; but the practice "made me mad." True I had a few boys to teach, and the sixpennies of those who did pay were useful; but others of them forgot to bring their pence on Mondays. Some of their mothers promised to pay another time; perhaps they may, but as it is now beyond the "limitations," they need not fear an arrest from me. Again, I had to encounter direct opposition in my new line, from the Orthodox. It was charged against me, that I refused to *beat* the boys because they could not " say their spellings," and that, with such mildness, the boys would be saucy, and overbearing; that those who did read under me, read their books more like reading a play, than the Bible; that by teaching them to read " poetry, and stuff," the boys would, at some future time, all run away from their masters, or parents, and turn players. With such reports current, my school was soon at a discount; I struggled on for a time, but the school returns were insufficient for my family. By necessity I kept the school, until prejudice prevented it from keeping me. In vain I looked around for some means of support; I could discover none, except by a return to my former vocation in the Theatre.

In January, 1826, my late manager, Mr. F. D. C., called upon me, to inform me that he had made arrangements to join in management with Mr. H——d, and had come to offer me a situation in their Theatre. They were then at Bolsover, a small market town in Derbyshire, remarkable for its castle, and anciently famous for its manufacture of buckles.* The offer was accepted, and the small preparation necessary for the

---

* Ben Jonson celebrates BOWSER BUCKLES in a Mask, provided by him, at an entertainment given to King Charles and his suite, at the Castle of Bolsover, by the Duke of Newcastle, in 1634.

campaign arranged. On a bright sunny morning in the young year, we started on our journey, through a knee-deep snow. The distance was considerable, and our attenuated condition ill fitted us for a long journey through deep snow drifts. As we approached Bolsover, the country was naturally wild, and the snow was piled up in fanciful mountain ranges, one o'er-topping the other like a mimic model of the mountains of the world. To plunge through them would require an effort beyond our strength; to skirt them was often difficult and perplexing. About three o'clock P.M., the sun was suddenly obscured by a dense pall of hoar; it fell so thickly that we were soon encrusted with it, and it was with great difficulty that we could track our way. With all our care our infant daughter was nearly benumbed with cold; our concern for her comfort increased our anxiety, lest on such a night, in such a dreary place, we should be worn out with fatigue, and perhaps perish with cold, as we had been now two hours walking without any assurance, nay, with scarcely a hope, that we were in the right direction. We at last observed, at a short distance from us, a labourer apparently returning from work; we called to him, and he immediately came towards us. We asked him to direct us to Bolsover, as we were strangers in that country, and being baffled with the hoar, and stiffened with the cold, we were now completely lost. The old man stood a few seconds before he spoke to us, eyeing us over with a glance of suspicion, then with a full-toned voice asked "Where dun ye come from?" "Tickhill," was the reply. "Tickhill, God help you—hum! Why you an come full three miles wrang!" exclaimed the old man. —"You wunna get there to neet," he continued, "for it's a dang'd rough road to begin we, an it's up t'ot huggins in snow. What trade may you be, an its fair to ax?" I answered him, "A comedian, and that, if possible, we must reach Bolsover that night, as we had to *play* in the first piece." He appeared quite calm at the expression of *comedian*, perhaps unconscious of its meaning, but at the word *play*, the old man started, as though he had encountered a sprite; he paused a moment, then raising his broad-brimmed hat, and looking sternly from under his large arched eye-brows, he loudly exclaimed, " Why, Lord bless—the Lord bless us!—why, you belong to them player-chaps wuts at Bowser? No wonder ye've lost! By'r leddy, I alwus reckoned as how you player fellers knew ivery thing, afore last Sunday, when th' Ranter Parson, wut preached at Clown toud us, as not one o' us as vallied his soul wur to go near ye at Bowser, for youn wur a soor lot o' chaps wut had lost God—aye, an that he'd a given you up to the devil altogether, for ye were aboon his hooks—an it looks loike it, or you wud na been lost on a neet loike this." I hinted, that the Ranter's knowledge of our being given up to the devil, was a revelation peculiarly his own; and, that he might also have known, if he had a Testament of his own, as I had never seen any such thing in mine, which professed to be of the authorised version. However, as he was a Christián, I would again appeal to his charity, to point us out the right road. After a speedy aspiration that we should quickly renounce our devil-trade, and imploring a blessing on us, he pointed out the most accessible way. Thanking him for his prayers, and this desired information, we started onward with new hope, and at length reached Bolsover.

As our names were announced in the bills for the evening, despite of our fatigue, we took a cup of tea, and thus refreshed, we at once prepared for the theatre. The play was the "*Castle Spectre*," in which we groped our way through "Hassan" and old "Alice."

Our associate manager, Mr. Charles H——, was one of a "long line" of strolling managers; and he combined the various professions of tragedian, printer, dyer, and stenciller; so that, however bad the business of the theatre might be, the old actors declared it was indeed "a bare common where Charley could not bite." It was no uncommon thing in the "good old days" for a strolling manager to print his own bills, and as ours claimed "kith and kin" with the renowned Baliols of the North—not the mighty Scot, pray do not confound them,—but, the celebrated Baliols, who so long ruled in buskins in the north of Yorkshire; Charles duly respecting those hereditary possessions, kept together the various branches which had descended unimpaired to him. Could you but peep into our manager's lodgings on a non-play day! He was always well lodged; no "little room up stairs," or "sit by our fire side," was of any use to him; he must have a good room, and a large one, on the first (ground) floor. Such a scene of bustle, unparalleled, perhaps, in the sleepy days of '26. The *melange* might be equalled *now*, at Gloucester, where the horrid Gauges "break," and piles of boxes heaped together in glorious confusion "mock Olympus"—where the "confusion of tongues," unknown before the rails, make the famed Babel of old a type of silence: such a scene might give an indistinct idea of his room. Enter the *sanctum sanctorum!* see the "mighty engine"—"the press"—that prints our bills; mark! how he turns out "*John Bull*" (in worn out letters, badly inked), and "*Devil to Pay,*" for to-morrow night! Nor is Jobson too proud to play the *devil* (for this time only), to the pressman, Dennis Brulgruddery. Time must be improved, and here the physical and the mental are both attuned.—" A pretty blusteracious night we have had of it, and—Charles, my lad, this *letter* gets worse for wear; if we go near to Sheffield, we must recruit, my boy." Mark with what force he pulls "home" the lever,—"the sun peeps through the fog this morning for all the world like the—bad ink, my boy, bad ink! Confound this inking business, Sir, its a greater bore to me than studying Jobson." Sings—

> " Over hills and high mountains,
> We'll drink dry the fountains,
> Until the sun rises again, my brave boys."

" How is the ink, Sir ?"—

> " Until the sun rises again."

In careless regard are strewn wigs, swords, satin gowns, dye-stuffs, stencil patterns, paper, ink, and play-books; amidst them all our manager stands by the press, and pulls, and blusters, until the " hurly burly's done," and Charley's himself again. Our manager likewise possessed another property, of greater value than those he kept in boxes for the stage,—that was, a warm heart: he was frank and honest, ever ready to share his purse with a pennyless brother of the profession. This company was well stocked with actors, but, as usual in small concerns, the actresses were few. The business at Bolsover was tolerably good, and the pieces decently got through—for a strolling company. From Bolsover we travelled to Alfreton; there we opened our theatre in the large room at the Angel. The business was good, our company in good repute, and all things smooth, until the end of the season. Our old strife-breeder, Mr. Lamb, was one of our company; and it appeared to be a part of his business, when no one gave offence, to " take offence without giving;" so when our season was about to close, he contrived, by his machinations, to dissolve the joint management of Messrs. C—— and H——.

Mr. C—— was now to take us forward on his own account. The towns in that part of the county were thinly cast, and thinly inhabited. Until our half-company could be again filled up, we removed to Crich, a small town that buttresses the High Peak of Derbyshire. The place is famous for its lime-stone, of pure white, and the scenery around it is very romantic. On the summit of a large limestone rock, stands an ancient round tower, of considerable height. At the time of our visit it was rather dangerous to climb to its top; we had to ascend by a stair of oaken beams, which were set transversely into the wall; many of them were rotten at their ends from extreme age. The view from the summit is exceedingly fine, commanding an extensive range of undulated country, with the blue crested High Peak range, resting themselves upon a pillow of clouds. I inquired amongst the villagers for what purpose the high "stand" had been erected; but they did not give me any correct information. It has the appearance of being a beacon-tower, of ancient time. Some assert it to be of druidical origin; others, to be *Cael's Wark*.* This lofty tower differs materially in construction from the many druidical remains which abound in the Peak; the masonry is regular, and the timbering somewhat modern. It is a striking object to the tourist, and may be seen for several miles around the place. From its dilapidated condition, it was in contemplation to take it down; but I am informed there is a project started to repair it, and conserve it as a relic of past ages, to astonish and delight succeeding generations. A week or two was passed at Crich, and as there was no *joint* manager to quarrel with here, Mr. L. was obliged to quarrel with the only one we had: Mr. C. had no appetite for these disturbances, and Mr. L. was consequently discharged. Our small concern was then removed to a neighbouring town, called Ripley: and from thence, to Cromford, near Matlock. At Cromford our manager had an offer of a partner, who was anxious to embark in the business: he was one of that large class who "live by their wits," called Quack Doctors. This gent. was famous as an *Aroscopist*, and he had a practice amongst the miners of Derbyshire which, for extent, many a surgery keeper, with his little room hung round with certificates, and

"A beggarly account of empty boxes,"

---

* The inhabitants of the Peak generally attribute every gigantic work of nature, or of art, for which they cannot otherwise account, as the work of the Gauls, Celts, or other ancient inhabitants of the island: hence the denomination " *Cael's Wark.*"

might almost sigh for. Still this man's notoriety was nowise an enviable one. If to believe that a doctor *can* cure you, be to effect the cure, W——r D—— gave his patients room to exercise their faith. But what is there that credulity cannot tolerate, particularly amongst the illiterate? You shall behold our Doctor holding one of his Sunday morning levees, at his residence, in the neat little town of Belper. Look at him seated in that large arm chair; is he not a great man? Have you seen the Æsculapius that Lord Elgin sent from Greece?—Have you seen Henning's restored cast of him?—What grace! how majestically he grasps the subtle type of his prudence and forethought,—and how venerable he looks! Our Doctor is not so old; he is in his prime; but he is as great, reckoning by the stone avoirdupois. It is said the ancient was exceedingly skilful in discovering the medicinal power of plants; our doctor dealt in herbs too. His attire bespeaks his importance. His large dressing-coat of plaid,— red plaid; do you not see it reflected in his face? Buttons,—every button, Sir, upon his coat, is solid silver, and worth five shillings each; indeed, all of them are current five-shilling pieces. Do you doubt it, there is the head of old George to attest his loyalty,— or, his vanity! Then the bunch of watch seals, and *the keys*. Of the seals—they are seals, not those little fragile things, washed with gold, and cut with doves and roses, that mincing misses pass over a gilt edged billet: no such things; they are seals, which, if melted down, would fetch something. Are they not too large? —humph: No. How would Goliath have looked, supposing him to have wielded a Field Marshal's baton, instead of a spear, like unto a weaver's beam? And the rings on his fingers,—they are as massive as the seals. They would not go round an oyster-barrel, but they do fit the Doctor's fingers; and they are all "solid gold," the Doctor "affirms it." And the big slippers; they are red too,—the second of the primary colours prevailed with the Doctor from his nose to his big slippers; some of the poor mountaineers used, by way of distinction, to call him the *Red man*. See him surrounded with bottles of all sizes, from half-an-ounce to half-a-gallon. There are some of a peculiar mould, each carefully sealed with red, and containing worms tape and taper; and oh! how long, taken from— who knows who? They were taken,—our Doctor "affirms it," by himself, from poor creatures, that, but for him,—might have got better. And there are the jars, white and brown, filled with pills and unctions; bundles of herbs, gathered (perhaps) in the "night's dank dew." Boxes, by the dozen, of snuff, aromatic, and capable of curing the most stinging head-ache; and if your head does not ache, this snuff can make it ache—it can do either, the Doctor affirms it. There is a "powerful grace" lies in the herbs whereof this snuff is compounded; they were gathered beneath the young moon's influence, by Mrs. D——: she was very particular, and never permitted Madam Luna to fill her horns before she had gathered the snuff plants. Mrs. D——, whom the Doctor familiarly called Mis-the-riss, was made a Doctress all at once, not by *degrees*—the Doctor could affirm that also. The Mis-the-riss was a clever woman, and not too proud to be useful: she could pound, and mix; besides, *she* understood the

Doctor's Latin,—a matter of grave consideration, for mistakes in pharmacy are often serious. You would be lost in surprise could you be allowed to witness our Doctor in his room, study, or surgery; he did not care so much for names: and your wonder would be excited to hear him examine a patient. One case is a fair sample of them all—though our Doctor did not believe in fixed principles. You shall hear a case. It is a fine morning in early June—a Sunday morning, when over-wrought machines are allowed to rest a few hours to rub up the muscles, and put them in order for next week, and to otherwise dispose of what there was not time to do during the six slaving days. The sun was above the horizon by the third hour; but before the half-closed eye of day had glanced his enlivening ray down Monsal Dale, yon miner was footing it sturdily to Belper, to secure the first turn at the Doctor's. The Doctor was no respecter of persons; a miner's guinea was as good as a Lord's; so when they " came in a ruck," he " tuk 'em by rotation." He is always an early man—when he is sober; he opens at six on Sundays, when the days are long, because, when the folks come from Castleton, it is a long way for them, especially if they have to return the same day, and carry a three-half-pint bottle of stuff with them. The Doctor is seated for business; the miner has secured the first turn: he approaches the Doctor, he trembles (no wonder), he strokes his hair, he bows—that is, he nods his head. The Doctor accosts him in a voice as mild as the infant thunder that sports around the craggy-browed Peak at midsummer :—" Well, me man, what's the mather we a?" The patient replies—" I don't know, but I've been about a week this way." "O, I no," says the doctor, "ha' you browt your bottle?" "Yees, Sir, theyn toud me as you'd want it." And here the miner presented his bottle. The doctor places it between his large eye and the light, shakes it up, uncorks it, smells of it, and exclaims, "By'th' hookey, me man, but yer d—d bad: I'll just bet one guinea that yu'll dee, however." The man looks pale. "Don't faint, me man; put out your tongue." The man obeys. "Hey, I see your d—d bad, Sir; do yer know that you're a gotten the *Tout-ma-lowrie!* Yur trubbled with phlem and mucus, aint you?" The man nods, and stares upon vacancy. "Your disorther is what we call the *Ki-i*, and the *Cal-a-bang.*" The man trembles. The Doctor says, "Don't ye be feared, me man, I can cure yur,—what wages ha yer?" The man revives, but makes no reply. "How mony bairns ha ye?" "Seven, Sur." "Ecod," says the Doctor, "you've a lot,—Mis-the-riss, empty that fellow's bottle—and see yur, Sur—dy'e hear, you must bring it full again next Sunday,—and Mis-the-riss, bring two o' them half-pints, and sum pills?" Mrs. D—— is dutiful, and the things appear. "There, Sur, you mun drink a big cupfull, neet and morning, out o' the bottles, and take two pills three times a day, —I can do you, sure, wi' six bottles!" The man nods, and says, "Thank you, Sur—wuts to pay?" The Doctor ruminates. "Let's see, seven children; bottles shud be fifteen shillings, and th' pills half-a-crown— seventeen and six—I reckon you can't afford it?" The man shakes his head. "Come, then, fifteen altogether," says the Doctor. The man then reaches down to the bottom of his pocket, and draws up a small bag of sheepskin, out of which he presents the Doctor with a sovereign. The Doctor laughs (not titters), and says, "Come, yur'e a tight un to plead poor—here, Mis-the-riss, give change—take fifteen, the feller says he's poor!" The man takes the change, the bottles, the pills, and bows;—nods, as before,—and retires. The doctor calls, as he retires, "You mun cum next Sunder, and mind and bring yer morning's w——." The man, who kept backing out, was in the street before the last sentence was finished; he has turned his face towards Monsal Dale again, and ponders as he goes, upon his strange disorder, his bottles, the pills, and the fifteen shillings.

I once met with this quack-doctor at Heage; he invited me to the White Hart: we had liquors and refreshment, but, alack, when the landlord hinted at "the shot," the Doctor's purse was empty; he tried to sell his pills, but there was not a purchaser; he recommended his snuff, but there were no buyers. He swore "the people wouldn't be bad." At length, the landlord, finding that *both* his customers were pennyless, thought that the sooner he stopped the tap, the better for himself. This Doctor was not a stranger to him, albeit he preferred his money to his credit. As necessity often forces hard bargains, the landlord took a dozen boxes of the snuff as a pledge, that the Doctor would, as he promised to do, call *some* day, and pay him. The quack had what he called "grand days,"—those were, when he wanted his purse replenishing, or when he was canvassing a fresh place: when he succeeded in the latter, he called it "breaking new ground." When he was "breaking up," he made a great parade,—was particularly nice to display the plaid (red), buttons, seals, key, rings—all but the big slippers; but to atone for slippers, he hired a man-servant. He sent John (especial man-servants are always Johns,) "over" the day before with a quantity of bills, containing a lot of specifics, and how many yards of worms, or, as the Doctor called them, "wurrums," had been by him destroyed; each case was attested, or, in his own phraseology, "affirmed." John put up at the Inn, where he was met by the Doctor (the Redman), in full dress, with his polished mahogany box of "wurrums," his gamboge, elixir of vitriol,—and water, plentiful in Derbyshire; so the three-half-pints, which John had in a basket ready, if wanted, could be readily filled if anybody would "come down;" their health, or the duration of their disorder, mainly depended upon their "coming down." The large number of his patients was comprised within the pills, snuff, and worm-cake range; sometimes a bad case "came down" for a bottle, for which the charge of ten or fifteen shillings was demanded.

The amount of money that he gulled out of the people by this Ki-i and Cal-a-bang mummery, almost exceeds belief. This quack's house, during his popularity, was often crowded, upon the Sunday mornings, from six o'clock, until twelve or one, by the incredulous, who sought him from every nook within the Peak range, and consequently, money poured in upon him.

Wealth, so unworthily brought together, was soon wasted in riot and drunkenness, which brought their characteristic train of evils, decay of health, and waste of substance. Even gullibility at last failed with this —so called—Doctor. He had drained the cash from many a poor family; how many of them he cured, or killed, cannot be so readily ascertained. He escaped a verdict of manslaughter; perhaps his stuff was so nicely compounded, that if it did not good, it could do no harm: an objection may be taken to his gamboge, but if he only used so much of it as was necessary to spoil the colour of the water, such an homœpathic dose could not destroy life.

While we were acting at Cromford, the quack I have just sketched was taken with the strange infection of turning player; and calculating upon his power to raise any amount of money which might be required of him to enable him to embark in the management, he now offered himself (no small offer either,) to Mr. Campbell as a partner. One evening, during the performance, Kraken had gained admission behind the scenes; the liquor was ascending within him; he was momentarily impressed with his future prospects as an actor, and was determined to try his hand at the business. He rushed upon the stage, reeled to the foot-lights, and being drunk, fell across them, and from the effects of the liquor, he was unable to rise again. The audience came to his rescue; they took the Doctor, and charitably carried him down stairs, and thus our manager escaped—at once and for ever—from the annoyance and further entreaties of the quack-doctor—the Emperor of *wurrum* quacks, W———r D———n.

How strange it is, that men, who have to wring out their few shillings by excessive toil from their handicrafts, while their whole life's-flood is ebbing, in continuous drops, from the fountain of their brow—how strange that they should be so reckless of their better selves, as to shorten their lives by casting their brains as so much offal upon the consuming altar of ignorance! How long will it be before we rise up in our tens of thousands of thinking men, instead of, as hitherto, crawling instinctively over the commons of animality, and devouring its brutalizing garbage? When shall we hurl the sophisms of the mammon-loving quacks "to the dogs," despising the carcase-feeding dominion of those who would fatten upon human vitals? When shall we accept the advice of that mental physician, who offers it gratis, for the elevation of body, and the salvation of soul—the mighty Doctor of Education?

It was now the season when invalids visit the baths of Matlock, and lodgings were not only scarce, but dear. My wife and I had to tramp it to a neighbouring village—Bonsall, each night, to sleep; it was distant about three and a half miles. It was excessive toil for us to return after the play was over, to climb the rocky steep, each taking a turn in carrying the children. The burden was increased by the disturbed state of our stomachs, which gave us sundry twitchings and gnawings for want of more provender. Our theatre was next removed to Bonsall, until we could fit up a theatre at Matlock. At Bonsall our beginning gave promise of a short, but remunerative season; but after two nights' performance, the Clergyman put his ban upon us: no unusual thing with us to be stopped by those well-fed and State-paid teachers of the people. In company with our manager, we waited upon him, to see if persuasion could win a few nights for us.

No; he was very marble :— he could not sanction such wickedness. Was it not presumption in us to ask such a thing? To desire to act "filthy plays" within the dominion of a Rev.—shocking! Have not the dramatists themselves been very doubtful characters, and the actors still worse? Do not history-books say, that Warwickshire Will stole deer? that Rare Old Ben got drunk? that—but, oh dear, what is not said that is bad of the play-writers and actors? Perhaps it is the especial duty of the saints below, to put their veto upon the dissemination of such wretched profane stuff; only the pure in this vile world of our's should do it; and whoever heard of a Bishop poaching venison, or a ghostly father being "half-seas-over"? Our manager grew tired of this foil: one day, lacking decent sustenance; another, and the ghost of a steak would be haunting your stomach, yet, before you could grasp the substance, some sleek priest, whose larders were greasy with the profuse abundance of tax and tithe-bought viands, would give a righteous shrug, and cry, "It is better you should starve, than gain a loaf by reading poetry to the people—to *my* people." Mr. C—— determined to give up the stage, our little knot was dissolved, and again my family were stranded upon the shoals of disappointment. Again we had to pause before we let ourselves loose upon the waters of adversity, for we knew not how to shape our course to make a haven. In our dilemma, we heard that a small company had taken up somewhere in the neighbourhood of Derby. Rising early one morning, I took the road, and paced along, until I reached the village of Mickleover, where I found the company in question, under the management of Messrs. Spencer and Kennedy, containing four gentlemen and three ladies: this, also, was a sharing company. I explained to them my desires, and at length engaged for myself and my wife. Of this company report spoke well. Again filled with hope, I trudged back to my family with the pleasing intelligence. The next day we packed our box off by the carrier, to Derby, and started ourselves for our next situation with a knapsack of properties on my back for present use, and with our two little children, the one in its mother's arms, the other, now walking a mile or two, and then, poising upon the knapsack on my back, his little legs hanging over my shoulders, to rest his young, but laggard limbs. Thus disposed, we jogged along over fieldway and roadway, until we reached our destination. After procuring a lodging in the house of an aged and toil-furrowed peasant, we partook of tea; and when snugly seated in the ingle-nook, we could once more afford to laugh at old care and weary bones. Our new friends were aristocratic strollers; they "talked large," and affected to look down upon "the people that had just joined." Time is a sure leveller of wiredrawn distinctions, and he,—good old fellow,—admonished the great ones, that we were all brothers and sisters of adversity, and they were forced to believe it. Mrs. K—— our tragedy heroine, now a burley, claret-cheeked dame, who, but for her sex, might have played Falstaff without stuffing, was, as report said, a Highland lassie, as wild, yet as lovely, as those heather-clad rocks, whose feet bathe in the shining lochs, and whose brows kiss the heavens. In the wild glens that diversify that land of mountain grandeur, Mrs. K——, while yet a "wee lassie," is said to have been surprised one day by the *bell-woman*, who, after her usual prologue, declared that "a play, the *Gentle Shepherd*, would be ocit a neet i' Sandy Comerford's barn, by ane Davy Ray and Jammy Crainstones." The lass went to see the play in Sandy's barn, and her sloe-black 'een struck, like barbed darts, deep—deep into Davy Ray's heart. Davy's inward pain was only to be cured by the possession of the syren that struck him. He made her his own, and soon after he introduced her to the stage. Her first essay is reported to have been in "Elvira," in the play of "*Pizarro*." When she was told by Davy that she was to make her appearance in that part, she exclaimed, "Hoot Davy, mon, I'll no do that; I'll never be able to do the speech about the boiling leed, and the sockets 'o the 'een." In Davy's time, even as now, necessity would not be over nice, and our heroine made the trial; she was encouraged onwards; she ventured at the speech of the "sockets 'o the 'een," and thenceforth became an actress. Mr. K—— was also a singular old man, but warm-hearted, nevertheless. It was laughable to see the old fellow, as he stood at the wings during a play, his eye intensely riveted upon the speaker on the stage. If an actor was not quite perfect, or a pause took place, for which he could not readily account, then the old gentleman grew furious; with hurried step he would pace along the sides, his head bowed to the ground, and beating his forehead violently with his fist, he would cry out—often loud enough to be heard by the audience—"Come to Hecuba, Sir,—d—n it, Sir, why don't you come to Hecuba!"

The first play we had to take part in here was the tragedy of "*Romeo and Juliet.*" I was to personate the gay "Mercutio," and my wife the "Nurse." Our tragedy queen was to play the "hopeful lady," who had

"Not seen the change of fourteen years."

In spite of all her trimming she looked more like Queen Dollallolla, than a girl whose age, "be it spoken,"

"Come Lammas-eve at night, shall be fourteen."

About the hour to commence the play, several of the "gentlefolks" of the place entered the theatre, which being reported to Mrs. K——, she affected to faint at having to play before "such company," with "that creature for a nurse." "O! I shall be so cut up," exclaimed the armful of beauty; but she was obliged to try her fate. Our Nurse had scarcely uttered, "What, lamb!—what, lady-bird!"—before our manageress changed her opinion, and at the end of the first scene, "Jule" declared she never had a better Nurse! The piece went off smoothly, and "the gentles" complimented the talents of the company. The great merit of this company was, that the pieces were always perfect before they were put upon the stage.

We remained here a few days, and after a fortnight's stay at Etwall, a neighbouring place, we removed to Castle Donington, in Leicestershire, where we remained about a month. At Donington our business was wretchedly bad; very few of those who attended appeared to appreciate the plays: farces, burlesque, and dumb show seemed to be more to their taste. After a month of hunger was passed, we removed to Shardlow, in Derbyshire, about four miles distant from the former place. Here our success was as great as our want of it was gloomy in the last place.

To a " traveller at home," nothing is more surprising than the difference of taste and of manners in the inhabitants of adjoining villages. Sometimes I have observed this marked difference in the short space of two miles; and without any outward thing whereby to indicate the cause, you might find the people at one place seeking their pleasure in the ale-house, and making bets upon the next prize-fight, while they had to pledge their coat, or hat, " to fasten the stakes;" in another corner a group might be found playing at cards for a quart, and laughing at having bilked the policeman so nicely, by each pocketing his hand of cards as the limb of the law entered the door; others would be earnestly debating the age and qualities of a bull-dog, or quarrelling over the bets upon a cock-fight; while in one corner, propped up by the chimney-breast, a solitary one, nearly drunk, with closed eyes, his head fallen upon his breast, is grunting out a filthy ballad, not one of the company present caring to notice him. In such places the inhabitants generally show an utter contempt for everything associated with literature: they can find amusement in coarse oaths, in insulting and harassing, by every means in their power, anybody who professes to love literary refinement or science. In a neighbouring village, or hamlet, on the other hand, you may find the bulk of the inhabitants fond of reading, and conversant with the poets,—panting to gain a better acquaintance with our Shakspeare, and quoting his writings,—singing out the songs of the Ploughman Bard,

"A man's a man for a' that,"

having their occasional music-meetings, and taking pleasure in the theatre, because they can appreciate the author's work, and can find religion beaming in the soulfulness of his expressions. True, that in such places, a reckless few may be found, but they are the pitied outcasts, whose education was too often furnished in a prison, where, for certain offences, they had been at once punished and refitted for the next depredation. It is not less true, that where the people are better informed, there they are generally honest—there they are more independent, in every sense of the word; there, too, they are better fed and clothed, seldom troubling the workhouse, and always spoken well of by their employers. If it be desirable to have a happy and contented people, begin to use the Christian precept, "do unto them as you would they should do unto you," and the people will respect you. Any one who has travelled in our country, and would open his eyes and his ears to the things passing around him, must have observed these facts. Will the opposers of the people's education believe it? They had rather not. Serfs can be whipped to their duty, say they? Happily, no: we thought once it was our destiny, but the Testament we have read has taught us to shun such a creed.

Whatever the cause, we found auditors at Shardlow, but four miles from our former place, most interested in sterling pieces,—those whose object was to reach the soul, rather than to amuse an hour, were always the best received here.

We made a lengthened season at this place, and were well remunerated: we had each good benefits, and we enjoyed the good opinion of the inhabitants. My wardrobe was reduced when we visited this place, but one by one I replaced it—trousers, waistcoat, shirts, hat—until I was entirely new rigged, except my very "seedy coat." After my benefit, which left me some two pounds ten shillings—a world of riches—I started, accompanied by my wife, to walk to Nottingham, to purchase a new one—second-hand. It was a sweating day; the bright sun was dancing over us. The day was unusually hot, even for a summer's day. The player is bound, hand and foot, to conventions, particularly the one of *looking respectable:* for if he is not well dressed, how can he understand the " study of mankind ?"—To be a player, he must be a gentleman; and to be a gentleman is to be well dressed! So necessity made it imperative upon the players always to put on the best appearance. Yes, that vulgar notion which makes poverty despicable, was plentifully visited upon the strollers; albeit, he is like the poet—proverbially poor. Well may the adage run, " that to be poor, and to look poor, is indeed, to be miserable."

We were now to enter a large provincial town; and, as far as appearance was concerned, I was a " dandy" in all things, except a coat. I could not be expected to disgrace my profession, by entering the town of Nottingham in a seedy coat; so I kept up appearances by walking into the town in my shirt sleeves, the old coat nicely folded, and hung over my arm. In such trim, and under such a frizzling sun, I could pass unnoticed, particularly on the market-day, when roughs of all degrees congregate. We wandered from place to place, looking for a likely shop whereat to get decently dressed. At length we reached the shop of Mr. Gresham, the pawnbroker, in Weekday Cross. Mr. Younge, who was with me, had himself made good bargains, in similar situations, and he advised me to walk into the shop now at hand. I did so: there I was supplied with a new—second-hand, olive-green surtout coat, for twelve shillings,—made a *gentleman* of for twelve shillings. Only twelve shillings! What a pity it is that any human creature desirous of making a man of himself, should ever be so very poor, that he should writhe under

"The proud man's contumely,"

when just twelve shillings current would make him a perfect gentleman. I donned the new coat from Gresham's pawn-shop, and in order to " look big"—for pride, like typhus fever, is intermitting, if ever you get within its pale—so I, to show how I could endure the heat of that broiling day, or else to show my new coat, strutted proudly along the streets of Nottingham. It is said that about two o'clock P.M., is usually the hottest time of the day. I am not certain it was so on the day in question; but this is certain, that it was just two by the Exchange clock as I promenaded the Long Row, and I did not feel the heat more oppressive with my new (second-hand) coat on, than I did in the morning with my " seedy one" off. It may be, that " what will keep the cold out, will also keep out the heat." My new coat would. I left Shardlow in the morning, a three-quarter sort of a *fellow*,—I entered it in the evening every inch a *man*. It was done for the low price of twelve shillings. Again, I say, what a pity we have so many "creatures," and so few men, when we can earn as much in one day as would set us up; yet, in consequence of labour being one thing, and capital another, thousands cannot receive that sum in a week.

The next day, with feelings of regret at leaving such friends as we had found in Shardlow, we bade adieu to them; and the next morning we packed off to Duffield. We stopped for several weeks in Duffield, but our receipts were scarcely enough to furnish our existence; we struggled on, but a good meal was a luxury we seldom enjoyed while there. To add to our want of comfort, the importance of our tragedy Queen was not a whit less off the stage than upon it. Our necks began to ache with looking up to her Mightiness; each day the crick in mine was more severe, and we began to think seriously of getting another situation. There were great difficulties to be overcome before I could do anything, with even a small theatre, on my own account. The want of dresses and scenery might be surmounted, if the requisites for purchase could be furnished. But the great necessity—that of supplying myself with actors—would prove the greatest obstacle; for the stage had been so badly supported, that those who really were attached to the profession had been driven from it.

The Theatres throughout the country were deserted. Every week the newspapers supplied advertisements of Theatres in the provinces to be sold, or sometimes of paragraphs, that they had been converted into chapels, or other purposes. In London alone the profession could maintain itself—there it flourished. And from 1826, to the years 1844-5, we have witnessed the anomaly of the Theatres being honored, and crowded with auditors in London, while they have been deserted in the provinces; and the actors have been starved out, or forced to seek other employment. What, then, has driven this source of pleasure and instruction away from us—our poverty, or our friends? National prosperity or depression may—indeed they must, affect the Theatre, in the same ratio as they assist to depress other places of recreative instruction; but poverty has not been the sole cause of the decline of the drama in the small country towns. The great cause of failure may be found in the prevailing ignorance of the artisans and peasantry. The drama will never be enjoyed and appreciated by an ignorant community. They may make gamblers of themselves, and be able to understand the jugglery of betting-books and horse-racing,—they may arrange pugilistic encounters, or play at bagatelle for gallons of ale—all this, and more of such like man-lowering amusements they can understand, and support;—but such a class cannot descend, with our own Shakspeare, deep into the human heart, nor can they fly off with him, upon the wings of imagination, " from earth to heaven." No; they belong to the earth, and are " of the earth," most " earthy."

They can plough, and drive steam engines, but they have no spirituality. Their region of thought lies like

> "An unweeded garden
> That grows to seed; things rank and gross in nature
> Possess it merely."

How many of those who profess to make it their life-business to analyse the human heart, while in a mass they would bind you to their opinions, have a word of approval to give you of the theatre, or concert-room? Rather do they not tell you to shun recreations,—above all, to shun the players, as you dread sin and the devil? Some of them do not confine their maledictions to the theatre alone, but they attack the sciences: they believe—or they tell the ignorant so—that the Devil is the author of the best book on Geology, and ascribe many other good things to him. Many of them, who certainly ought to understand the ability and power of his "brimstone Devilship" much better than the "common people," ascribe the drama to his authorship, and give him the Theatres as so many town and country houses into the bargain. Is it not pitiful that men who make their education their boast, should thus attempt to despise the revelation bestowed by the Universal Parent upon those High Priests of mind? HE alone inspired them with the power of prophecy. HE it was that bid them draw aside the prejudice-veil of dulness from never-thinking men, and to reveal unto them

> "The form of things unknown."

V 2

Yet we are to be forced to believe that these men are the children of the devil, and, as a necessary sequence, that they hold their commission direct from the evil one. Let us pause before we take for granted a creed so dark—so much at variance with God's revelation in external nature, that never-tiring teacher of the ways of Omnipotence!

We were wearied out by vain attempts to keep in tune with our manageress; so with the close of the business at Duffield, I left that company, together with Mr. Younge. I was now in business on my own account. My stock-in-trade was important, to begin with. Of scenes I had none; and of actors, myself and my wife, and my little son,—who by this time had begun to sing songs, give recitations, and play the juveniles when required. He was considered a prodigy of his age; and, as far as "drawing" went, he often proved the best man in the company. The old comedian, Mr. Younge, completed our number to begin with. A gentleman, of the name of Stevens, and an acquaintance of his, a lady, Miss West, joined us soon afterwards. My first scene I painted upon printed calico, being a number of old gown skirts sewed together. I next added a few wings, painted upon calico, and, with a few dresses, our little affair solicited the notice of the villagers. In the late autumn of 1826 we commenced operations, at the little village of Quorn, near to Duffield, and there, for a week or two, we were well rewarded. From thence we visited Long Eaton, Basford, Bulwell, and several other villages in that neighbourhood, until we reached Kimberley. At most of the former places our receipts enabled us to procure something like a living; it was a mean one, but it might be tolerated. At Kimberley, we were reduced to a miserable existence—a quart of buttermilk, which was charitably given to us each morning by the landlady of the inn where we were lodging, and a penny loaf, divided between two of us. This quantity, which we were compelled to measure out as carefully as a " fat overseer" measures out the dietary of a Union workhouse, formed our daily rations for a fortnight. Of course we had but one meal per diem, so we usually breakfasted about seven o'clock at night. Before we could purchase our supply of bread, my wife had to earn the money to buy it with. This she did by knitting night-caps, muffatees, comfortables, &c. Those articles, when sold, returned from fourpence to eightpence for profit, or rather, for labour. After the articles were sold, I or Mr. Younge, or more frequently both of us,—for company is soothing in adversity, had to walk to Nottingham to purchase the material to work up into the before-named articles; for every twopence was well saved, although purchased by a walk of sixteen miles, in stormy weather; for, during our stay at Kimberley, the ground was deeply covered with snow. On one occasion only had we the luxury of tasting a flesh-meal during our stay at Kimberley; then an extra produce in the knitted articles left us sufficient to indulge in the luxury of a dinner: we had surplus fund sufficient to purchase half a peck of potatoes, with a few pence to lay out in flesh. Mr. Younge and myself sought out a butcher, and with a degree of assurance which nothing but *wealth* could impart, we asked him to supply us with a quarter of a pound of mutton. The butcher looked at us very sternly, and taking his knife, as if to serve the chop, " A quartern, you said, didn't you?" and away went the knife through the loin that was laid upon the board. " A quartern?" said he; " aye, you are the player fellows, that are starving to death upon the hill yonder —poor devils!" He saw it in our faces; the compliment was not less unkind. After supplying us with the meat, and demanding a fraction extra for the " small cut," he allowed us to leave his shop for a few yards. It was about noon-time of the day, and three or four stocking-makers were taking their usual lounge, to enjoy a mouthful of fresh air: to amuse these men, the butcher called upon us to return. Unconscious that we were to furnish merriment for these men, we returned. " I say," said the butcher, jeeringly, "are both you lean fellows going to dine off that *lot?*" This taunt struck like iron into Mr. Younge; the wild blood rushed up to his cheeks, and gazing angrily upon the butcher and his mates, he grumbled out a curse at their heartlessness, and then hastened away from them. I coolly replied, " Yes, Mr. Butcher, two lean fellows are going to dine off the lot, and four other persons also;" and I followed my companion, with the mutton wrapped in my pocket-handkerchief, while the butcher grunted a solo, and the stockingers laughed out a chorus. There are seasons when seeming trifles make a lasting impression on one's memory: this was one of those occasions. It was not that I felt deeply hurt by the fellow's sneers; still the form of that butcher has haunted me ever since. There are the groups, as perceptible now as they were at that moment,—butcher, knife, stockingers, and their jeering halloes. Hard fare had accustomed me to such dinners. I have had many such since that time. I hope the butcher has fared better, and has not been tied down to such a joint as made up " that lot."

I was in Nottingham on one of the snowy November days in that year, and upon my usual worsted-purchasing errand, when I met an acquaintance—Mr. Morley, who was commissioned to engage some comedians for a gentleman who had taken the Riding-school, in Nottingham, as a minor theatre. I thought this was a favourable opportunity to endeavour to better our situation; for the severity of the weather, and scanty food, united to chain us down to Kimberley. The gentleman who was to open this minor theatre was Mr. Batty, the proprietor of a circus. A circus! There was another impediment; for a player to hold communion with a horse-rider was rank heresy in the profession. And better is it to be starved orthodoxly, than heterodoxly fed. What conventionalist will question it? Mr. Batty said, above all things, he wanted a scenery painter. He declared I was just the man, and if I would engage with him, a trifling addition to my salary should not part us. Queer times, when you are forced to be listening to promises of salary, and yet afraid to take the offer. Very perplexing. My duty to my starving children, to my creditors, to my bowels —all said, " Take it, man." " Think what the profession will say," whispered Honour. " What! mix with the vile profession of saw-dusters? Never! never!" The struggle was short, but long enough to make my bowels grumble like the dying strains of an organ. They conquered. I had a respect for both profession and stomach, and the gist of the argument resolved itself into an opinion, that, "like unsevered friends," they ought to dine together. It was evident I might defend my honour, until Honour would bring in a verdict against me of " Died by starvation;" so I bolstered profession for the chance of a month's feeding. Mr. Batty gave me a sovereign to bind me to the bargain, and I gave him a pledge that I would return the next day, and commence painting. I was half crazy with this business. I was now bound to him; the sovereign had done the business. Would it become known amongst the actors that I had joined the horse-riders? If so, would not the very fact be "trumpet-tongued" against my future progress? But my starving family—my dreary prospects—the sovereign; thus I went on soliloquising, until I caught my eye upon a pile of bread-loaves, in a shop window,—that put the finishing-stroke to the business. I went into the shop, purchased some bread, and changed my sovereign. I then felt more easy. I hastened back to Kimberley, repeated to them my adventure, but it only brought momentary relief; the same objections as I had taken had to be overruled by *them*. Again we marshalled all the host of professional conservatisms, and they appeared in numberless array. Gaunt Hunger was there also to oppose them, and fiercely he fought his "battles o'er again;" and in making the last onslaught, he seized one of the bread-loaves I had brought in with me,

"And thrice he slew the slain."

We soon had the tea-kettle boiling, the tea made ready, and congratulations were mutual. We made a feast, that for heartiness would have given a fair challenge to a Scotch breakfast. We discharged our bill for lodgings,—we had none other to meet; for, thanks to the kind-hearted of Kimberley, they kept us out of debt, as no person would give us credit. The next day saw us pack off to Nottingham. There I was scene-painter and stage-manager to Monsieur Batty.

Our Monsieur might be French; he talked a good homespun dialect, but he *might* be a Frenchman. If he was not born a Frenchman, I dare say it was necessary that he should call himself one, because many English persons know that all good actors—whether of the Circus or the Opera—are foreign. The prefix of Monsieur, or Signor, gives powers to a performer. I am not singular in my opinion here, for Dick told me himself "he was always applauded twice as much when he was Signor, as he was when only an English Mr." Dick used to say that mustachios were worth twenty pounds a year to a man; but as he had to be the Clown so frequently, he never could wear a pair long enough to get much by them,—to make the best of it, he had a beautiful pair of false ones for out-door business. If you are required to play in the orchestra as well as the circle, then a prefix of Herr is useful, and enables an Englishman to give a peculiar relish to the tones of a cornet-a-piston. Dick was a wag in his way. He used to say he was forced to have his wife called a Madame—he did not like your Madams, but it was profitable, he said; but if he had a daughter, she should have, said he, a tail to her name,—a *le*, or a *lest*, as a finishing syllable. Dick said a lady could always appear to more advantage with a finish to her name. He had been long enough in the craft to know the exact market value of Mr., Monsieur, Madame, or Mrs.

Monsieur Batty intended to engage the Riding School as the most commodious place for his circus and stage. He was out-generalled in his plans. Mr. Cooke, of circus popularity, had agents at work with the proprietors, and got possession of the place before my master. This was a misfortune, as the School was the place of repute. Failing to procure the School, Monsieur Batty fitted up, at a considerable expense, a large wooden building at the bottom of Chapel Bar, and commenced operations. There, all the day, and half of the night, I was employed painting scenes, or superintending rehearsals: now, fire-eating in "*Ali Pacha*," or spouting "Angerstoft," in the "*Floating Beacon*," or mimicking a dance of savages.

Mr. Batty remained at Nottingham until the middle of December, and then removed to Derby. Our Governor—so called in saw-dust parlance—thought it would be more profitable to have the town of Derby to ourselves, during the Christmas holidays, than to stop at Nottingham, and share them with a rival. So holly-wreathed Christmas saw us at Derby, blazoning forth scenes in the circle, melo-drama, farce, and spectacles, mantled up in sulphurous robes of red and blue fire. The business at Derby was a losing affair to the Governor. The January of 1827 welcomed us to Ashbourne, with many fair promises of support. The Theatre was taken as the most likely place; there we had the usual routine—with the exception of the horses—of melo-drama, farce, ballet-de-action, fence combats, and rope-dancing. The receipts at Ashbourne were not sufficient to support so large a company, and keep the "Grand stud of horses" standing idle in their stables, with hay at ten pounds per ton, and ale, for the grooms, at eightpence per quart. Monsieur Batty was now tired of the "mumming system;" the fairs were more congenial to the tastes of the "moulders;" they would not be bothered with studying plays, and "the d—d nonsense about feeling and expression, and all such-like patter." There was also a not less important consideration with Monsieur—it did not yield him money enough. The fairs were "the things" for them; the roar of brass band, the parade of horses, and glitter of spangles, with the wood-cut of Monsieur H—— on the tight-rope, and the real acrobats done in oil, upon show-cloths, with the bawl of "just a going to begin." These things usually bring down the "blunt" at the fairs, and that is "the be-all and end-all" with the riders.

From Ashbourne Mr. Batty intended to travel southward, to be ready to commence his out-door business at Lynn Mart. My engagement was now at an end with Mr. Batty: even the dread of short meals in the country could not induce us to accept the money-temptation of travelling to the fairs. We had a few weeks in the Circus, and all that could be said well of it, was, that we had a good salary, which was punctually paid. For the rest—but education has reached the riders of this time (1847) I should hope. Twenty years ago their manners were repulsive, and to talk to

W

them about circumspection and propriety of conversation before females, was to get yourself offended by them, and to be charged with assuming a mawkish sentimentality. Sanatory reform will wash out the slang from such places, along with the filth that it drenches out of St. Giles's, that famed college for teaching a living language to the showmen.

Expecting that my former engagement was to finish with our business at Ashbourne, I had opened a correspondence with a gentleman resident at Alfreton, whose *professional* name was to be Mr. Wells; his amateur amusements in theatricals had, at last, grown up into a desire to make the stage his profession. He had a good stock of scenes and dresses, and I thought our united property would make up a passable affair for the small towns; Mr. Wells receiving a dead share for his part of the concern. I now determined to travel to Alfreton, and complete our arrangements. Having packed off my boxes by the carrier, I and my family determined to walk thither, and to husband the few shillings we had saved with Mr. Batty, expecting that we should have a pressing necessity for all we could get. It was a nipping winter morning, and the journey a long one; for when it is considered that we had two children to carry such a distance, each mile of road, in such weather as we had to go through, became painfully longer as we became weaker with the exertion required for the task. But on we struggled, my wife pressing our little daughter more and more closely to her bosom, to impart additional warmth to her child; I, too, huddling the boy, or pressing his little legs to my sides, to cheer him onwards, as he was poised upon my shoulders, or riding pic-a-back, and clasping my neck. The cold was too intense for him, and despite of all our cheering, or coaxing, he was at last so benumbed and cold, as to cause him to cry and sob aloud with pain. Hope came to our rescue at last: approaching the town of Belper, we came to a rocky knoll, where two or three cottages were clustered together; the door of one of them stood wide open, and a blazing fire was curling up into the spacious ingle-nook. As we were nearing the door, an ancient dame, in grey woolsey petticoat and blue printed bed-gown, a large mob-cap, bound closely to her head by a black ribbon, with a turned-up nose, and her face flushed like a "bloody-wall" in June, waddled hastily up to the door; then, placing her arms a-kimbo, contrived to block up the whole of the door-way. I had anticipated comfort, as I saw the red fire reflecting on the white snow from the cottage door-way. I was too sanguine in my expectations: before I could speak a word to this mountain-hag, she froze my blood; for, despite the rose-pink of her arched cheek bones, it was evident that uncharitableness was enthroned in her heart; she looked as hard as the ice-robed crags over which we were walking. I implored her, in Charity's name, to allow us to warm our children at her fire. The old beldame curled up her nose a little more into the murky hoar, as if to sniff in a sufficient quantity whereby to test it, and then forcing her toothless gums into her skinny lips, grunted out, "Ney!" Again I begged the favour, and again she answered, "Ney: I henna noot to gi youn!" I told her I did not wish her to give me anything; but as we had a long way to travel before we could get to our place of destination, I only wished to warm the children, and I would pay her anything she required, as I was not without money. She again pressed her knuckles more firmly into her fat sides, and fanned out her grey woolsey, at the same time biting her lip, and exclaiming in a tone of bitter firmness, "Ney, I shanna!" In vain my wife proffered to remain on the outside with the young one, if the old dame would but allow me to enter with the boy; or if not, to allow the little fellow to go to the fire and warm himself. No: it was evident the old madam had drank more of buttermilk than "the milk of human kindness," and she now summoned the gall from her bony heart to aid her in her last reply— "Ney, I tell youn, I wunna ha my house-floor weeted wi' snaw for noother you nor your brats, sa gang yer way to Bilper!" and with the close of the sentence she threw the door to with a bang that re-echoed amongst the rocks like thunder. I was too much troubled with the desire to procure warmth for my children to complain of the old woman's bitterness; the words struggled with my utterance, but pity restrained them. Was it that this woman did not possess a benevolent heart, or that she belonged to an age when the inmates of a lonely wayside cottage fancied that they saw a thief or a burglar in the person of every broken-down looking wayfarer? Happily this woman's conduct was an exception to the frank and generous hospitality that half a century ago characterised the inhabitants of the Peak.

I remained at Alfreton a few days to plan my future operations, and to draw together the persons with whom

I had corresponded. The ladies were, as usual, the great difficulty. I had only one: Mr. Wells had promised to himself a wife that was experienced on the stage; but she was not with him, and some days were yet to elapse

"Till holy church incorporate two in one."

As I was near to Bolsover, and had made several friends there, whilst I was with Mr. Hillyard, I fixed upon that place whereat to open again. There I concentrated my little corps, and my scenic trappings, and on the 1st of February, 1827, we commenced operations. During the first week, after announcing our opening, I never took a sixpence. Four days after our arrival, the future Mrs. Wells joined us; and I expected thereby to be able to take a wider range of pieces. In this we were sorely disappointed, for the lady proved herself a novice in the drama; she had performed for a few nights only in an amateur company. It was now too late to alter our arrangements. Mrs. Wells was engaged with her husband, and we must now make the best of the bargain. Strange things are of every-day occurrence.

Marry, that rascally tormentor, Cupid, doth sometimes drive poor mortals over very hobbly roads! He would not let Mr. Wells have it just as he could wish it to be during the honey-moon. On the first Sunday morning after our arrival, while we were seated at breakfast, an elderly lady presented herself at our lodgings, and demanded of me her daughter! I expressed my surprise at such an extravagant request. I told her that I had no one under my care, but my own family. When her rage had subsided a little, she told me that she was the mother of the young lady who had come to act in my company; and that the lady had been kidnapped away from her home. I accompanied her to the inn where her daughter, with her husband, was lodged. Mr. Younge was also, for the time being, a lodger in the same inn: to economise their limited means, those three persons had agreed to board together. At the time we entered the inn, Mr. Younge was engaged as cook. We had taken a few shillings on the Saturday evening; they had provided Mr. Younge with meal sufficient to bake into cakes for their breakfast, and he was then busily enployed tossing them round in a frying-pan. I explained to Mr. Younge the nature of our visit: he said, as the "young couple" had not yet come down to breakfast, he would show the bride's mother to the bed-room. She ascended the stairs, and was not over choice in her modes of expression when she met with the bride and bridegroom. Mr. Wells was indignant at such intrusion, and claimed a right over his spouse as her true lord and master. The bride's mother was positive; her voice was loud and shrill; she declared that nothing would satisfy her anger but the restoration of her daughter. She had no faith in Gretna marriages, or run-away matches. She would *see* the Priest, and *hear* the bells, or it should be no wedding with her. In vain the husband pleaded regularity—the old woman could not be appeased; she would have ocular and auricular demonstration; and her daughter Mary should, in her mother's presence, answer to the Priest's question of "wilt thou have this man?" nothing short of seeing and hearing that, should ever reconcile her to her daughter becoming a *Mrs*. In a rage she bid her daughter "to pack." Then came the recollection of the fellow below-stairs, with his jokes and pancakes, which stung her to madness, she raved at the thought of her daughter being forced to eat cakes baked in a frying-pan! I tried my powers of persuasion to induce her daughter to sue for a divorce; for I told her if she could not eat cakes prepared in a frying-pan, she was not fitted to be the wife of a strolling player, for such a dish would afterwards prove a luxury! Married or not, she had come for her daughter, and she would take her home again! She would have a second wedding; she would give her away after the fashion of her own heart. Again she declared that she would see the Priest, and hear the bells. The poor husband was forced to consent to the new arrangement,—after twenty-four hours of connubial bliss, he was doomed to mourn over twenty-four weary days of gloomy widowhood. Verily, Cupid is a bold-faced tormentor! On the twenty-sixth of March, the Priest again consigned Mrs. Wells to her husband's care, and gave him a protection in black and white against all future intruders.

I remained twenty days at Bolsover, with bad business: since my former visit the trade of the place had fallen off, and poverty and gloom had seized upon the inhabitants. I cleared about thirty shillings by my benefit. The play was the notorious "*Weare*." However strange it may appear, such morbid spectacles pleased such a people. It drew its units in

Derbyshire, even as it drew its thousands in London. In the first city in the world the crowds drew forth their shillings to be allowed to feast their eyes upon the "real gig" of the murdered Mr. Thurtell; in the country they threw down their pence to hear the gig talked about.

I travelled a few miles southward, pitching my camp at a pleasant village called Pleasley. We continued there for five weeks, and our acting satisfied the expectations of our auditors. We contrived to live tolerably well; the average amount of our shares was about five shillings each per week, and the chance of a few surplus shillings if a benefit-night succeeded.

Our next town was Sutton-in-Ashfield. We fitted up our machinery at the Swan Inn. The trade of the town—stocking-making—was at a low ebb; and, at that time, the taste of the inhabitants was not very poetical. We remained there a month, and the history of our doings may be summed up in a short sentence. We narrowly escaped death from the effects of hunger. Mr. and Mrs. Wells were now well satisfied of the amount of pleasure that belonged to a stroller's life. There was no under current in the chance-blown sea of theatricals that could bear them above the materiality of the world of bread-loaves;—if there was no biscuit in the locker to glut the savage maw of hunger, there were no viands in Imagination's profuse bill of fare that could invigorate their prostrated bodies. They preferred beef and pudding enjoyments to those of the stage; and they now left us, to return home to Mr. Wells's legitimate trade of manufacturing queen-cakes and sweetmeats.

A trifling circumstance occurred during this visit to Sutton, which was the precursor of my career as an artist. Already I have said that at this place Hunger had marked us for his own; he mocked us daily with breadless breakfasts and meatless dinners. To make his sport complete, we were lodged in a room, the walls of which were hung around with bacon flitches—real pig's-flesh. Every time our yearning bowels gave a roar, the fiend pointed to the flesh that was hung up; we might look at them, he said, but that was our share: a pretty sore temptation for hungry mortals. Hunger may tempt us, and threaten to upset our philosophy, but Hope is ever at hand to check him, and to bid us bide our time.

A gentleman, named Oscroft, was a resident in the town, he possessed considerable ability as a painter and a musician; he was likewise a lover of romance and poetry. He often visited us, and sympathised with us in our sunken condition. A temporary acquaintance grew up between us, as we appeared to possess kindred taste. Mr. Oscroft had some patterns for stencilling walls, which he had purchased, but which he considered were not adapted to his trade. These patterns he offered to me; and they were the very things I had long desired to possess, but which I had neither the chance of procuring, or the ingenuity to design. I soon found a customer for my new trade; I began to work in right earnest; the mode of application was to be blundered out: but perseverance, and a little thought, soon overtopped every difficulty. I worked onward; my progress was, necesarily, slow at first, but the job I had undertaken yielded me twelve shillings when I had finished it,—a very acceptable sum in such a strait. It served to pay for our lodging, which was sauce enough for all the pain and temptation we had suffered in our hall of bacon-flitches.

To estimate the amount of joy that results from being enabled to pay your liabilities, and partake of one meal,—potatoes and salt if you like, you must first be without a meal for several days together, and have to exist in a room where the incense from roasted beef and savory viands steam up to your nostrils two or three times a day,—to have your sitting-room hung over with pictures of salted bacon, with conscience whispering to you, "if you cut a single rasher off those flitches you will be guilty of felony; and if you wish they were your's, you covet your landlord's goods." When you have experienced so exciting a situation, and are suddenly ordered to eat of the good things before you, and to pay your debts out of the cash in your pocket, then you will taste of real bliss.

It has been my lot, through life, to always observe the sun, even through the storm-clouds. If the rain was pelting me, and for a moment had forced me to press my head into my bosom, I never was afraid of being wet through by it; for, let it pelt its hardest, or blow its bitterest, I was always cheered onward by the sun of Hope. I may have been too sanguine; but if I have occasionally lost the substance while grasping at the shadow, it has taught me a not less useful lesson. Let the morbid ones tell us this is a life of misery, they will find it tough work to induce me to preach, much less to practice, their creed. God's world is fair and pleasant; Mammon may warp it, and Hypocrisy try to veil its beauties;—let them: undaunted I shall still hold on my way, despising alike their evil teaching; and as I struggle onward through life, my battle-cry shall be—"TRY AGAIN!"

No wonder, then, that I found alchymy in those coarse stencil patterns: I saw gold in them ready to transmute whenever there was a long rent-roll, or a dearth of food, which the returns of the theatre were insufficient to meet. I felt myself on the road to independence, enabled to earn my own living when circumstances dammed up our regular channels of subsistence. It is true independence to hold your head erect in the world,—to be enabled to exclaim, that all you enjoy of temporal things, is but a just and equitable return for the labour of your own head and hands. I would that every man in Britain could boast of such an independence!

We filled up our time by "gagging" each evening in the villages surrounding Sutton, while I was slowly, but surely, earning money by the stencil pattern, to pay our way out of the place. The run of bad business we had lately experienced drove away all my fair-weather actors. Mr. Younge and Mr. Manuel were the only persons, except my own family, that remained with me. The greatest loss to me was the want of scenery and properties which belonged to Mr. Wells, and which he, of course, took away with him.

Our next place was to be Blidworth. Before we could open at that place, we wanted more scenes. Mr. Campbell had stored up a portion of his at Ripley, in Derbyshire. Mr. Manuel being his relative, thought it would only be a family favour if he was to use some of them: accordingly, we started to Ripley. We were too poor to employ a carrier, so we each loaded ourselves with as great a quantity as we could support, and marched with them to Blidworth. Our returns were small ones, but enabled us to live moderately. We were at Blidworth in Passion-week. Easter Monday being a general holiday, we expected to have " a bumper;" to our surprise, it was a total failure. Mr. Manuel was a Catholic by profession, and he attributed our failure on Easter Monday to the fact of my having eaten some broiled bacon to breakfast on Good Friday morning.

My little knot of " village-hunters" were too poor to waste time by an endeavour to arrange for a place to move to before we left the old one, so we had to pack up our scenery, and other properties, in a bundle, and to set out upon a voyage of discovery. Three shillings was the united capital that we could muster amongst four of us—the children excepted. We travelled onwards to a large village called Oxton. The landlady of the principal inn in the village said she had no objection to our acting in her large room; and further, that she believed our acting would be received with favour by the inhabitants generally; but before she could give her consent, I must wait upon the magistrate, and have his permission: "for," said she, "our magistrate is very particular." That was an answer sufficient to dash away the faintest glimmering of hope. My experience with clerical magistrates had taught me to estimate the *advantages* to be derived from such applications; they were mainly a series of contemptuous refusals. I only met with three exceptions during my season of strolling. One gentleman—the Rev. Brooke Boothby, with the charity that is expected to adorn the religious profession, condescendingly discussed with me the hardship—he might have also added, the tyranny—that bound the poor stroller over, hand and foot, to the merciless—that made him "a rogue and a vagabond," in our boasted land of freedom—in this "home of the world." But with the exceptions already named, the most courteous application that could be made to that class, was treated with contempt.

There was no quarter for us at Oxton: we were forced to travel onward. Wearily we passed through Calverton; there was no resting-place for us in that village. A landlady of one of the inns "thought," she said, "that we should do well in the place, but"— oh! the trepidation that sometimes waits upon a but!— "but," said she, "a gentleman was dead in the neighbourhood, and she dare not let us stop, as all the *quality* had gone into mourning!" Her announcement put us into mourning also. A single glance at our brows would have testified to their looking black.

Well! on we must pack: the road grew wearily long; our feet were sore, and our spirits sinking, as we descended into the populous village of Arnold. As we approached each public-house, in rotation, we asked to be allowed to stop at them; but, "No! no! no!" was the ever-depressing answer. We had almost walked the length of the long dirty street, when another sign-board, whereon was inscribed "The Horse and Jockey, Joseph Read," again lit up our pallid countenances. Another trial was left to us; one more chance of success or failure. Before, we had sent some one of our party into the house to reconnoitre; besides, there was economy in it; one half-pint of ale was alone required, and each had tried his persuasive powers in turn, with non-effect; but we were desperate now. The last public-house in the village was before us, and should this chance fail, there was no hope left for us but to pass the night in the lanes, or to creep under the lee-side of some hay-stack, supposing ourselves fortunate enough to meet with such a make-shift bed. Again, we were to make a trial of the strollers' supposed pass-word to the heart of Utility—appearance. We determined to throw high for this one chance of a night's shelter; we ordered a pint of ale, and to support appearance with a becoming dignity, we determined to pay for the ale in ready cash! Adventure aid us! In such a crisis threepence was about to be sunk in ale. Oh, poverty! The important question was put,—"Can we sleep here to-night?" and the answer was, "I will consult with the master. Let me consider; you are players, are you not?" "Yes, madam," I answered. She saw it; our shabby-genteel appearance told the tale. "Well," said she, "I will inquire, and let you know; but I do not know how it will be, for we have had some players here lately." She retired to consult with her husband. She had told us the names of the players she had alluded to, and we did not think that our present request was strengthened by the patronage of the before-named gentlemen to the Horse and Jockey. Courage for sinking hearts!

The landlady returned with the welcome answer—"You can stop here if you like."

Too frequently one difficulty courses another on the heels. We had promise of beds, but how were we to pay for them? Threepence was already gone. We might fairly expect that the price would be demanded before we were allowed to couch our harassed limbs in Mrs. Read's bed-linen. We took the stock of our ready cash: we could raise sixpence in copper amongst us. I had twopence halfpenny, and two farthings; Messrs. Younge and Manuel three-halfpence each. It was expected that such a sum would not suffice to find sleeping accommodation for six of us; so it was charitably settled that I should take the whole amount —sixpence; that would provide a bed for my family, and the other two gentlemen were to re-consider what could be done for themselves. After a short deliberation, they resolved to travel back again to Blidworth, where they had reason to believe a bed would be cheerfully offered to them. After a day's fatigue— one of hard walking and hunger—they imposed upon themselves a turmoil of eight miles, over dreary heath roads, to secure a bed for my family. How would the nightly revellers in down—the despisers of the "vagabond players," act under similar circumstances? Would they "go and do likewise?" Who but the poor would make such a self-sacrifice, to turn out, under the dark-hooded night, with bleeding feet, pennyless, and supperless? Who but the poor, to serve the poor?

Usage, and the books on arithmetic, both say, that two farthings make one halfpenny. I had two farthings in my sixpenny-worth of copper coin: but what would "appearance" say, if the manager of the strolling company, just come in, was obliged to offer fivepence halfpenny and two farthings for his bed? Sixpence current it might be, but would it look like a real respectable silver sixpence? No: such a meagre tender would operate against my future prospects, and would at once stamp me

> "Bare, and full of wretchedness."

The thought stung me. A night's rest would be but momentary relief, if my poverty was to drive me away the next morning. Some means must be devised to avert such misery, and, if possible, to prove my respectability. I hastened out, and paced the dark street, until a twinkling ray brought me to the window of a large shop. I looked in; its multifarious piles bespoke it the store-house of some village money-maker. An old, grey-headed man, with spectacles resting upon a rather large nose, was poring over his day-book, or ledger, by the aid of a farthing dip, whose twilight threw the greater part of the large room into an awful gloom. All within was as still as the pillowed glade of a deep-robed forest at midnight, when the lazy winds have sunk to sleep. This, thought I, is the place wherein to effect my barter. I approached the old man, and asked, with all the politeness that my embarrassment could afford, "if he would favour me with change for two farthings." This dealer in all sorts, whose name was Jones, was reputed doubly careful in guarding against loss in this world's dealings. He was scrupulously nice in all accounts of profit and loss; and in my case he could not see that a fraction of advantage was to be gained by the accommodation. After a long pause, he declined the favour, saying, "I would rather keep my ha'pence." I was rather anxious for the exchange. To expose my poverty was not, under present circumstances, a thing to be proud of, so again I modestly pressed for the change. "Are they good ones?" cautiously asked the old sugar-plum. The answer was "yes." "Well," said he, "I must try, but I do not see what I'm going to get by you; but I suppose you must have the halfpenny; I hope I am not going to do myself any harm by this transaction." I thanked him, buttoned down the money, and hastened back to "*my Inn!*"

During the evening, the landlady entered our room to look to the candles, and trim up the fire. She took a seat, and became very communicative. She talked with us about the business of the stage, and expressed her fear that the inhabitants of Arnold were too sensual to enjoy our acting, or to support our entertainment. She, however, wished us success; and by her kind and affable manner, she expelled the dark foreboding that was making the night seem long to us. I began to tremble about the payment of our lodgings, and consequently introduced my new stencil decorations to her notice, and gave myself an excellent character for their execution. Before bed-time I had the pleasure of receiving an order from her to "slap-dash" her parlour. Tired bones, avaunt! the lodgings are already paid; yes, and a smell of the frying chop, to be purchased out of the surplus money, is already expanding our collapsed stomachs! We retired to bed without our hostess demanding the pay; we slept comfortably, and dreamed of bacon and tea-cakes. The next morning we were joined by our two companions from Blidworth; the sixpence furnished all of us with an excellent dinner.

We tried the theatre at night; but, alack! the landlady was right in her conjectures; not one person "darkened our doors." Night after night succeeded, and still the same results—nobody cared to visit the "play-folk." Finding it hopeless, we abandoned our acting for a while, and betook ourselves diligently to the stencil pattern and paint-brush. Messrs. Younge and Manuel grew tired of such horse-in-a-mill sort of work, and so they left me. I continued to live right bountifully upon the proceeds of my labour; replaced my wasted wardrobe, paid occasional visits to Mr. Manly's theatre, at Nottingham, and spent the summer very agreeably. But the longest lane, it is said, has a turn; as the autumn approached, my business in cottage decoration began to fall off, and I had again to prepare myself for another stroll.

My farewell effort at Arnold was made by bringing my friends together,—at least such of them as I thought would patronize a play. The one selected was the "*Castle Spectre;*" the parts of which were mainly filled up by amateurs, from Nottingham. The part of "Osmond" was played by Mr. Harrison, from that town, and it was delivered with great taste and judgment. Two or three of the leading families of Arnold, and Mrs. R——, who kept a respectable boarding-school, together with fourteen of her boarders, and several others, honoured this benefit. The play was got through smoothly, and satisfied my patrons. After paying my engagements with my Nottingham friends, I had an useful sum remaining—about thirty shillings, which I considered a very good share. Miss Foote played three nights, at the Nottingham Theatre, the same week; her share, it was reported, amounted to the modest sum of ninety-five pounds sixteen shillings. I hope she was as well rewarded at Nottingham as I was at Arnold. Her share was rather more than the stroller's week's work. It is our English custom to do business by gluts; we like to mark our generosity by forcible contrasts.

My next co-partnership was with a gentleman named Mills, who had been strolling in Mr. Abbott's company, in Yorkshire; but having some good scenes, and other properties, was anxious to make the best use of them. Mr. Mills was reported to be a good actor, and his wife to be a clever actress. About the middle of November I engaged a large barn, at Farnsfield, Nottinghamshire, and fitted it up as a theatre: there I was joined by Mr. and Mrs. Mills, my old friend Mr. Younge, four other gentlemen, and one lady. After a few days' experience with my new partner, a night or two of playing soon told us that his ability, as an actor, had been over-rated. Although, in external appearance, he was consumptive, he was not without lungs;

"He would drown the stage with tears,
"And cleave the general ear with horrid speech."

Yet many of our bumpkin critics were mightily tickled by such bellowing. They liked, what Richardson used to call "*a howld spaiker*"—an actor that could "move storms," and "roar you an 'twere any nightingale." To this class, acting reveals itself like the lightning, which tells of its power by the loud thunder-crash that follows the flash, before you can say, " it lightens."

For a month we did our best to draw audiences at Farnsfield, but we had up-hill work of it. Two or three of the richer families bespoke plays, and we had a few good nights; the bad ones reduced our average amount of sharing to four shillings and sixpence each per week, exclusive of the bits of candle ends that fell to our lot in the general scramble. Although our reward was meagre, we discharged our bills, and relieved ourselves from the bodily fear of duns.

Early in 1828 we removed to Edwinstowe, a little village eight miles to the northward. There, for a fortnight, we tried our mimic power, with better success, at least, in the money way. A small knot of the reading and inquiring class in this village were constant play-goers. I paid "my way," added to my wardrobe, and saved eight shillings. We next journeyed westward, to Warsop, a large and populous village, but in the main the inhabitants were extremely ignorant. We remained about a month at that place, and all the while we were discussing the strollers' problem,—upon what minimum of food can a human being exist, yet be able to walk about, to talk, to make people believe he is well fed, and that he has money in his pocket? There was much discomfort while we were trying to unriddle the affair, and before we reached the solution, Famine forced his keen teeth so firmly into our vitals that we were fain to accept the charity of a kind man that lived in the village, whose name was Kertchveld, and the business of whose life was to do good. Since our visit, this Christian has been summoned to a "better world," to enjoy the reward of his labours on earth. He enjoyed a moderate fortune, and he bestowed it liberally upon the lone widow, the hungered, and the desolate that moved around him. He had money in the funds: the day preceding his death, he felt that the hour for the up-turning of his glass was at hand; life's sand-grains were nearly outrun, and he expressed his readiness to meet his Father in heaven! During an interval of rest from pain, he remembered that on the following day the interest of the money he had in the stocks would become due. For years he had given the whole of this interest-money amongst the poor, whom he was wont, while in health, good-humouredly to call his pensioners. He was yet of the earth, although within sight of heaven, and he prayed his Father that he might be allowed a few hours more to again relieve the destitute. The God of Mercies heard his prayer: he lived to receive the money, and to be assured that it had been distributed amongst the poor of his neighbourhood. His work was done; with Christian resignation he gave his body up to death, and his soul was borne on the wings of angels to the throne of Him who gave it. His memory is embalmed in the hearts of those who knew him here below.

Again we packed off our paraphernalia to Bolsover. I know not what drew us to that place on the present occasion,—certainly not our good fortune on a former occasion, neither were our prospects brightened now:

it might be that Hope prompted us in our forlorn condition, to throw ourselves amongst persons who were known to us, rather than to seek aid from strangers, when our empty pockets forbade us an introduction. My wife was seriously ill, and expecting every day to add to the number of our family; she was, consequently, anxious to be amongst persons with whom she had some previous acquaintance; for, in her present situation, there were daily indications that her travail would be severe. We were fortunate to again procure lodgings with a kind old lady who had, on our previous visits, furnished us with shelter. After our run of bad business at Warsop, we were ill-provided against a storm of neglect at Bolsover. I was already so poor, that it was with great difficulty I provided "the bills" for the announcement of our season. We struck up "drums and trumpets." No; the *flourish* was with fiddles and clarionets! It was of no avail; we had not a sufficient number of auditors to pay the incidental expenses, so we were forced to dismiss the few that obliged us with their presence. Saturday evening promised better things; again our village band rattled the roof with a "louder strain," and we drew the curtain; and after its fall we shared just twopence halfpenny each. The season lasted three weeks, and our average weekly sharing was tenpence. On February the 2nd, 1828, my third son was born; my wife's extreme illness—extreme even in such cases—and our total deprivation of food at such a time, filled my cup of grief brim full with anguish. Hopeful as I have ever been, my heart quailed within me at that time.

The uncertainty of my wife's recovery, and my inability to provide her with necessary comfort, were tugging hard at my heart-strings; and I frequently stole away from my business and my home, to seek relief in tears. Thus troubled, I have paced the lonely platform that surrounds the fine Castle of Bolsover—talking to my inner self, and cogitating upon the future, until my heart was charged to overflowing, and thus forced up to my eyes a banquet of brine, which assuaged my anxiety. Troubles are but for a season.

On the 20th we had the "young stranger" christened Frederick. The name was selected in compliment to my manager, Frederick D. Campbell. Although we had hitherto been so lonely, two or three of my old acquaintances now rallied around me, and determined that we should have a christening party. Accordingly, from the church we adjourned to the Anchor Inn, to wash "the young Christian's" head. The priest, the Rev. Mr. T——y, made one of the party; he was not above mingling with his parishioners; on festive occasions, he thought the best homily was to "take a little wine." Many a ranting story was told of his Reverence's respect for his cups. He was not the first to break up our party at the Anchor; and for the nonce, we were boon companions. We forgot our empty cupboard, and the priest his gown. Whatever were his faults, he had not the one of hypocrisy to add to the catalogue; for, amongst his holiday texts, he did not disdain the one,—

"Go fuddle all your noses."

The morrow broke, only to bring back our former woes. We had still to batten upon grief. I and my wife took a benefit conjointly; and although it was by far the best house of the season, we had not the heart to take the surplus, when our brother and sister performers, like ourselves, were besieged by starvation—so we divided the spoil equally amongst our numbers.

I could earn only eight shillings with my stencilling while at this place; and to secure that sum, I was indebted to my kind friend, Mr. Kertchveld, of Warsop; so that I had to go to Warsop, and return again to Bolsover, during the progress of the job. After all, I could not pay my way out of Bolsover. We were obliged to leave the best portion of our wearing apparel, as security for our return to discharge our liabilities, at the earliest opportunity.

Mr. Mills now left me; from the first he had been an unpleasant partner, and it was a relief to my mind to be separated from him. My next place was Whitwell, in Derbyshire. My company was reduced to my old friend, Mr. Younge, and two young men, who had joined me on my re-commencement, at Farnsfield. Whitwell proved worse to us than the last place,— starvation drove the two young men away from me. I was now reduced to Mr. Younge, and my own family. We could not venture from this place: my scenery was all pledged for rent, and we were once more reduced to abject poverty. To render our situation still more distressing, the weather was exceedingly stormy. The rain fell night and day without intermission; it was rare to enjoy one hour, out of the twenty-four, of fair weather. Necessity, it is known, is a very peremptory master—his will is his law; and when he has the power, it is useless poor mortals attempting to resist him. Hunger could brave storms, as readily as he could "break through stone walls." We were forced to a neighbouring village called Cresswell, to try if we could raise a few shillings to soften our hard lot. We carried with us a calico scene, and two or three dresses in a handkerchief. A little barn was offered to us by the landlord of one of the inns. This barn was half-filled with hay cut up into trusses; of the hay we formed our gallery, truss upon truss, and covered them with boards, to preserve the hay as much as possible from dirt and spoliation. The inn stood upon a piece of low ground, a few yards from the bed of a sinuous river, called the Wollen. The continual rains which had fallen had swelled the little silver river into a large and muddy lake, and raised itself up to the very threshold of our barn, on its front, or river side. The back of it was buttressed up by a steep hill, which formed the base of a famous rock, known there as the *Crag*. Within the Crag there is a spacious cavern, where, as tradition states, the ancient outlaws of Sherwood Forest used to secrete themselves, when the blasts of winter had denuded the greenwood. The cavern is large enough to shelter a band of fifty or sixty men; and there are smaller caverns, large enough to serve as store-rooms, and would accommodate a good store of venison, and sack, if need be. Those places are still known as Robin Hood's Bed-room, Friar Tuck's Cellar, &c. In the days of our Henrys, or Edwards, this rude place would have served as an excellent dining-hall for the bold forest ranger; and from its singular approach, might well disarm the suspicion of the paid hordes that were commissioned to bring this outlawed chieftain to the King, either dead or alive.

When our gallery was arranged, and our scene nailed up to the wall, we sat down upon the threshing-floor of the barn, awaiting for the coming evening, now humming a tune to drive off despair, or wondering if, in our forlorn situation, we should again be enabled to redeem our pawned properties. The rain continued to whiz and patter down in torrents, and the Wollen gurgled aloud as it hastened past our lonely house. Experience had taught us the importance of having music on all occasions, particularly where there was something needful wanting to entice the notice of the indifferent ones in our location. We tried our persuasive powers,—for we had neither silver nor gold to tempt with,—so we tried our feeble eloquence to draw a clarionet-player, that lived in the village, to assist us with a pipe from his instrument, hoping thereby to draw the natives; but we could not induce him to accept our humble coin of " thank you;" it " would butter no parsnips." True, we had no lack of *music*, for the organ-voiced wind was pouring forth harmonious chords from the rocky-piped ravine that lay at the foot of the Crag near to us; the rain sang a wild song as it was played upon by the fitful storm, and the unbound waters laughed and shrieked as they leaped madly over their rocky bed. There was a mournful pleasure in this elemental trio, and it was questionable whether it would not retard, rather than entice the villagers to our intended entertainment.

The night came, and with it inquiries of what the "show-chaps" were going to do? That was a grave question. In such times, however, an inquiry is sympathy, and as such we enjoyed it. By-and-by, a boat-load of farmers hailed our barn; the storm had flooded the street, and enabled a flat-bottomed fishing craft, that had come to the wheelwright's to be repaired, to float over the stones. To enjoy the fun of a fresh-water voyage, a jolly crew had embarked on board this *Dreadnought*, determined to have "a lark." Here was fair promise for our clamorous bowels. Oh! charitable storm! Is it not "an ill wind that blows nobody good?" Five or six of the crew paid down a shilling each, while the commander put off for a fresh cargo. Drunk with joy at the prospect, we ordered candles to light up our theatre, and bread, cheese, and beer to lighten our withered bodies. We played to them as much of Tobin's "*Honey Moon*" as we could connect with our limited force. Sometimes we "doubled" the scenes, and occasionally blended others. During the scene with Lampedo, the Doctor, one of our front-row customers started from his seat, rushed up to the lights, and fixing himself in a serio-comic attitude, he beckoned his hand, as if for us to pause awhile. He then turned his burly frame to the auditory,—he was a fine study for a picture of a "laughing audience,"—his cheeks were as red as the sun-ripened side of a Siberian crab-apple, his well-fleshed lips were at full stretch, and his black diamond eyes were ready to leap from their confines, and dance the hay round our thrashing-floor stage. Thus gleeful, he turned to his fellows, and shouted with a voice, that for power, for a time completely drowned the storm's rattling—" By'r leddy, lads, but ween cum ivvery neet if't storm houds, speciously an we can cum by't water—shunnut we lads?" "Ween shall! ween shall!" was answered from all present, amidst a roar of laughter. "Ween come," continued to be re-echoed amidst the laughter-peal which had now taken possession of the house, audience, and players. Laughter was the future lord of the night. A moment's pause ensued, only to give breathing time, and to allow them to hoop their sides with their hands. How far we were guilty of setting on those "barren spectators to laugh," I cannot so readily tell. Whatever the cause, laughter had taken possession, and he showed no desire to be put aside; so, in very sympathy, we, forgetting, or never caring about the "cunning of the scene," laughed as hard as they did. I believe Dame Nature was that evening trying over some of her chemical vagaries, and, to test the potency of her funny compound, she gave each of us a drachm of her LAUGHING GAS. To us, it was not the least part of the merriment, that we shared five shillings each, after paying for the lighting and our refreshment.

Five nights more we played in that barn, and were well paid; our scenery was released from pawn, our pockets were replenished, and a surplus remained to enable us to pay the first instalment of our debt at Bolsover. There was but one trifling drawback to our pleasure,—we had to travel each night to our quarters, at Whitwell, the water being often knee-deep in the vallies, and we had to plash along under the "dark blanket" of the storm-shrouded night. Our way, by the foot-road, lay over the summit of the Crag, and the fear of precipitating ourselves into the deep ravine below, often filled us with fear; but caution, and the guiding hand of Providence, led us safely through the seeming danger.

We continued our "village-hunting" during the summer, visiting Tuxford, Kneesal, Moreton, Blackwell, Shirland, Riddings, Kirkby-in-Ashfield, Selstone, Lowdham, Fiskerton, Lambley, and Arnold. An every-day struggle for rations absorbed much of the instruction that may always be derived from an intercourse with men of all grades; and during this flying campaign we were often at starvation point. The labour, too, was severe: having to care each day for the necessities of a family, made it trying heart-work.

The precarious profession, and, as some have it, the *idle* one, of the strolling player, is not, as many suppose it to be, all time mis-spent, or thrown away. Oh no! even in its hungriest form, there is to him a morality in its privations. There is an ever-heaving swell of human passions riding over the sea of life, which is constantly awakening his attention, and stirring him to new thought. The daily phases of human life are to him Nature's preachers, exhorting from practical texts, upon the ugliness of vice, and the God-like purity of virtue. As a mere business matter, he must look into the beating of the great human heart; his profession is not, as many assume it to be, a mere bread and cheese question; if it were so, he need but renounce it to-day, and pick up a better one to-morrow. Let him but set up for a Professor of Cant, and, with a trade "idle" enough, he shall have his "bread buttered on both sides." No: the player has aspirations far above such mere loafing propensities! To-day it is his business to hold pleasurable converse with men who can look beyond the narrow present of local pride, or cast into the deep soul of universal brotherhood. It may be that he finds but few such men. Does he despair? No: the few do live; they savour the earth, and it rejoiceth him that they are a growing class; for every pure thought that the good man casts upon the fallows of humanity, like the grain of mustard seed in the parable, shall germinate, and throw our its interminable branches, which will one day be large enough to shelter the whole family of man from the blasts of ignorance. Again: he has to mingle with the dull and sensual;— and must he shun them? No; he cannot shun them: they, too, are God's children, however frail, and they do but bide their time; they will yet awaken to new life. The stroller cannot despise them; even their "form and pressure" is food to him. They, too, are the tools by which his imagination has to hew its way to the hearts of his auditors. To the player, the ways of men are the manifestations by which he is to shadow forth the divinity that dwells within his craft. In them he recognises the in-dwelling of "the invisible spirit that works in nature," and makes her ways "boundless in significance." Yet the purists deny the player's mission, and call his trade idle and mischievous. It is of no avail; they may throw down the stumbling-blocks of hypocrisy, but they cannot stop the car of Truth. Such trimmers have no faith in Nature; they will not condescend to look at her, except through their smoked glass of universal depravity. They can mask, and antic, and cry aloud; but alack, for them, there are no "sermons in stones." Nay, half afraid lest a moral lesson should be found astray upon Nature's highway, they bid all men desert it, and dally not to worship in such a temple. They will not hear a psalter in the breeze, nor see an altar on the mountain. Because the stroller will not mock the heart with "mortifying groans," they would stamp his sermons with the bile of " outward hideousness;" he cares not, assured that even his texts of cheerfulness are a balm for care-worn hearts; he still sings on, and will continue to sing—

> "Why should a man, whose blood is warm within,
> Sit like his grandsire cut in alabaster?
> Sleep when he wakes? and creep into the jaundice
> By being peevish?"

Wearied by poverty, we halted at Arnold, and I re-commenced my old trade of stencilling, but found that the demand for it was not so great as on my former visit. I had succeeded in improving my patterns, which enabled me to introduce them amongst a class of the inhabitants who despised my former ones; so I had still hope of partial success. My improved patterns were (in 1828) scarcely equal to many of the paper-hangings that are now (in 1847) sold at one penny per yard. However, as they were considered superior to the general run of such things at that time in use, I got several excellent jobs thereby. From the cottages of the poor stockingers, I was elevated to the parlours of the "tradesmen," and the boarding-schools.

From Arnold, I was recommended by my friends to Nottingham, and my first *grand* job in that town was at a boarding-school, in St. Peter's Gate. The lady of that school also solicited me to paint her school-room windows; and, considering they were of the Elizabethan character,—plain chamfered stone mullions and transom—the performance was not much to boast about. I had, notwithstanding that, no confidence in my own ability as a painter in oils, and I politely declined the offer. My patroness was determined that I should be a painter; and whether I would or not, I was forced to provide the paint, and do the work.

As the famous Goose Fair approached, I got several good jobs. I had to stencil a room in a large house in Park Street. The housewife wished me to paint her two or three doors a plain chocolate colour. Although I had tried my hand upon a more difficult operation in St. Peter's Gate, simple although that one was, still I durst not undertake the present one, of painting a plain battened door one of the simplest colours in use. The lady intreated, but I excused myself. When I went to my job on the following morning, I found her hard at work upon the very doors that I was afraid to undertake. I felt ashamed of my want of self-confidence, and a consequent degree of embarrassment attended it. The lady laughed heartily at my situation, and she continued it, at intervals, during the day. I felt plaguily annoyed at the jeering, although I could not but admit that I deserved it. Toward evening I finished my work, and received my wages. As soon as I was clear away from the house, I ran over to myself the whole of this adventure; and I determined never again to lose a job because I had not studied how to paint.

The remainder of the time that I spent in the neighbourhood of Nottingham was filled up by closely watching the proceedings of the painters, when they were at work upon shop fronts, or other commodious places. Indeed, so anxious was I to observe the various methods of graining, that when I noticed a piece of work that appeared ready for the finishing process, I have often walked out from Arnold to Nottingham—four miles each way, to observe their processes. I have often had to experience disappointment from my miscalculation of time, and from other causes, when the finishing had been put off, and have had to go again, and again, to secure the opportunity. My prying, walking to and fro, and seeming officiousness, soon rendered me obnoxious to the workmen; that I was forced to brook; for I was afraid, if they really knew my intentions, that I should meet with a summary dismissal from them; so my extreme anxiety was made to absolve my policy. From the date of my working in Park Street, I began to consider myself a house-painter. Instead of refusing such work when it was offered to me, as I had done heretofore, I solicited for it on every occasion, and undertook all that came in my way, without even questioning my ability for it. Although such a ready-made way of commencing a trade may not be a good one, neither to be advised, or relied on, still it was beneficial to me. I was determined to be a painter, and zeal fastened my attention upon the necessity of surmounting every difficulty that lay in the way of becoming a respectable decorator; hence I was prompted to secure any chance that could administer to my desire.

Seeing no prospect of my profession providing me with anything beyond a miserable existence, I—as has been already stated, we but barely escaped death from hunger—I was, therefore, doubly anxious to grasp at anything to eke out my present uncertain livelihood. It was evident that theatricals were at a discount in the provinces. It was not likely that the prevailing ignorance of the people could be set aside at a tangent, neither was it likely that the persecution of the stage would be given up by that class of men whose interests depended upon its condemnation. They had set "the mark of the beast" upon its objects, and the people were forbidden to think aught but evil of it. Such of the people as did venture to give an unbiassed opinion that it was harmless, or might be made useful, were branded as *Free-thinkers*, which meant, that they dared to question the opinion of those they had hitherto paid so well for thinking for them. In those days, every person who dared to think anything that was not found in a certain conventional chart, was a *Free-thinker*; and by the chart-makers, a free use of thought—God's best gift to man—meant all sorts of bad things, from disobedience to doctors, down to *Infidelity!*

Again I contrived to live at Arnold tolerably well, until the rains and snow of winter put an end to the painting business for a season; we were then thrown back upon our starving profession of strolling. In the month of November, a company of players, under the management of Messrs. Lewis and Bryce, visited

Arnold; they engaged myself and my wife to play with them during their stay there. From Arnold they removed to Bulwell; there we accompanied them also. Reckoning according to the sums generally realized by strollers, we were tolerably well paid; our average shares amounting to six shillings each per week. Mr. Lewis solicited me to join with him in management. If I did so, he was agreeable to confine the company to two dead shares, himself and Mr. Bryce taking one of them, and I to take the other. However, I declined Mr. Lewis's proffered kindness, for there was nothing in common in our dispositions and modes of thought. With him *money* was the "be-all, and end-all;" the utility, or the dignity of the drama, had no place in his calculation. If money could be made by that miserable system, yclept by the swell mob "kite-flying," it was just as welcome to their pockets as if it had come through a more legitimate channel. No matter how the season might have paid, it was still a part of their business to "fly a kite," or, in plain English, to send a note to each person in the town or neighbourhood, who was known to be either wealthy, or charitably inclined, and to solicit money from them, urging poverty as an excuse for the liberty taken. Such conduct, although not rare amongst the strollers, was, happily, by no means general with them. Nay, so much was everything in the shape of eleemosynary charity dreaded by the player who honoured his art, that he would rather perish with hunger, than bring disgrace upon his profession, by making himself a public beggar! It was quite enough that the law made him a vagabond! There were a few of those martyrs to their craft left upon the stage during my short "day of sextonship;" but persecution had nearly done its work, it had driven the greater part of them away from the Theatre. Although I wanted an auxiliary trade to aid the hunger-craving struggle for bread, I had not yet drunk the lees of the histrionic cup, and I had hope, even yet, that fortune would give a brim-full bowl of comfort; I had, therefore, no desire to attach myself to a company where such unprofessional means were used, as my new friends were said to be guilty of practising. Then, again, as actors, they were devoid of merit. The lady, Mrs. Bryce, was exceedingly fond of showing off her symmetrical frame in such parts as are facetiously denominated "breeches parts," on the stage. Mrs. Bryce was most happy when starring such parts as "Rolla," "Richard the Third," "Young Norval," &c. Whoever joined the company, she claimed those heroes as her prescriptive right. I know not why she preferred the *inexpressibles;* most lady performers tried to avoid them, and they were generally repulsive to them, even when forced, by circumstances, to put them on: but Mrs. Bryce liked them; she would have them; not that she could read them, or walk them, better than other people, for her gesture was truly bombastic; neither was she a second Olympic goddess,—oh, no; she had no *Vestris's leg!* yet she preferred the breeches. Strange taste! Our country audiences were not, as she must have imagined them to be, such noodles, as to prefer the counter-scream of a mad-cap flirt squeaking out, "My kingdom for a horse," to a burly good fellow, with a full round voice, sternly proclaiming—

"A thousand hearts are great within my bosom."

Such an embodiment might be understood; but for a mincing lady to go striding about with Lilliput gait, in fleshings, moustachioed and corked, with half a sheet of pasteboard and a rusty rapier, it was "villanous," and "a most pitiful ambition in the fool that used it." Sometimes ladies, as well as gentlemen actors, will play "fantastic tricks" before frail mortals here below! Besides these, there were reasons manifold why I could not join Mr. Lewis as a manager.

Amongst my village campaigns, I can look back with some degree of pleasure to those at Bulwell. I met with several warm friends, and some of them were not niggards with their social comforts. From the Rev. H. E. Herbert I had many kindnesses; from Mr. E. G. Pickering, who conducted a boarding-school at that place, also solaced me with many civilities. Amongst other useful things, he gave me my first lesson on velvet painting: if it was not much in itself, it was an unit in accomplishments, and it has often proved useful when hard times forced me to be nibbling upon "short commons."

It has been, and yet is, one of the pleasures of my life, to muse upon the various stepping-stones that have helped me, dry-shod, over the impetuous stream of necessity. It is not less pleasurable, after having crossed the river, to sit and rest upon a grassy knoll, made fragrant by the blossoms of the yellow agrimony, and spangled with the snowy bell-flower, and there leisurely to tell over my grateful thanks to the willing hearts and hands that threw the crossing-stones into the pool, and whose only reward was, that they might bear the slip-shod wayfarer comfortably over the flood.

If atoms are concreted into mountains, and the pearly drops that trickle down the hill sides meander through the vallies, until they swell on, and make an ocean broad enough to bear proudly the bark of commerce to every clime, so every atom of useful information piled up in the mind, and every drop of intelligence rolled onward into the ocean of life, all tend to swell the vast sea of inventions, over which the mighty engine of labour bears forward the wealthy of the world!

As soon as we had finished our business at Bulwell, I parted with my late *friends*. I had been previously solicited by a party of amateurs at Nottingham, to play one night for them. I agreed to do so; and on Monday the 19th of January, 1829, I starred the part of "Job Thornberry," in the comedy of "*John Bull*," my wife playing the part of "Mrs. Brulgruddery." The place was crowded to suffocation, and we were well remunerated for our trouble. I then drew a few performers and amateurs together, and took the field once more, commencing a short season at Radford (adjoining Nottingham); from thence we removed to Warsop, afterwards to Edwinstowe, Tuxford, and Collingham; but I had my usual fare,—I was wedded to poverty, and closely it stuck by me. At Collingham I was completely stranded; my company, one by one, fell off, until Mr. and Mrs. Storey—who had joined at Radford—were the only persons left with me, and they were anxious to try some other part of the country. It was not unusual for the strollers—particularly when several towns in succession had failed—to remove to a distant part of the country. It was usual to imagine that any other place would prove better than the present bad one. We constantly shut our eyes to the real cause of failure, which was occasioned by ignorance on the one hand, and a bigoted persecution on the other. My numbers were now reduced to my own family; and we were forced to the village of Norton, in Lincolnshire, to give an entertainment. Although it was our misfortune to "dismiss" only three persons visiting our place of performance, our journey to that house was not altogether in vain; for, during my conversation with the landlord, I managed to impress upon him my ability as a painter, and succeeded in getting from him an order for a new sign, for his public-house,—the subject to be the Sportsman. We were returning home rather moodily—(the certainty of retiring supperless to bed, after a ten miles' walk, had not much about it to make us merry); still, in the most distressing situations, kind Nature has ever a solace, if we can but attune our hearts to receive it. There was one here for me: the nightingales were singing, and this was the first time I had ever heard those lovely creatures, that make the night glad with song. I had often longed to hear them; Milton had blessed them with his line—

"Most musical, most melancholy,"

and now in my sadness they had come to bless me. It was an unbought pleasure, which, if it stood not in the place of a substantial supper, awakened the heart to gladness, and enabled me, for a season, to forget my troubles. We were not discomfited with our failure, for we travelled over again the next evening, and realised about three shillings, to find us with bread. I painted the sign, received a sovereign for my labour, and then removed to Beckingham. During my stay at that place, my father came to visit me. He had not seen me since I took to the stage; he had only heard of me by report, which had not been at all times correct. No wonder, then, that he was anxious to behold his runaway child once more, before old age, and the every-day infirmities that were stealing upon his frame, prevented him from seeking me out. He had heard that I was in the neighbourhood of Gainsborough; thither he started, then following in our wake from place to place, he at length found us at Beckingham. Our meeting was a wild one,—it might be expected to be such a one. When the momentary transport was over, we were reconciled, and enjoyed mutual comfort.

For some weeks I continued to travel about that part of the country, up as far as the Cliff road, and back again to Lincoln, which place I reached in the beginning of July. Upon my arrival in the city, I heard that Messrs. Huggins and Clarke, then at Mansfield, were in want of a scene-painter. I determined to set out immediately, and try if I could procure the situation. My wife and family were to stop at Lincoln until my return. With sixpence in my pocket, to defray the expenses of the journey, I set forward. It was a broiling day, and for temporary relief I was often forced to walk without my hat—now and again stooping, or lying down, to drink at the water brooks. The concentrated rays of the sun darted powerfully over my head, and I was not philosopher enough to understand, that my black hat was gathering up the heat, and centering it on my cranium. I was afraid to spend any part of my money on the road, for I expected to have to pass the night at Mansfield; and if I had to pay for sleeping, there might not be much left for luxuries. Toward evening I reached Edwinstowe, where I ventured to call upon an old friend, whose acquaintance I had cherished on my former theatrical visits to that place. This gentleman was by trade a shoemaker—his name, Trueman. I knew him to be kind-hearted, and was anxious to call upon him, as my way lay through the village. My business being made known to him, he invited me to stop and take tea with him; he saw that I was already fatigued with my walk, and it is also probable, he guessed that my pocket was not over-stocked. Feeling that his invitation was kindly meant, I readily accepted it. In the course of our tea-table conversation, he persuaded me to rest all the night at Edwinstowe, and on the morrow he promised to accompany me over the forest to Mansfield. The next day was the fair at Mansfield, and the old gentleman had been for years a regular attendant at it. Although extremely anxious to see Messrs. H. and C., as I was sadly distressed with my journey, I was easily prevailed upon to stop until morning. We were early prepared for our journey the next day; it was again very hot, but our progress over the moor was a light one. My companion was an intellectual man, far above the ordinary range of village shoemakers. He was a zealous politician, and he knew by past converse with me, that I took a deeper interest in political matters than players in general were wont to do. Thus agreed, we lost no time in preliminaries, but began at once to settle the affairs of Europe! We had seven miles to walk over a billowy forest of gorse; and I dare say, that under ordinary circumstances, over such a dreary heath, the miles would appear long ones. Indeed, the neighbouring villagers now call them *good miles;* and they compute them by the country standard of seven miles *and a bit!*—the "bit" usually measuring as much as any one of the preceding miles! Be that as it may, to us, that morning, the miles were not tiresome, for we had scarcely time, before reaching Mansfield, to assure ourselves that the passing of the Catholic Relief Bill would not end in seating the Pope snugly in Lambeth, and so place the Church in danger! In 1829, Birmingham had not quite decided upon the Reform Bill; we, however, determined to pass that bill that morning,—" the whole bill"—aye, and more than Lord Grey afterwards gave us. My friend's faith in governments was not over strong; he knew, that up to that period—even as to now—the people had been bamboozled; and many a time, during an earnest debate, he had to "down 'em to hummer," and express his fear that they would drive the people to desperation—for, it will be remembered, revolutions had not gone out of fashion at that time! My argument was, "That the people were awakening, and would have the bill." We were somewhat in advance of our peers that morning, for we did carry the bill *unanimously*—two to nothing!

On my arrival at Mansfield, I learnt that the company I was in search of had gone to Worksop. I was unable to follow them further; I had not the means to do so; besides, I was fearful that my family, whom I had left, had not wherewith to find them with food. For once, despair really seized me. I had often had troubles before, but they were momentary. Now, my heart sunk, and a cold shivering ran through me. I was a long day's journey from my family, and at least ten miles from the company which I set out to find; scarcely a faint hope of succeeding with them if I started onwards; the weather very oppressive, and but sixpence to support me on the journey. In such a dilemma, I knew not what course to take. I sought out my friend, Mr. Trueman, and acquainted him with my misfortune. He advised me to return to Edwinstowe, and try if I could not get a living there, as a house-painter. I liked his idea, but could discern no prospect of its realisation; notwithstanding, I resolved to go back with him, and try if there was a chance of success. When my friend's business was over, we took the forest path homeward, renewing our political converse, and before night-fall we were again at Edwinstowe. While talking over our breakfast table the following morning, a gentleman entered my friend's house; Mr. T. communicated to him our desire, that I should commence a painting business at Edwinstowe. Mr. Joseph Peatfield, the gentleman just named, and to whom I was partially known as a comedian, agreed with us, that in the present state of things, it was desirable I should, if possible, settle in business; he, therefore, kindly offered me his house to commence upon. This was an inducement for me to try my fortune in trade, and I resolved to make the venture. After breakfast, I set off with a light heart for Lincoln—not with a light heart only, but with a full purse—for my friend had, unsolicited, lent me half-a-crown, and I always regarded that loan as the most opportune act of kindness I ever received. I hastened back to my family—the sun was still sending his lines of fire through the unclouded space, but I cared not for it,—I gathered the big drops from my forehead, and dashed them upon the parched turnpike road, and kept my way right joyously. I felt not the road—I was drunk with delight, and oblivious to everything save the prospect of living at Edwinstowe! Only one day was allowed to pass before we started for our proposed home. My wife, and my goods were packed upon the top of a felmonger's waggon that was bound for Ollerton, which was but two miles distant from our resting place.

I soon found friends and a moderate trade at Edwinstowe, and for a while I appeared to "sail before the wind." It is true, that my trade did but barely furnish the means of living; indeed, we were often upon short allowance; but, with an increasing family, a settled home offered more domestic comfort than I had found upon the stage. For several months, we were content to remain in lodgings; but we afterwards rented a house, and enjoyed the consequent advantages. I readily found sufficient employment to keep my family during the summer months, but the winters were severe trials; still, bad as those winter seasons were, the worst of them was luxurious when contrasted with many of our theatrical summers. If I had more of "the substantial" enjoyments of life in my new situation, I had not a contented mind. There was a strange chaos around me. Surrounded by the most beautiful scenery, of a peculiar character—for there nature had indeed been prolific in her bowery grandeur—the remains of the old forest of Sherwood were within bow-shot of my home—around me beautiful spots of greenery were diversified by the splendid mansions and choicely stocked gardens of the wealthy, whose clustered magnificence has won for their locality the euphonious appellation of *The Dukery*—still this profusion was a blank to me. I could not see it, for my heart was yet upon the stage, and many a sigh for my old profession stole from me, when to all outward appearance I was surrounded with worldly comfort. Time, which softens down many asperities, did but increase my longings. Day after day I looked abroad upon the glory around me with a distempered gaze; the landscape appeared sickly, and the sun red. Night after night I mingled with my village friends, but their social converse was like a mid-day sun in December, thawing all within the compass of its oblique rays, while, beyond its influence, under the shade of the unsunned north, all was bleak, cold, and icy! Thus it was with me: the sun of conviviality warmed me for a moment, but it set quickly upon my hopes, and left me, like a scathed and blasted oak in the forest, withered and dead to myself.

No wonder, then, that with feelings so opposed to my situation, I determined to try the stage again. A long winter, with a scarcity of employment, seemed to furnish me with a sufficient reason for leaving my trade. From the early part of October, 1831, to March, 1832, my receipts were only twenty-five shillings, out of which materials and tools had to be deducted. True I had many benevolent friends; but in my most abject condition; my heart withered at the thought of living upon charity. I had half-promises of jobs that might be got at some distant period, but they were not attractive enough to keep me at Edwinstowe. I entered into correspondence with several actors, and engaged to open a theatre at Sutton-in-Ashfield. I solaced myself with the hope of better success than before. Fancy persuaded me that things were generally better in the country, and that consequently I should do better. I determined to gather up a good company; my scenery was re-painted, and several new ones added, and this time I thought all would go well. Thus prepared, I began my theatrical experiment at Sutton, in March, 1832. Things did go tolerably well at that place: I had an attractive company, and enjoyed a good season. Strange to state, however, I was not so comfortable on the stage as I had expected to be. My residence at Edwinstowe for a period of nearly three years had in some measure ruralised me, and I now found that "your own fire side" was no mean consideration. Then again, I had underrated the opposition to the drama, which I foolishly imagined had been lessened by the rapid strides that the country was every day making toward general education. There was the double mortification, too, to find that my companions in the "sock and buskin" were still as jealous of each other's ability and comfort as ever they were.

From Sutton I removed the company to Alfreton, where we renewed our acquaintance with distress: there we had bad houses, and increasing disaffection in our company, with little prospect of amendment. At the end of our short season, I was forced to part company with some of my performers. I soon supplied their place with others, and travelled to Duffeld, where, as usual, poverty kept close at my elbow. I found it difficult to get a town of sufficient promise to induce us to take it, and thus we were forced upon the village of Draycott, hoping there to procure bread and water for the company, whilst I took a journey round about, to try for some likely place to move on to. During our stay at Draycott, I received a letter from a friend at Edwinstowe, Mr. Henry Russell, expressing an opinion that if I were to return to that village, I should find sufficient employment as a painter, as two of the large jobs I had anticipated were nearly ready for painting. So without further loss of time, a return to Edwinstowe was resolved upon, and my profession of Comedian renounced. My company was already reduced, and to those who remained, notice was given of my intention to give up theatricals with the close of our business at Draycott. It was evident, during this short trial of three months, that if I was to persevere in following the stage, it could only be attended with severe privations, which, if individually, I was disposed to endure for the sake of the profession, I had still a duty to discharge to my family, and, if possible, to provide them with the means of living; and assuredly the stage could not do that. If to me the love of strolling was a palliative for the pangs of poverty, their zeal might not be so warm as mine; and if I refused the proffered inducement, should I not be guilty of indifference to their comfort and happiness? Assuredly I thought so. Hence my theatre was dissolved; and without further correspondence, or question of success, I set out once more for Edwinstowe.

Stern necessity now forced me to take " a long farewell" to a profession that I loved and honoured. I could have endured privations in it, but, unfortunately, they were extreme enough to be called miseries. It was my misfortune to enter into it at an inauspicious season. My individual amount of money-support from the stage never averaged as much per week as " the poor stone-breaker," who follows his monotonous vocation by the road-side, generally receives for his. Ignorance, poverty, and bigotry, had waged unceasing war against us, crying with their merciless tongues—

> "The world is not thy friend, nor the world's law:
> The world affords no law to make thee rich."

While social progression will proudly date her birth from the commencement of the nineteenth century, dramatic representation will have to look back to it as the dark age in which she was forced to cower down, and weep tears of blood under the cowl of debasement.

No one, however enthusiastic he may be for the drama, will set up to defend all that has been done in its name, notwithstanding it has wrongfully, I think, been subjected to a wholesale condemnation. I say it advisedly, for tens of thousands have been taught to shun it, without being allowed to ask themselves a question as to its use or abuse. Are there not thousands who can testify to the truth of my assertion?

men too, who in other matters possess considerable knowledge, yet know no more about the drama, and its claims upon their attention, or of the theatre, and its uses, further than they have *been told*, that "the theatres are the sinks of vice, and that plays are wicked poems." We are not so content to take our literature upon credit, or our music, our pictures, and our newspapers. Our theatres, when properly regulated, are great news of the world, where hundreds at once can scan the page of humanity, and read the ways of men as intelligibly as we can read the weekly digest in the Press! We despise all seeming in the other arts, yet we take the drama as so much "sounding brass." Will not the people have their amusements? Ought they not to have them? Few will deny their necessity. True, they say, but we can have amusements quite as moral as the drama! No doubt of it; but that is not a sufficient argument for the uprooting of the theatre, and driving the drama into the closet. Shakspeare will not be cribbed; he will laugh or weep with you in the closet, if needs be; but he had rather reveal his soul-filling poetry through such living embodiments as Macready, Phelps, Faucit, Mrs. Butler, or the Cushmans. We have no species of amusement that can teach, at one and the same time, the great lessons of the ever-varying mind, so cheerfully and so practically as the drama; and if denouncers had been as active in its purification, as they have laboured for its extinction, we should now have had our great national amusement what its Master intended it to be— a world-large "mirror," wherein we could

"See ourselves as others see us."

To this consummation it will come; for as Englishmen are declaring in the most emphatic manner, that they will become as well educated as they are already commercially great, an educated people will not be less chary or forgetful of their ancient boast of " merrie;" they will assert their right to enjoyment, even as they freely give their bodies to labour, and claim for their country its title of *Merry England* once again! Are, then, the vast imaginative faculties so necessary for the perfection of the drama, to lie uncultivated? Can we find no instruction in witnessing that perfect delineation of character which the great art of dramatic action cherishes? Has not such delineation often delighted, and refined us? and shall we now, because an illiterate and outworn age allowed the theatre to be prostituted to bombast and dumb show—shall we now allow it to be blotted out by inky superstition from the page of regeneration? No: already has the infant Education, as yet but a span long, begun to ask, who is this William Shakspeare, of whom the sages boast, and whose texts our preachers quote? " Some folks tell us," say they, " that he was born in England, and delivered lectures on Humanity, to admiring thousands, in the reign of stiff-ruffed Bess! How is it that we, the artisans of his country, know him but indistinctly?" " Ay! and how is it," asks the wondering peasant, "that I have never heard of him?—I who toil long days at the plough,—who till your fields, and raise to perfection the stuff that furnishes you with bread loaves,— how is it that I have never heard of such a man? I have heard how that great jugglers came to our country from afar; I have heard of most of the foreigners,—

of one Mr. Jupiter, that would not help a man out of a deep rut, unless the waggoner would put his own shoulder to the spokes, and give the first lift,— and I have heard of good King George, that had guns fired off, the bells rung, and bonfires made upon his birthday, because he was the Father of his people; and I have heard of that great man who came from abroad, called Mr. Thumb, who improved the people by kissing above a million and a half of ladies, and received one hundred and seventy-eight times his own weight in gold for so doing, which, as the calculators say, would make three thousand one hundred and twenty-five statues of silver of the same weight as himself; and my young mistress has shown me her *card*, which Mr. Thumb presented to her as a token that he had kissed her,—and she says that she would not lose it for the world: and I have also heard of Great Wizards, and Mountebanks, but I never before heard of William Shakspeare. You now tell me he has been a preacher two centuries and a half, and above all, that he was born in England. If so, where can I hear his sermons?" This rustic is the type of thousands whom I have met and conversed with, who never heard of Shakspeare; and some hundreds who have heard of him, fancy he belonged to the fabled few who lived on Mount Olympus. This country thrashing-machine had never heard of the moralist. No, not he; but he had heard of a play-house! He is now told that the poet's sermons are plays, and that his pulpit is a theatre! Mark you! at the bare mention of that word *plays*, how the cold blood rushes to his cheek; see, his lips quiver, and his eyes look wild.

He wonders how the WORLD'S POET could have been so foolish as to have written a *play!* They must be wicked things; he has been told so over and over again. Prejudice has his time-withered fingers firmly in his collar, and stares upon him with jaundiced eyes, lest he should doubt and halt; yet the man could have wished that a genius so god-like had chosen a better name for his discourses upon everything, than *Masques* and *Plays*. O! what a pity that the great drama of life should be likened to a revel,—that a magician should be chosen to let the sublime curtain of poetry fall over his picture of sublunary actors, who, even as he "foretold,"

> "Are melted into air, into thin air:
> And, like the baseless fabric of this vision,
> The cloud-capp'd towers, the gorgeous palaces,
> The solemn temples, the great globe itself,
> Yea, all which it inherit, shall dissolve;
> And, like this insubstantial pageant faded,
> Leave not a rack behind. We are such stuff
> As dreams are made of, and our little life
> Is rounded with a sleep."

And can language so sublime be ever uttered in a so-called wicked play-house? Ay! and it is our boast that our own great dramatist has given it to us. Artisans of purse-proud England, take courage; Shakspeare and the drama shall be again our nation's boast. When universal education casts off his swaddling-clothes, then will he be strong enough to bring the dramatist to your own doors; to you, factory-workers, whose right to earn a scanty supply in ten short hours, in your miasmatic atmosphere, is questioned by brassy capitalists; to you, poor earth-imprisoned miners, doomed to your long night-day of toil; to you of the workshops and counter, will education bring back the recreative pleasures of the drama. Learn to value the wealth you produce, and your labour-share thereof, then shall there spring up an army of Macreadys, bringing the moralist to your Theatres, Athenæums, People's Colleges, and Temperance Soirées; they will steer you to an ocean-wide mind of philsophy,

> "Deeper than e'er plummet sounded."

Yes! and for you, poor neglected rustics; you, of whom it has been said, that it were better you remained in ignorance, lest, by getting knowledge, you should break your plough-shares, bury your mattocks deep in the earth, burn your flails; then, filled with strange airs, make unto yourselves wings of wax, and fly into Lazyland; Shakspeare sang for you. Then be no longer strangers to his "prick-song;" he is willing to harmonize you if you dare but listen to him. Arouse ye! instead of sitting half demonized at the ale-bench, maddening your senses with

> "Hot and rebellious liquor,"

awake! and quaff the cup of poesy. He offers you a brim-full bowl, as sweet as Hybla's honey-drops, and pure as the fount of Helicon! Ask you for "sport," he offers you a forest—all Arden if you like,

> "More free from peril than the envious Court."

There you may roam to the full of your bent, nor fear a six months' vice-training upon the tread-wheel, for trespassing in "my Lord's" preserves. He has pleasures for you, more heart-warming, better far, than excitements of cock-fighting and billiard-playing, which, instead of amusing you, do but blunt the better part of man, and sink you deeper into the sloughs of vice. The day has arisen, when this Shakspeare will visit you; in your verdant homes he will soon be with you. In the meantime, seek him in the nearest library, he will not mock your poverty; if you cannot afford him a morocco case, he will not despise a paper cover. Yes, I have faith, that in a few more years, the spread of Education and Science will break down the barriers that Bigotry, Prejudice, and Conventionalism have been studiously building up in years past, and patching, again and again, as the breezes of knowledge have weakened them. They are now going down with a fell crash; Progression has examined them, and pronounced them rotten. The day-star of religious fraternity is risen; in it all shams and hypocrisies will be tested in the furnace of Truth. For such an age was Shakspeare specially ordained. Try him; you will find him

"One entire and perfect chrysolite."

CHAPTER VIII.

"OUR VILLAGE."

In the latter part of June, 1832, I returned to Edwinstowe, resolved once more to try my hand at business. As my sole dependance was now to be on trade, it became absolutely necessary that I should fit myself for it by diligent study. Although I had been for the past five years sedulously gathering up every scrap of information that opportunity threw in my way, as yet I had not had sufficient experience to warrant me in setting myself up as a master painter. As I could have no opportunities of oral instruction, the only alternative left me was, to make the best use of such as I could obtain. There appeared to be three methods, at least open to me, from which I might draw forth information:—First, to diligently improve, by close application, the little knowledge I had already acquired; secondly, to study the best books on the subject which

I could procure; and, lastly, in my imitations of woods, or marbles, to go directly home to nature, whenever that was practicable. With such means I set to work, determined to make the best use I could of them.

Shortly after my settling down here, I was casually introduced to a gentleman, who was enjoying a tolerably prosperous business as a house painter, at Ollerton, two miles from my residence. Despite of my real inability, this man took especial pains to inform his neighbours that they had better not employ me! Report was already rife with his jeers about my impudence, and inability. He appeared to think that our present meeting presented a favourable opportunity for him to damage me as a tradesman. He asked me "if I thought the people wanted scenery painting on their walls and window-shutters?" and exposed me, thus publicly, to a severe "roasting;" then wishing, with exceeding charity, "that I might succeed." I gave fulness to his desire, by telling him, I had already determined to do so; for although young in the business, I had given myself up to three masters—Nature, Books, and Application; and I felt myself quite safe under their tuition. My rival—for such, in truth, he felt himself,—ridiculed such abstract teachers. I asked him to allow me a three years' apprenticeship under the above firm; also promising, if at the expiration of that term, I was not prepared to compete with him upon any works he chose to name, I would then leave the field of action clear for him, and seek my livelihood elsewhere; and he very readily accepted the challenge. He thought such sentimentality all very well to furnish small talk for a "player," but too air-brained to be reduced to practice as a painter. He had forgotten to take into his account, that Necessity will be obeyed, and stern though she may be, often presenting her volumes of instruction written in mystic characters, she has also the talismanic power of imparting knowledge; and to those who will profit by her lessons, she generally proves a good mistress. So Mr. Ben. H—— found in my case. Adversity had long been working in my brain, and it had wonderfully sharpened its powers; and in less than three years' time from my pseudo friend's desire " that I might succeed," he resigned business to me, with an acknowledgment, that in the higher branches of the art he could not compete with me. This circumstance would not be worthy of record—mere vain boasting, were it not that too many resign themselves to their (so called) hard fate, often without an effort—too frequently without arming themselves with the determination to better their condition. "Ay! all very well, Mr. Artisan," I hear some timid one exclaim, "but what is a fellow to do when he is down; is it not all down with him?" Do! I will tell you what to do; battle bravely with Necessity; stick to her, and when she finds you are resolved to prevail, she will turn round, and become a kindly helpmate. It will help you to weather the storm of circumstances, take the helm when you are on the adverse tack, and steer you into the harbour of prosperity, where you may safely anchor, and perhaps ride out through the voyage of life. Determination has often aided me; success is yours also, if you will it. To prevent mistakes, however, do not suppose that I measure success by ounces of gold, troy-weight. I have hitherto had little of money-wealth, yet have had riches manifold,—hearty beef and pudding meals when I required them, earned a fair reputation as an artisan, and well content to labour on, always hoping for comfort and domestic happiness.

My trade grew steadily, and became tolerably remunerative. It has not, as yet, ordered for me a banking-book, but it has enabled me to pay my creditors twenty shillings in the pound. If, by industry, I can continue so to pay them, I shall look with greater pride upon my *ledger*, than I should do to a register in the *Heralds' office*, or to be rated to the *Income Tax*. While I feel, as every honest heart should feel, a due respect for, and grateful recollection of, the favours conferred upon me as an artisan— whatever their amount or degree, I am proud of them, and thankful to the donors. As long as I claim for myself the full right to exercise all the privileges that pertain to a man, I trust ever to feel the responsibility of the duties that belong to a man; and so feeling, to endeavour religiously to discharge them.

It would be nothing short of base ingratitude, if, in the present narrative, I was lightly to slur over the thanks I owe to one, who, with no other object in view than to reward exertion, and make happy the home of a stranger, used her influence and rank to introduce me, in my capacity of an artisan, to the notice of the wealthy in the country around me. It was my good fortune, soon after settling here, to find a true friend and a patroness, in the Countess of Scarbrough. Her desire to procure me employment, and to administer comfort to my family, has been, and still is, of essential service to me; and to her I am indebted for the respectable connection that has so materially aided me in my business. Whatever may be my future lot in life, I cannot be unmindful of the many favours I have received from one who, in all truth, I may call my patroness. But there is another pleasure—one far above all selfish considerations—the pleasure of recording, that the Countess of Scarbrough has been the friend of the distressed of all conditions, in the village and its neighbourhood. Possessing, as her Ladyship does, a truly benevolent mind, distress has always found in her a foster-friend. She has now attained a ripened age, and deservedly enjoys the respect of the peasantry around her home. The earnest prayers of hundreds are daily offered to the Universal Parent, that she may yet be spared to succour them; and whenever the summons of death shall call her from this world, to enjoy the reward of a well-spent life, " in another and a better world," tearful eyes will bedew her bier, and the fervent bosoms of those who know and venerate her worth, will have a monument of gratitude to her memory graven on their hearts.

For a long time after my settling at Edwinstowe, my leisure hours—particularly the evenings—were spent in the flower garden, and in dramatic reading. As I could no longer act in the theatre, I had select audiences in the workshop of my friend, Mr. R. Trueman. Many a boisterous laugh have we sent pealing round the plastered walls of that little shoe-manufactory,—it was not mere titter, but right musical roaring, capable of making every last within the rails dance to our piping. You know, already, that my friend was a politician; he was also a warm educationist, and devoted much of his spare time to teaching in the Sunday Schools; he was also religious, but Christian enough not to care whether the church he heard a sermon in was crowned with a spire, or covered with tile or slate—and whether the preacher did duty in a black silk gown, or a blue coat; so long as there was charity in the discourse, he cared not for strict conformity; nevertheless, he had been taught that plays were bad things, and as a sequence, had many a struggle with himself about them. Often, after an affecting passage had been read, the big tears would course each other down his manly face, until he heard the climax—then, with great earnestness, he would frequently exclaim, "Don it to hummer, but any man might get as much good from that, as they do from many a sermon!" Whatever may be the opinions of others, I have reason to suppose that some little good has sprung up from our readings, inasmuch as they are often spoken of with pleasure. If none other was done but relaxing the sluggish minds of the hearers, and stirring their souls with the harp of poetry, I have a better faith in their expansive powers, than in the best regulated melancholic shake of the head Mr. Very-sedate could make.

At a time like the present, when the thoughts of all good men are fixed upon the great social problem, of how the working classes of this country are to be placed in self-dependance; how they are to live by their labour, having therewith sufficient leisure time to educate, and fit them for the discharge of their duties as citizens;—in such an age, I trust, that a retrospective glance over the last twenty years, of the doings of a village, which, considering its ruralised position, and the avocations of its inhabitants, now ranks amongst the foremost in education and morality; now that we are calling upon all benevolent persons, and asking the aid of Government to extend the means of domestic comfort, and to diminish crime, with its myriad contaminations—I trust the slow, but not less certain advance of a rural population, will not be uninteresting—particularly when it is considered, that the close of this narrative must be intimately connected with their advancement.

Half a century ago, the people of this district retained many of the privileges which anciently belonged in common to the inhabitants of Sherwood Forest. Here the hays of Birkland and Bilhagh, comprising $1487\frac{1}{2}$ acres, were open to them to range in, and indirectly to profit by;—true, those woods were under the control of appointed forest rangers, verderors, agisters, and woodwards—still, almost undisturbed, they could supply themselves plentifully with firewood, during the whole year, out of it. In autumn, they cut down the brackens, burnt them, and then sold them to the alkali manufacturers: this process was mainly carried on by the women and children, and sufficient was earned to pay off the years' shoe bill of the family, or the grocers', tailors', or other tradesmen's bills, and thus the comforts of the peasantry were advanced. Again, they could turn their swine into the forest, where they were allowed to fatten upon the mast. Many a laughable story is told of the manner in which the hogs marched in swinish order to the forest in the morning, and returned again at night, without the aid even of a swineherd, each grunter going direct to the night-shelter provided by its rightful owner; so regular were those hoggish wood-rangers in their habits, that their masters never troubled themselves about "jackey's" safety; their return with a bellyfull was a matter of certainty. There was no lack of amusement either, as well as gain; the villagers residing on the forest skirts, could go forth with their guns, and kill the young jackdaws, starlings, or small birds, without having the fear of gamekeepers and trespass warrants before their eyes. Indeed, the jackdaw season was one of great jollification: a day was set apart—the villagers invited their friends from a distance; a band of music was in attendance—the party previously preparing themselves with bread and beer, and other luxuries, sufficient for the day: all being ready, the amusements began, and at intervals they regaled themselves; the bowery oaks circumscribed their dining-room—the sward of the green wood was alike their table-cloth and carpet; through the windows of the fretted roof, they caught glimpses of the blue heaven; whilst the band feasted themselves, the daws, starlings, blackbirds, thrushes, ring-doves, and the various small warblers, joined to the fitful music of the winds—all played a jubilant more heartily, and harmoniously too, than the best trained, and bread-loaf payed, barrack band ever played "O the roast beef," at an officers' mess. Yes! these rustic revels were toil-relaxing; no sugar or daylight was taxed for their support. But the privileges just named, great as they were, are not a tythe of those which they enjoyed. How is it with them now?—are not the forests still left for their enjoyment and profit? Oh no! no ranging for them now-a-days; they are given over to those who know better how to take care of the rustics, than the crown was wont in days gone by. Of course, it is said, that in the various exchange and inclosure acts, the PEOPLE'S RIGHTS are always respected! In this boasted land, "the pride and envy" of all others, as it is our custom so to roar it out on public days, and in public houses— in this land where even-handed justice is a national brag—surely, in such a country, with the afforestation, the people would have their commons converted into parks and parterres; or, if a subdivision took place, and there were, by inadvertance, an extra acre or two thrown in, they would be given to the million, to the people, without whom all the broad acres and parks of England would be worthless. Alack! talk we of equal rights, of people's parks, and the commoners' lands—where are they? Echo replies, where?

Amongst people enjoying such advantages as those villagers enjoyed to a late period, it was not unreasonable to expect, that some portion of that brave spirit which animated the band of Forest Outlaws, whose names are linked with the history of our country, should have descended to the more humble natives of Sherwood; for here, in particular, the history of his (the head of the band) resistance to oppression, and his love for, and protection of, the poor, has been transmitted with veneration from sire to son. What else could you expect in a locality where every nook, primrosed dumble, singing stream, or crag-roofed grotto-cave, is dedicated to the memory of Robin Hood? or to his first lord, Little John, the Maid Marion, or the Outlaw's merry men?

> " And to the end of time, the tales shall ne'er be done,
> Of Sherlock, George o' Green, and Much the miller's son;
> Of Tuck, the merry friar, which many a sermon made
> In praise of Robin Hood, his outlaws and their trade."

In this village the very houses still remain, where the King's huntsmen trained up the hounds, which years ago chased the sleek deer in Birkland Hays. Those are now converted into a couple of cottages; the dormer windows peep out of their low roof, and lilies, marigolds, and wall-flowers, bloom within the two-yard wide garden, in the front of them, and apricots ripen on their old grey walls. Only one generation has passed, since the last huntsman was consigned to his tenement of clay, upon the hill hard by. The old church tower, whose ashlar courses seem to have been thrown together at random—but yet, with perfect method—is crowned with a beautiful crocketed spire, which calmly watches over the forest worthies who lie entombed at its base. The spire, which tapers far away into the airy space overhead, mystically tells the spirits that hover within the hallowed mound, that yet a little while, and the Archangel's trumpet shall call them again to new life! Every thing is green with the forest days. Even at this late period, despite of the pains that have been taken, to rub off the mould of ages, you cannot stand upon this spot, and muse upon the past, without seeing those " merrie men" before and around you. There are the huntsmen, that made yonder glades re-echo with their wild "Yeo ho boys—forward!" Even now, you hear it melting into the breeze, and dying away far down yon tangled greenwood aisle! There lie the maidens, and here the youths, that a century ago were dancing* "a merry May" around yon sturdy oak; although his locks are grey, and his branches

> "moss'd with age,
> And high top bald with dry antiquity!"

See how he laughs at the remains of frail humanity. It is but a hour, by his reckoning, since those maidens, once so beautiful, were gathering up the mossy cups, all bright with pearly dew, and wreathing them into a garland. They were for love tokens, and ancient usage had decreed, that they should gather them before the burning eye of day could dry up the mist. They have filled their "osier-cage," and lightsome feet are tripping it back again to the wild notes of a village clarionet player, whose innate science scorned to hamper itself with the set crotchets of professors. Like the flowers, they have perished; but the spirit of their beauty still haunts us. Every step we take is over the earth-bed of those who gloried in freedom.— Peace be with them.

---

* Amongst the many poetical customs of a by-gone age, this was a pleasing one. It was usual here, on May mornings, for the youth of both sexes, to hie them to the forest, and gather token-flowers before day-break, and return with them to decorate the doors of their lovers, before they were up in the morning. This is one of those rural customs, which, like well-flowering, and dressing, and the depositing of garlands in the churches with the dead, as is yet the custom in some parts of Derbyshire, which, in this age of mere utility, we might well have retained.

In all ages the collar of thraldom has been brazed securely, while the people were drunk with blood. The degrading wars of the last century ended by crippling—nay, by nearly destroying two classes, the yeomen and the peasantry, both of which had been our nation's boast. True, these classes are yet talked about; but where are we to look for the true spirit of independence, which was once associated with them. Go to the review, after eight days' "playing at soldiers:" shall we find it there? Or is it written upon the soup and clothing tickets? Think you, shall we find it on the "show-days," where the premiums are given for the best labourer? the one who has struggled with starvation wages for a long term of years, and who, during that time, has worked early and late on the week-days, and given in a few hours on the Sundays, and brought up eight or ten children without "troubling the parish?" Shall we find this once boasted independence upon the labour-deserted hundreds up-heaped acres' farms, or does it sit with its head buried in its hands mourning with the ruined cottiers? I am afraid we may seek it in vain at any of those places. Sterling independence, which dare be honest at all hazards, finds no home where the creature, which might have been a man, groans spirit-broken beneath a dominant class-master. Nor can true liberty dwell with ignorance. There is an independence babbled about at election times; and another that thrives upon beef and wine, which tries to be civil to the diners "below the salt," who, in the height of their enthusiasm, imagine for the moment, that they are the brave hearts spoken of. Alack! follow the gaping crowd home, and dwell with them a few days, and there observe what sort of a thing this holiday independence is! What, but a gradual sinking down of manliness, until every principle of true self-dependence, once the peasant's dower, falls down, down, down to serfdom! and at last the beggar believes that the law that enslaved him ought to throw a bread-loaf to him whenever he is hungry. Give us, the Artisans and Peasantry of England, but another half-century of such independence as the "heaven-born" minister, Pitt, and his servitors cut out for us, and we have been in consequence enjoying—continue it but a little longer—and you shall behold the United Kingdom one vast Skibbereen, or Connemara; you may then convert the factories into charnel-houses, and the parks into Golgothas.

With the rise of the demoralizing "volunteer days," the self-dependence of "our village" began to wane, and the few who still held stoutly the quarter-staff of freedom were sorely tried. For a time, the wars threw the dust of high wages in the people's eyes; and the tax-chains, that were to bind down provisions, were forged, before the labourer had rubbed off the film of riotous living. A class winked at the spread of drunkenness, which, they imagined, was better worth encouragement than education. Was it not better to get "gloriously drunk" two or three days a-week, and mind your work on sober days, than to be always sober, and regularly to work eight or ten hours each day? Many of us remember the brutalising cry of "What did poor people want with education?" Aye! what, indeed? for there is no *breed* in them. Yes, no breed! for often, with our vaunted advancement, I hear the blood-rousing argument held, that certain men, like curs and spaniels, are born for menial purposes; hence the assertion, that they were never intended by the Great Disposer to be lawyers, officers, or clergyman. Enough, then, for them, basely bred that they are, there, in their thousands, for enraged foreigners to use as a self-made regimental target, to practise glory upon. We pretend to wonder, and to grieve, that all Ireland has become a beggar-land,—why should we wonder? In any country or clime, do but trample humanity into the dust, write "boon thrall" upon his neck, and when pistols and torches fail to procure the shred-man with bread, he falls self-debased into the "slough of despair," gazing sullenly upon the labour that does not ennoble him, and thenceforward regards exertion as a curse. A nation of bondmen will ever be a nation of beggars! Do but tighten the cord of serfdom, and assuredly you shall behold "free-born" Englishmen a nation of beggars also! Who, then, will keep the "free-born" beggars? Shall we not, locust-like, spread over the fair acres, and devour up every green thing? Will breeds, and feudalisms, find workhouses for us then? Count the cost; and if we must be million-fed with beggars' broth, come then—

> "once we'll pray, and then
> We'll all go building workhouses, million men."

Thanks to the god-like attribute that adorns labour, we cannot be long enslaved in commercial England; without labour, commerce cannot exist; without labour, there can be no corn-waving acres. Labour can fashion spinning-jennies, and fly over railroads. If, then, the labourer is content to remain withebound, it is his own fault. While he can subdue the elements, and bend them to aid his productive powers, he can surely break the cobweb threads of thraldom, whenever he chooses to begin right earnestly to brush them off. The car of Time is winged with progression, and were a nation of Titians to hurl down their stumbling-blocks of stand-still policy, thinking thereby, to crush the claims of labour, the

> "Million million men"

need but to stop the loom, and let the plough stand still; and the Titian idlers would soon pray the hitherto despised pigmies of labour to take to the mattock and mill once again. While the nineteenth century has enshrined itself in learning and science, so shall it emancipate and embalm the holy cause of labour. The millions now look with abiding faith to the God of Truth, who gave them "the earth for an heritage;" to Him they cry aloud, "We will labour, and shall we not eat?" Yes, they shall eat! for the God of goodness hath willed it! All who now look calmly upon the population problem, doubt the policy of attempting to chain down the mind.

Perhaps, in no part of Sherwood's wide range, has that uplifting spirit of freedom which animated the patriots, Robin Hood and his "merrie men," whose name will be venerated by our countrymen as long as the principles of liberty for which they struggled shall be cherished amongst us; nowhere has that spirit been more fondly nursed than in this village. Until a very recent period, the distinguishing characteristics of those foresters have been theirs. Those outlaws,—so called,—for it was not difficult to gain the honour of outlawry, in the " chivalric days" of the Henrys and Edwards,—the outlaws were sworn enemies against the perpetrators of public injury, or private wrongs. It was to me most noticeable on my first visit to this place, that a number of old persons living here, some of them seventy and eighty years of age—those men, when speaking of virtuous actions, of love to all men, protection of the weak and lowly, of warm-heartedness, hatred of oppression and tyranny, of their thorough detestation of meanness and base conduct, however exhibited, of their love of jollity and good fellowship in whatever phases it might present itself; when speaking of any, or all of those things, they were invariably associated with the doings of those "merry men of old," and as they told their tales, a generous burst of indignation would arise, or a glow of self-approval reveal itself, as they exultingly exclaimed, "Aye! those things are our business, a part of our duty, for we are the real Robin Hood's men—the true Foresters!"

It may be expected, that amongst so large a number, at a time when education was at a discount in universal opinion, that now and then an exception of a roguish character would be found amongst them; there were a few such, which, when compared with the others, might be called a half-degenerated class. While they possessed a nobody-cares sort of dislike to oppression, they were content to enjoy themselves—if revelling with Bacchus was an enjoyment—with a never-ceasing praise of " nutty brown" ale, they gloried in a good joke, and were not very choice about the rank of the persons they chose as their butt; yet their maxim was, "Do nobody harm." They enjoyed a fair stand-up fight, whether with cudgels or fisty-cuffs, they cared not which: fight with you, or drink with you, they were ready for either, yet all " for love!" Another good feature with them was, whether "in their cups," or "solid and sober," they were always willing to share their last crust with a distressed brother. A rare specimen of this class still survives; he may be considered the last of the "hard heads,"—a race who were constant by day and by night in the service of Sir John Barleycorn. He is now old and decrepid, his lameness, no doubt, being accelerated by sleeping night after night in the woods, or the straw-yard. For years this veteran has enjoyed the distinguished appellation of "His Honour!" A few years ago the curate of the village called upon the old man to converse with him on religious matters; after some talk with him, he promised to send him a Bible, "his honour" also promising to read it after he received it. Shortly afterwards the curate was passing the cottage-door, and observed the old man employed with the book. The curate accosting him, said, " Well, Isaac, I am glad to see you reading your Bible." " Oh yes;" replied Isaac, in a gruff tone of voice,—gruff, but not intentionally uncivil. " Will you tell me what you are reading about?" said the clergyman. "O, to be sure I will," was the answer, " I am reading all the wars of the rascally Jews, and all that sort of thing; why, what a blood-thirsty race of men they were, Sir." "Oh! Isaac," said the curate, "you have strange ideas;

you must remember that you only notice the histories; you must turn to the New Testament, it will give you comfort and consolation, and strengthen your belief—for I hope you do believe." "Do believe?" said Isaac, with great earnestness, "aye, to be sure I do—do believe—do believe—to be sure I do," he kept muttering for some time. "Well," said the Rev. Gentleman, "I am glad to hear that." Will you tell me what you believe in?" "To be sure I will," replied Isaac, stopping short the clergyman's conversation, "to be sure I will; I believe, Sir, in everything; in all the kit of them, Sir;—believe?—to be sure I do." No wonder that the curate, who took a deep and serious interest in the religious education of his flock, felt pained at such ignorance, for he knew the old man was in earnest, and was greatly astray in matters of such moment to his future welfare. As soon as he had recovered the shock, the curate continued, "I am grieved to hear you talk so lightly upon such a serious subject; you know it is my duty to warn you against continuing in your present careless state; and when we meet together, as we one day must, at the bar of judgment, you cannot say that I never warned you of your danger,—you cannot then blame me." This was too much for the old man, who ignorantly thought that the clergyman feared to suffer peril for his misdeeds. The veteran then summoned every serious thought within him, and clearing his rusty thorough-bass pipes to give effect to his utterance, replied, "I won't, Sir,—I won't, Sir, depend upon it; no, Sir; I'll never mention your name upon that same piece of business!—I won't, Sir." This was too much for the pastor to bear; it struck a chord too deep for words to express; and he left poor Isaac, with the intention, however, of renewing his visit in a few days, hoping to meet him next time under more favourable auspices.

Now, although this old fellow was completely lost to the spiritualizing influence of the book that lay upon his knees, as he sat at his cottage door, he was not, consequently, an evil-disposed man; no, he was charitable, and brave too, in his own way. Was it impiety that called forth those unlettered replies to the curate's questions? He had never been able, in his younger days, to spare a single leisure hour away from the beer-house; and his drinking habits had scarcely met with a reproof from those whose duty it was to have checked such licentiousness. This man is an exception now-a-days; but, half a century ago, the follies of such a man were preferred to the sober meddling of a working man with self-elevation, and political economy. Then, it was known, that the drunkard was never likely to trouble the law-makers with clamours for commercial freedom, universal suffrage, and a fair share of the proceeds of labour; and, with the class raised above the sot, to see a man "glorious" only excited their mirth, seldom their pity. It was enough that the wives had to mourn at home, and their sons, and their sons' sons, to be forced to beg their bread, through such false policy and recklessness.

The man who professed himself to be "his honour's" spiritual teacher—the curate of the parish,—who took his share of the tithes and taxes, as a reward for his instruction, was "his honour's" boon companion in many a booze—was present with him at many a cock-battle, and has grinned for a wager through a horse-collar with him. Did that priest ever direct "his honour's" attention to the New Testament? Well might the poor old fellow, in his characteristic lingo, while speaking of the "three persons" in his creed, talk about the "kit of them." Why wonder at the prevalence of ignorance in such an age of war and drunkenness? That very curate and boon companion of the old fellow's, has, on many occasions, while discharging his spiritual duties at the grave, been so drunk, as to require himself to be held up by a tombstone on one hand, and the clerk on the other, while reading the funeral service! Often, as might be expected, the most painful blunders were committed. The priest, who had declared he believed himself to have been called by the Most High to the cure of souls, was often so debased by liquor, as to commence the *marriage* service, as he met the sorrowing few in the church yard, who had come, heart-riven with grief, to consign a dear friend, perhaps a parent, to the last cold bed! What would be their pangs, forced to listen to such a mockery, at such a time? Yet this curate was "his honour's" spiritual adviser! and we wonder at the poor old fellow's ignorance, and call it impiety! Wonder, indeed! Pages of such disgusting recitals could be written of this curate, and all could be corroborated by living evidence in this village; but we shudder at the bare mention of them. Talk of the dark ages! Surely, in the world's history, we have not pages more black than those written in the last age's book of ignorance.

The evils attendant upon the long war, however they were to affect the classes generally, were destined to wreak their pauperising mischief upon the labourer. All Europe was drenched with human blood, that England's indebtedness might be swelled into a labour-drowning gulph, which the science of statemanship could neither sound, nor drain off. As the debt grew large, so also grew the Moloch of monopoly and capital; millions of money, hitherto unheard of, were piled up in masses, but not for the labourer to enjoy. During the debt-growing season, every article that the labourer had to deal with—from his porridge, shoes, coat, and everything even up to God's daylight—were taxed, re-taxed, and the taxes again ten per cented; and as this taxing was increased year after year, in the same proportion were his wages reduced, until at length the flesh-and-blood-machine, into which God had " breathed the breath of life," was compelled to exist, that he might work—not be enabled to work, that he might live thereby. Within the last half century, it is said, that not less than thirty-four parishes in the hundred of Bassetlaw alone have been inclosed;—how much richer are the peasantry who reside in those parishes for these said inclosures? Time was, when the humblest peasant enjoyed his right of " folcland,"—the land of the folks; but dare the peasantry of Bassetlaw set a foot upon one acre within those thirty-four parishes? Truly, some persons have been enriched by the mapping-out, and ring-fencing of these commons; but are they the " common people?" How many of the poor peasants are bettered by it? Doubtless, the peasantry are existing by thousands within those parishes; have the thousands been allowed to take the "lion's share?" Coeval with the inclosures have been the demolition of the cottiers, the allotting of hundred-acred farms, and the despoiling of homesteads. How have the labourers fared? Have they been spread over the monster farms, as the acres were multiplied by the hundreds,—or, have the labourers been employed in their tens, or their units? The prize ox feeders, the owners of thistle down, and couch-grass-carpeted acres, and the Union Workhouses, can best answer that. However, the poor have been cared for; the soup-ticket has been written, the clothing-club established, and the potato-plot set out; every thing that could be done to make them comfortable, has been done. There are many persons that entertain such an opinion, but very few of them are found among the labourers; they would rather enjoy the means of livelihood as a right, not receive it as a charity; they want wages, not pauperism, or the charity that induces it. Truly, charity covereth a multitude of sins, but its Divine Author never intended it to be made an instrument of demoralization and pauperism. And while there are honourable exceptions in the administration of the soup, clothing, and potato clubs, there are also lamentable proofs that the spirit of manliness has been broken by them. Cunning and hypocrisy have been engendered by them;—I have witnessed such mischief hundreds of times. The spirit of self-dependence, once broken, then the creature will resort to any cant or artifice to live by begging. I have seen those clubs made a condition that the recipient should attend a particular church; or again, that they should continue to live in the house of some particular landlord; or that the parties should send their children to some particular Sunday or week-day school, where certain tenets were taught, or that some certain obeisance should be tendered. I have seen, again and again, the deceit and cant that have been resorted to, to keep these "charities," and often the holders have become so debased as to glory in their deceit. If the charm of independence dwell not within the heart of the labourer, he cares not how he burdens society, so that he does but exist. Surely Ireland has read us a lesson on dependence,—such will ever be the ultimate fate of beggary. Continue to make dependents of English labourers, and we shall soon find an Irish level. Give us wages and freedom, and we shall show to all future time, that a nation of self-dependent men will ever be industrious and virtuous.

The man-sinking influence of depending upon other people, spread itself throughout the land; but it was destined to be checked, before the nation could be finally enslaved. In this village there were still a few brave hearts, who were forced, for a time, to sadly grieve over the wreck of liberty, and domestic enjoyment. Notwithstanding we are occasionally subjected to suffering and degradation, it is one of God's blessings, that the spirit of truth shall never die,—it may be persecuted for a season, but it cannot be destroyed. So it was in "our village"—the spirit of independence was yet alive in the breasts of the "true foresters;" and that spirit was again to arise, Phœnix like, out of the slumbering embers of an iron age—an age that brought forth a generation drunk with the blood of foreigners, who had been exalted into enemies, that we might slay them, and call the barbarity "Fame." Here, as elsewhere, drunkenness and ignorance, the foster parents of crime, were laughed at as playthings; and, as might be expected, depredations were as plentiful as the acorns of the forest. Edwinstowe had its share of crime: larders were plundered, and hen-roosts, sheep-walks, granaries, and farm-yards, were robbed; poaching, and its attendant train of mischief, was practised; all were as rife here as in other places, long after that glorious war which bedecked heroes with tax-woven honours, and filled our workhouses with paupers, and our highways with crime. Oh, yes! such a class were here, training for the hulks, and the hangman; they did mischief enough in their day, and brought disgrace upon the locality; but the wars, and the crimes engendered by the war spirit, were to have an end. A virtuous few were left; they were the missionaries of education, and moral emulation; and their reign of religion was destined to succeed the reign of terror. Let us pray, that the day may speedily come, when the blessing of freedom, knowledge, and virtue, shall make the whole earth a Paradise of Love and Liberty!

It was my privilege, soon after settling in this village, to make the two or three right-thinking men— the men who were anxiously looking for better days— my companions; and thus early we pledged ourselves mutually to endeavour to banish crime from the village, and if possible, restore it to virtue and freedom. From that time, we have diligently worked together, full of hope, that somebody would be benefited by our love-labour. Squatting down here, penniless, without a table, or three-legged stool, to furnish a cottage with, it may easily be imagined that I had tough work of it. My great want was books; I was too poor to purchase expensive ones, and the "cheap literature" was not then, as now, to be found in every out-o'-the-way nooking. However, Knight had unfurled his paper banners of free trade in letters. The "Penny Magazine" was published—I borrowed the first volume, and determined to make an effort to possess myself with the second; accordingly, with January, 1833, I determined to discontinue the use of sugar in my tea, hoping that my family would not then feel the sacrifice necessary to buy the book. Since that period, I have expended large sums in books, some of them very costly ones, but I never had one so truly valuable, as was the second volume of the "Penny Magazine;" and I looked as anxiously for the issue of the monthly part, as I did for the means of getting a living. I continued to be a subscriber to this periodical up to the publication of the last number; and albeit, but an unit, out of the tens of thousands that have been benefited by that work, I feel bound to tender my mite of gratitude, to its spirited and enterprising publisher. The "Penny Magazine" was the first intellectual mile-post put down upon the way-side, wherefrom coming ages may measure their progress towards a commonwealth of books.

In May, 1833, a few persons resident in this village established a Lodge of Odd Fellows, under the Nottingham Ancient Imperial United Order. Being known to many of the members, as a decent writer, and tolerable accountant, I was often solicited by them to join this Lodge, and become their secretary, but could not be prevailed upon to do so; for, in common with many others, I had prejudices manifold against Odd Fellowship; I knew not why, but I had them, and that was the only answer I could give to my friends, when importuned to join them. There was a world of queer things in those words, *Odd Fellows:* barguests, sprites, wizards, kelpies, swords, daggers, darkness blacker than pitchy midnight, were all within it, and cooking their "hell broth," and holding their wild orgies, to my mind's eye, within that bolted Acheron, the Odd Fellows' Lodge-room. To me, the pasteboard air-hunters and tempera-made owls, and demon kites with their atmosphere of red and blue fire, of the theatres, were things understood, and easily to be accounted for; but to be shut out from God's light, and given over to Odd Fellows, with swords in their hands, and daggers in their eyes, were more than common flesh, and thin blood, could hope to conquer; and so—for a time, at least—I dare not become an Odd Fellow! To an inquiring mind, prejudice, like the mists of Autumn, which are drunk up by the midday sun, flies away before the sun of information; and an every-day acquaintance, even with *odd things*, often plucks the terror out of them, and still closer companionship renders them agreeable. So it was with this same Odd Fellowship: every renewed conversation about it slew a demon, and raised up a mortal. After the Lodge had been established about eighteen months, I agreed with my friend, Mr. Trueman, to join the society—both being of opinion, that if we did not like it, after a trial, we could then withdraw; for after all my terrible imaginings, I observed most of my acquaintances, who did join the Lodge, came out again alive; nor did I hear that any of them were sent off to the sea shore, and there, at low water's mark, had a stake driven through their bodies, and left as a terrible example to all divulgers of secrets. Accordingly, in the Summer of 1834, an evening was fixed whereon to join this Lodge of Odd Fellows! The night arrived, my friend was present, but I was absent; I had not been able to overcome my prejudices against the society, and so was driven to a breach of promise. After my friend had passed the dreaded ordeal—pokering, it was called here!—I found him alive and well the next morning; he made a favourable report of their proceedings, and a week or two after, I mustered courage to join them. I soon became a warm advocate for the extension of the Lodges, and the promulgation of their principles. As I found them to be far in advance of the Sick Clubs (so called), it is true that I found them, in one respect, as I expected to do, enjoying a pipe and a glass; but this was not, as had so frequently been represented, their whole business,—they had other and more useful things to do. I found that an anxious desire pervaded the congregated brethren, to better their social condition—to lay up sums of money, that by prudent forethought, they might be protected against the pangs of poverty, when disease or misfortune assailed them. They were also storing up ample funds to provide for the decent interment of any of their members, whenever death should overtake them. They were likewise studiously asking themselves, how they could best provide for their widows, and procure a home for their orphans? All these pecuniary necessities formed the business of their meetings; and who shall deny the moral importance of such considerations? I am not ashamed to declare, that in the main, I found those institutions much to my heart's desire. Their Lodge has, unquestionably, been of vast use to our village; it has been the means of drawing a large body of men to provident and self-caring considerations, of checking drunkenness, promoting social concord, and sublimating, by intense fire-thought, gross lumps of ignorance into Christian men.

Those institutions have done much good,—they are still doing good throughout the country; but the good they have done is but as a water-drop to the ocean, compared with what they might do, if they would think more seriously about the matter. If they would but look abroad upon the numberless social evils which demoralize mankind, and reflect but for a moment, they would soon discover that their remedy lies in their own hands solely; and unless they head the march of improvement, ages may yet elapse before the well-fed, and well-clothed will see the necessity of doing it for them. Awake, artisans! from the death-slumber of "things are very well as they are," and live in the bright daylight of self-dependence!

One thing, however, must not be lost sight of, that while so much fault is found with those societies, the working men have had to fashion them, lacking, too, such information as was essentially necessary for their stability. The classes that might have helped them, have, with a few exceptions, stood aloof—content to stigmatise, rather than assist them. It cannot be surprising, if, under all the circumstances, many of them have been working upon unsound data. It is to be feared, that many who are flattered by present appearances of success, are not so secure as they imagine themselves to be; certainly not, if we are to take the tables as a guide, which are published in an excellent book, called "Contributions to Vital Statistics;" and a strong argument of the practicability of that work is, that its statistics correspond with the actual returns lately made from 3,682 Lodges in the M. U. of Odd Fellows. The financial condition of Benefit Societies has now become a question of vital importance to the masses, and it is likely to be well considered by them. Many objections are yet taken to Odd Fellows' societies; one of the strongest, urged by the religious portion of the community, is their frequent meetings at public-houses, which, as they say, not only countenances, but encourages drinking habits. This has led the executive of the largest dissenting body in the kingdom, to publicly denounce Odd Fellowship. This is to be regretted; for it should be considered, that the working classes have been driven to the public-house in very self-defence— no other place being open to them—and where else can they be admitted? They will still be forced there, until they organize themselves in a better way than they seem to be content with at present.

I well remember, that about eight years ago, several Odd Fellows, residing in this village, were anxious to have their own hall, or house, to meet in; this building they proposed so to construct, as to be generally useful for public purposes. To obtain the ground presented the greatest obstacle in this place; it was thought, that a nobleman, residing near to the village, and who had plenty of land in it, might, perhaps, assist us, if the necessity of the case, and the moral importance of the subject, were properly laid before him; with this view, a deputation waited upon the noble Lord's steward, to solicit his approval of the plan. Our visit was a fruitless one; instead of meeting with support, we were told that he could not encourage such schemes, "because, if they were carried out, they would ruin the publicans in the village." "Of what use," said he "would their large rooms be, if public bodies, such as Benefit Societies, and Odd Fellows' Lodges, met in their own buildings?" As we had reason to suppose our request, if prosecuted further, would not be promoted, as we could not get the steward's consent, we were reluctantly obliged to give up our project. I have no doubt, that in hundreds of other parishes, particularly in the rural districts, Odd Fellows would be similarly circumstanced, even were they as desirous of having their own hall as we were. It will be argued, that in the towns, the same difficulties do not present themselves; and, as regards the larger towns, I believe the argument will hold good, for in almost every town, ground might be purchased for such a purpose. These societies have already decided the question of meeting in their own buildings. Some of them have already built their own halls; others have rented extensive premises, converting them into committee-rooms, libraries, and schools, resorting to the public-houses only at their more numerous meetings;—this is, undoubtedly, a step in the right direction, and every year will add to their number. I have long advocated the necessity of the Odd Fellows having their own halls, away from the public-houses,—the advantages that must result from them, both financially and morally, are greater than they imagine them to be. There are thousands of them who do not see the necessity of such a change. Custom has its associations wound up with the public-houses. Whatever such persons may think, there is, undeniably, an under current sweeping through society, which is settling in that direction, and which it will be as fruitless to attempt to stem, as it was for the flatterers of Canute to expect that the ocean would stop its surge-roll, at the nod of an anointed King. Men now begin to ask themselves, what is the difference between enjoyment and drunkenness? and are careful not to place themselves within the vortex of temptation. Odd Fellows' societies will rise inestimably in favour, when the wives and mothers are assured, that they can meet at other places than the beer-houses. I make no war upon trades,—the inns are necessary; and as long as they continue so, they will be supported by the class that needs them, and no longer; but to maintain that societies, whose principal business should be to propagate the principles of economy and morality, must needs keep to the beer-shop, or the publicans must fail, is on a par with the argument, that railroads are an evil, because the coachmen want a living. In James's days, the sedan

2 D

chair-men petitioned against the use of hackney coaches, because they interfered with the vested rights of the chair-men. The day is not distant, when every Lodge, or groups of Lodges, will have their own halls, schools, and other social advantages. What they have done, will be an incentive to other social reforms; happily, the working classes are now awakening to a sense of their own power! Odd Fellows' societies have been eminently useful in convincing the working people of the advantages of union amongst themselves, particularly so in the rural districts. Even the new poor law has materially aided the progress of the Lodges, by forcing the poor to depend upon their own resources—and so avoid separation, death, and the "skilly" diet! By no other means would the rustic population have been brought, so speedily, within the co-operative circle. I look upon these institutions as the social axe, and paring-spade, which have been well employed in cutting down the brush-wood, and turning up the turf of the commons of humanity—preparing the weed-covered wastes of ignorance for a rich harvest of domestic comfort; and, I doubt not, but other, and still more important communities, will hereafter acknowledge, that without such pioneers as the Odd Fellows' societies, ages might have elapsed, before they could have persuaded the rustics to listen to their sermons of UNITY and LOVE.

The old Sick Clubs, in their palmy days, ridiculed the idea of the Lodges—then mere "free and easy" meetings—becoming benefit societies. When they were told that these Lodges meant to add Protection Societies for their widows and orphans, likewise schools and libraries, the old men thought that a voyage to Utopia might do the projectors good—then, if even they found their way back again, their wild notions would be somewhat modified by the trip. They have established Benevolent or Benefit Societies; hundreds of them are actively at work disbursing weekly sums in sickness, varying from eight, ten, fifteen, and twenty shillings, to each of their members. They have added other philanthropic branches, and they have worked well for the members, with every prospect of future success; and instead of taking a balloon for Utopia, as had been projected, the founders simply spent an hour with Misery in his breadless hovel, and then retiring home, asked Benevolence how such suffering was to be remedied? and the blue-eyed maiden answered—" By unity of action!" Philanthropy was at once astir,—no aërial voyaging for her—she took a cruise of milk and of honey, and went into the lanes and alleys, crying aloud,—"Up, ye sluggards! why hunger ye? Up, sallow faces! lean upon the arm of your brother,—link ye on, one to the other, and come with me, and I will teach you how to be happy; the plan is a simple and a sure one,—be united, and love one another!"

The Nottingham Ancient Imperial United Order, to which I belong, has, within the last five months (October to March, 1846-7,) independent of the weekly sick funds, paid the sum of £1553. 8s. 7d. for interments, to the survivors, the widows, and the orphan children; and the allowance is further continued weekly to the widows, and to the orphans until they severally attain the age of fourteen years.

Those branches of the Order have been faithfully discharging their benevolent duties since 1840, the year in which a branch called the Provident Society was added; in 1842, the Widow and Orphan's Protection Society was founded; and in 1845, a General Funeral Fund was established, in connection with the former funds; besides paying every-day demands, made by those branches, they have gradually laid up, by small savings, since 1840, the sum of £6302. !

If the working classes, connected with a few Lodges, have already done this, and more, why should they halt? There need not be one desolate hearth, or one unemployed hand, in the country, if they were but united by oneness of purpose. The miseries attendant upon starvation, the madness of oppression, the mischievous fabrications of over-population, and the thousand and one lip-made tortures, that are conjured up by disunion, to drive us to despair—we can dispel them all by a oneness of purpose. What shall we do? Unite and live happily, or "cut each other's throats" by envy and division, and reap the reward of a workhouse tomb? No; to work! to work! This is no time for social reformers to lie sleeping on their oars, while the life-skiff glides idly down the slimy tide of carelessness;—no; lay to—pull heartily. Mind was never so omnipotent as at this moment—sympathetic desire, for universal happiness is present everywhere; we cannot take up a book, or a newspaper, but the eye lights upon some new plan of progression, bearing upon the condition of the poor: labour has been long despised, but its enfranchisement is at hand!

Believing the Odd Fellows' societies to be capable of bettering the condition of the labourer, both financially and morally, I have devoted much of my leisure time, during the last twelve or fourteen years, to extend their usefulness. Within that time, I have assisted in the opening of from forty to fifty Lodges; and in my humble way, have delivered addresses and lectures, in favour of their principles, in England and Scotland, travelling above six thousand miles for that purpose; and in addition to those, have filled offices in my minor Lodge, and in the executive at Nottingham. During my connection with those societies, I have seen much good done by them, and I am not without hope that much more will be done. To those who take an interest in the elevation of the peasantry and artisans of our country, it is refreshing to note the improvement made by these institutions. I have observed persons, who, on their enrolment, were as rough and uncouth—particularly so in country districts—who appeared as wild and careless as the unpruned hawthorns, which bower the age-furrowed lanes of some sequestered hamlet; but visit those persons again, after experiencing six or seven years of this Lodge training—converse with them, and they will give you evident proof, that their minds, once as uncultivated as the wild wastes, have gradually ripened into thought, delighting in charitable works, and blooming in the brightness of true manliness; often they will express their deep thanks for such means of protection and improvement, and pour forth grateful acknowledgments to the founders of such useful institutions.

As a specimen of the schooling power of the Lodges, the progress of one man, connected with the Birkland and Bilhagh Lodge at Edwinstowe, is noteworthy. I have carefully watched the progress of this individual. Being a zealous supporter of the Order, and a warm advocate for his own Lodge, he was frequently in the habit of addressing the chairman; although he possessed a fair share of natural ability, he still wanted the polish given by education and practice, to make him tolerable as a public speaker. This man was, however, well aware of his own imperfections—but, as his heart was in the cause, he could not let his want of address deter him from labouring for the advancement of the society; he seemed to care little about refined sense, if he could only blunder out common enough to make himself understood. In large societies of men, where their abilities are upon a level, those with the most zeal, or assurance, are generally put into the foremost rank. Upon all public occasions, our friend, being of the zealous class, was mostly selected to preside over their assemblies, when visitors from other societies were to be admitted. Although our friend would have served as a sergeant, or a "full private," rather than a captain, on those grand days he was mostly pressed forward to the honour point. It was his custom, in the early part of his career, to draw together two or three of the best informed amongst them, and place those persons near to him, so that whenever his logic failed, he could apply to his friends to prompt him onward. I can well remember, that about twelve years ago, this individual could not deliver three connected sentences, without making a blunder. Often, when he had undertaken to detail the state of their funds, or the yearly progress of a Lodge, or the general advancement of the Order, he would, whenever opportunity served him, turn to his right or left hand friend, and ask them how he had discharged his duty? if he committed any mistakes that called for correction, or apology? and he usually concluded by asking, "What shall I do next?" Since his commencement, this individual has been constantly at his post, actively engaged in prosecuting the principles of the Order. He has, by determination and study, so far cultivated his strong natural ability, as to be enabled to address large audiences, fervently and fluently, for an hour or more, whenever his subject required so much time. I have frequently heard clergymen, and other well-educated persons, who have listened to his addresses, praise them for their philanthropy, plain sense, and eloquence. This individual is but one, out of hundreds, that are following in his wake, many of them exhibiting the same natural powers, and perfecting themselves by self-culture. Their advancement is, at once, a strong proof of the self-elevating principles of these Lodges. It is also a proof, that God hath not ordained an aristocracy of mind; but that he has given to all men an average share of intellect, which, if they improve not, they must content themselves to be dullards, and let others step before them in the march of improvement. They who desire to do good in their day and generation, must labour untiringly, laying hold of every opportunity to cultivate their mental faculties; then, assuredly, they shall shine amongst the galaxy of golden stars that gem the dark night of ignorance. Then they will rank amongst the benefactors of their race, and have the satisfaction of knowing, that by their endeavours their fellow men have been blessed. Such satisfaction will prove its own reward, and it will be more truly great than the gilded crown that circles the brow of the conqueror of kingdoms. To make mankind happy is alone true glory, and inward peace;— it will make life worth living for, and disarm death of his terrors;—an approving conscience will soften the close of life; and when you are ripe for the grave, instead of suffering the death-bed pangs of remorse for evil doing, guardian angels will fan you to sleep with their wings of love, and bear your spirit aloft, chaunting "Well done, thou good and faithful servant!"

The Lodge which has been established at Edwinstowe has been of essential service to the villagers, for it has raised the drooping spirit of the labourers, who saw no refuge for them in sickness or in adversity, save the Union Workhouse; by small savings they have purchased a certain dependence, and now they feel themselves rising into manliness. To the liberty-loving souls that here were waiting full of hope, that the spirit of their fathers would again stir the over-wrought and ill-fed ling-croppers to a sense of their own power,—to these men, the Lodge has proved to be a powerful lever, whereby they have roused the sleepy mass to new action. It is not less a proof that men, once made to feel the dignity of their position in society, will use every effort in their power to keep themselves, rather than to depend upon their neighbours for support. It is a gratifying fact, that out of the members of the Birkland and Bilhagh Lodge, numbering from one to two hundred, with only one or two exceptions, and of those, sickness was of unusually long duration,—with those exceptions, no members of that institution have troubled the parish for relief since their connection with the society. This ought to be a strong argument in favor of Lodges. Here it must have assisted materially to lessen the pressure upon the poor's rate, and superseded private benevolence. It has made the members comfortable in sickness, and kept their spirits buoyant and free, by the assurance that the money they received was their own. While the artisans and labourers have thus nobly struggled to help themselves, only one (Miles Webster, Esq.) out of the many gentlemen and farmers in this parish, has contributed towards the funds of this Society, although one of its first objects is to keep down the rates and spare the local funds. Surely, then, a people so circumstanced, will feel their own self-respect, and be true to the proverb which says, "God helps those who help themselves."

It is a notorious fact, that up to the establishment of the Lodge in Edwinstowe, and even for a long time after its foundation, crime was as rife in this village as it was in other parts of the county of Nottingham; for however sequestered the place, when a whole nation makes a trade of spilling human blood, and bids mortals get madly drunk with blood-gorged glory, the morals of such a nation must retrograde; therefore, it were vain to expect that "The Dukery" would prove an exception. Here, too, the debasing kill-time of cock-fighting* was a popular amusement—poaching was by no means a rare thing—drunkenness was a pastime, and education a thing not cared for; added to these, was the wild daring of the foresters, without the incentive which once made their firmness a noble thing. This daring, inherent in them, now the rather prompted them to evil deeds instead, as in the olden time, exercising its freedom in the maintenance of universal right, and the defence of injured weakness. This class, rejoicing in demoralizing practices, was here; and although a few of them found their way into this Lodge they were out of their element. Their nefarious practices soon caused their exclusion; they could not continue their depredations, and, consistently with the rules of the Imperial Order, remain members of this Lodge. Many of them were too confirmed in their vice to be easily made better men; but some were brought over to a serious consideration of their duty to themselves and their neighbours, and by admonition, suspension, and similar strictures, they were allowed to remain. Others again, warned by their example, abandoned their vicious habits, and for a season became probationists, proving their determination to give up their base practices, rather than be

---

* It is to be regretted, that this brutalizing sport is still carried on in the neighbourhood. When I was returning from Sheffield, in January, 1847, several persons from the village of Whitwell ascended the coach at Renishaw, where they had been fighting a main of cocks. Their recital of the sufferings of the poor birds, and their struggles with death, was told with a savage gusto, which seemed rather to be the language of demons, than of professing Christian men. These Whitwell men were the winners, and they gloried in their barbarity, again and again exclaiming with fierce oaths, that they had not left a penny in the place. Sport (?)

shut out from the communion of their fellows. Thus, step by step, the Odd Fellows' Lodge became a school of reform, and an asylum in distress. As the months and years rolled on, my friend, Mr. Trueman, and myself, were constantly labouring to introduce some plan of mutual instruction amongst them; we were patiently listened to, and our endeavours were applauded, but we found the mass difficult to awaken; however, we were nothing daunted by their apathy. I had felt, and still feel, the disadvantages of not having an early mind-cultivation, and therefore, I determined to do all in my power to lay the foundation of a better state of things in Edwinstowe, and my friend was ever ready to second my efforts.

In the year 1836, we agreed to try our hands upon establishing an Artisans' Library and Mutual Improvement Society. This I thought could easily be accomplished by a few friends joining together. I proposed that we should commence the work by taking shares of five shillings each. Two persons only, Messrs. Trueman and Widdison, were all I could get to join me in this scheme, and I was compelled to give it up. I then joined myself to the Mansfield Mechanics' Institution, and found it of great use to me; still I could not rest satisfied, without trying again and again to have a Library established at home. I was, therefore, constantly watching for a chance to carry out my views; but with the exceptions already named, every person I asked to become a member thought, that to pay down *five shillings to buy books* was the very height of extravagance, if not of madness!

Hope is a comfortable companion, and Perseverance a valuable friend; with their aid I made another trial. The most feasible plan that now offered itself, was to try what could be done by small payments. I accordingly suggested that we should try to get a few subscribers to pay one penny per week, and commence a reading-room with a few periodicals, regulating their number by the amount of our subscriptions. At the next Lodge-meeting, after the usual business was over, I made known to them my plan, urging, as well as I was able, the necessity of improving our members and their families by reading. After my short address, nineteen, out of the number present, gave me their names, accompanied with their pence. We proposed to meet on the following Monday evening, in the National School-room. At the appointed time we assembled, and in January, 1838, we began the Edwinstowe Artisans' Library; we resolved, that the subscriptions should be one penny per week; that both sexes should be admitted as members; and that all who should hereafter enter, should pay one shilling as an entrance fee. We commenced with Tait's, Loudon's Gardeners', and the Penny Magazines, Athenæum, Chambers's Journal, and the Visitor; these we thought would form the nucleus of a Library. We continued to add to our numbers, and in about six months we had fifty members. In addition to the periodicals, we added several of Scott's and Cooper's novels. We had also many presents of books; the most valuable one was several volumes of the Mechanics' Magazine, presented by O. Herring, Esq., of Southampton. The Earl of Scarbrough kindly patronised our little affair;

and for a time all was enthusiasm, and things went swimmingly on. By and by, however, the payments began to be neglected, and the numbers to fall off, and we were again reduced to twenty members; and where all was once animation, apathy had gained possession.

It now became a serious question amongst the few members that remained, how the society was to be revived and kept up in a healthy condition? As one means of resuscitation, I proposed that the villagers generally should be invited to our forthcoming anniversary, on new year's eve; that in addition to our usual tea party we should have a dance, which, to please some persons, we dignified by the title of a *Ball*; that our affairs should be laid before them, and if any surplus moneys were gained, they should be appropriated to the book fund. The evening arrived, and in addition to our few members, the villagers, men and maidens, mustered in goodly numbers. After tea, our report was made, and various addresses delivered upon the importance of education, and the necessity of keeping up the library, and our entreaties were kindly received. In due time the ball commenced; several of the members had grave doubts about the dance—it was a delicate business,—some folks thought there was harm in it—it was very wrong and irregular—and the polite conventions of the rueful were as plentiful as could be desired! However, all was well received, all were really joyful, and after our incidental expenses were discharged, we had a tolerable surplus to turn over to the society. To me, however, there was religion in that dance; and here I shrive myself by declaring, that I felt the spirit of beauty present with us, and saw it through the poetry of motion; albeit, I was too clumsy to take a fair lady's hand, and whirl her through the interminable circles and lines of beauty, still I could not, for one moment, believe that the Evil One had any business there. It may be that I am too earthy to perceive how things, seemingly harmonious in themselves, are made the instruments whereby mischief is effected; but I must confess I could not discover it at that meeting; every eye was bright, every eye bounded with delight, and each told his neighbour, that he never was more truly happy!

For a year or two afterwards, the library affairs rallied after the ball, but before the year's end, they generally relapsed again into the apathetic state; however, we trusted to a revival with the dance and tea party. Ridiculous enough, some persons thought, to lean upon such a staff; others thought it a good thing that we received the *money*, but contracted their lips, and looked down to the earth, then upwards again, and gravely shook their heads, exclaiming " That ever good books should be bought with wicked dancing money!" Perhaps it was wrong; but really a dance—that is, an innocent dance—cannot be so very, very wicked after all. I am sure they were happy at our innocent country dance. I am not singular in my opinion, that these meetings were joyous ones. We have been honoured with visitors on these occasions, both literary, sedate, and earnest progression men, who have met us here, from Sheffield, Nottingham, Mansfield, and other large towns, all of whom have joined in declaring that they never witnessed such a scene. Fun enjoyed himself without being faulty, where Intellectuality took Miss Harmony by the hand, and led her through the mazy hays, forgetting that they were the creatures of an outer world, where cant and discord reigned supreme. Our annual ball is now looked to as a means of spending one evening, at least, in the year, without the trammels of convention; and there, I believe, lies the secret of our pleasures; and if, as the townsmen assert, it cannot be done with them, it is a pity. Truly piteous are they, who might be happy, but dare not from fear of what Mrs. Grundy would say! We give ourselves up to innocent recreation, each heart being brim-full of desire to make the best use of one of God's good gifts. If, by any chance, a recreation, pure in itself, is contaminated by frivolity and vice, it is the fault of the abusers, and the evil should be placed to their account, and not set against the amusement. Rather drive the perpetrators out of the pale, than endeavour to exterminate a purely social enjoyment, and call it a vice—punish the vicious, but let life be, as its maker designed it should be, worth living for!

However people may disagree about the limits of amusements, I hope we shall be unanimous in our opinion, that whatever tends to the improvement of mankind, is of importance to society, and is a universal blessing. This library at Edwinstowe has been of service to the village. If but one person had been made thoughtful, it would have been reward enough for all the trouble it has bestowed upon the workers of it; but tens have been benefited by it, and have spoken of it with gratitude. After nine years of patient industry, we have piled up above 500 volumes of books. We cannot boast of an extensive collection; our progress has been slow, but not less sure; we have some really valuable books upon our humble shelves,—Knight's Pictorial Shakspere, Pictorial History of England, Penny Cyclopædia, and Goldsmith, Bloomfield, Scott, Byron, Cowper, and a few others—the prophets of all ages, from Homer to Elliott, bear them company. Amongst the periodicals, Tait's Magazine, the People's and Howitt's Journals, are the most read. Soul-refreshing as books are, we do not confine our Institute to them alone, but we have occasional lectures amongst ourselves—it may be that some of those discourses are not over logical; what then? they are still useful to us, and we cannot afford to be over nice; if one new thought be struck out during our evening's muster, or the value of an old one made clear to any one present, then our meeting has not been in vain. We have had, also, lectures occasionally, from a few of the master-spirits of this age—the foster-parents, who give intellectual milk to the up-grown babes, in this young day of thinking for yourself. These men, sympathising with our poor, but earnest endeavour to help ourselves, have come "without money, or price," to assist us, and we thank them for it,—we are poor, our thanks are poor, yet we do thank them. Amongst those who have aided us, we must make mention of the late lamented Francis Fisher, of Sheffield—Spencer T. Hall, the poet and mesmerist—George Searle Phillips, the poet and fellow labourer in the field of education—and Messrs. Franks, Johnston, &c. &c.

In addition to the use of our books and lectures, we have likewise weekly classes, five nights in each week, from October to March; those classes are open to all the villagers, whether members, members' children, or not; they are free to all, with this trifling exception, that they provide their own fire, candles, and books. At those classes are taught reading, writing, arithmetic, music, and drawing; we have also a class, which, for want of a better name, we call a Conversation Class—it is so called, because we discourse upon any subject that first presents itself to our minds, at the commencement of the evening—hence, the subjects are multifarious, as history, both ancient and modern, social progress, natural history, geology, geography, &c.—so it will readily be perceived, that we have not much trouble with the sermon, after the text is fixed upon. Every subject is illustrated with chalk upon a black board, also the names of persons and places written up, which the pupils are made to repeat aloud, and after an hour's conversation, they are questioned as to the subject which they have been discussing. I am proud to be ranked amongst the teachers in those classes, having the pleasure to superintend the drawing and conversation classes. The average attendance at those classes have been, male and female, as follows: to writing and arithmetic, thirty—music and drawing, ten—conversation, sixty. The attendance at the lectures has varied from twenty to two hundred. Such is a brief history of our village library; to me, its prosperity is a matter of deep interest. To those who cry aloud about the ignorance of the boors, but who never lift a finger, or give a sixpence, towards their instruction—to such persons, one hour at our classes would teach them a lesson which they never would forget—they would find out that ignorance was the result of neglect, and not the inborn curse of a caste. I have been well repaid for all the trouble the attendance upon them may have caused, by looking around upon the assembled class, to see the village youths, of both sexes, anxiously pursuing their studies—to see boys in their clean smock frocks, who, during the day, had been toiling at the plough or the flail, now sitting with a black board before them, and a piece of chalk, sketching flowers, animals, or geometrical figures; or again, to hear them in the conversation class, discoursing about Cheops, Raphael, or of who invented and perfected our steam engines, and spread our commerce over every clime; or again, telling over the burden of a song first sung by our Shakspeare, Burns, Byron, Elliott, &c. Who, then, shall say that our time has been mis-spent? May we not hope that, at least, one twinkling ray of information has burst upon the minds of these rustic scholars? It will be remembered as the years of life roll on, and which, gathering lustre from reflection, may light its possessor to knowledge and virtue. They, perhaps, lacking these means, might have studied in the beer-house, the cock-pit, or the prize-ring, and eventually have qualified themselves for a prison, or the hulks. Ignorance is a living death!

In the summer of 1840, a severe affliction interrupted my studies, and for a time damped my hope of being useful to my fellows. A violent attack of amaurosis suddenly deprived me of the use of my eyesight for several months. In my distress I consulted several physicians of accredited ability—they all, with one exception (the late Dr. Fielden, of Hull), pronounced my case a hopeless one. This reverse was a serious blow to my growing prosperity; with seven children around me, one an infant, and all mainly dependent upon me for support, the visitation was to me a matter of serious concern; the pangs I experienced when unable longer to distinguish them, except by their voices, were too acute now to describe. Painful as my situation really was, I dared not despair; and although I had resigned myself to outer darkness, and was, in mind, cogitating upon my future lot in life, even in this extreme, hope never forsook me—and while believing I knew the worst, I calmly determined to wait with patience God's pleasure.

I cannot forget the debt of gratitude I owe, for the skill and attention of the surgeon who attended me— J. W. Lilley, Esq., of Ollerton, Nottinghamshire— whose judgment and treatment of so desperate a case met with the cordial approval and admiration of the various professional gentlemen I consulted in my affliction; for not only professionally, but by consolation and sympathy, was I benefited by that gentleman,—his advice and services are most thankfully remembered. To those who can imagine my situation at that time, I leave the pleasure of feeling the joy I felt, when, after a few weeks of gradual recovery, I was enabled to make out the letters that compose the heading to the *Nottingham Review* newspaper. I had no words, but tears of gladness, wherewith to express my feelings on that occasion. From that time up to the present hour, my restoration has been slowly going onward,—a partial dimness still obscures my right eye; but for all the useful purposes of life, I have to bless God for his merciful care and protection.

I have already said, and I trust I have proved, that Odd Fellowship, notwithstanding the many revilings with which it has been assailed, has done some good; for here, in our village, it may be said, that out of the Lodge grew the "Artisans' Library, and Mutual Instruction Society." If the co-operative spirit, which binds up and fraternizes the stray children of toil, had not already begun to unite the scattered fragments of humanity within "our Lodge," I should have experienced the same degree of disappointment, when I recommended its formation, that I experienced at the onset, and during my canvass for the five-shilling subscribers. Hence, then, arises the necessity, that every individual should try to improve his neighbour, so that while they may be merely the teachers of a few rustics, yet their sons, and their sons' sons, may, by their teachings, become the instructers of a county, and through them be raised up a generation of teachers to improve a kingdom, and so " shall righteousness spread over the earth." It was this spirit of enlightenment that made the Lodge useful, and which modelled its tempered clay into the more beautiful vessel, the Library— united the advantages of both, and brought about those intellectual meetings called "The Sherwood Gatherings."

A desire had long possessed me, that it was worth an effort to try to make our "village feast" more spiritualizing—at least, that it would be well to make one day out of the week a day for intellectual training, instead of the whole week being a beef and pudding business; for here, as with the rest of the rural population of England, the old-fashioned revelries of feasts, and wakes, were highly esteemed. It is true, that they were no longer the jollities that existed

"Ere England's grief began."

We were no longer enjoying the days in which true Saxon blood made the Foresters' hearts beat merrily. O no! those days were changed for the all-work and all-taxes' days, when such horse-work, and empty pockets for half a bread loaf, had made the sons of Johnny Bull very melancholy boys indeed. Our ancient "feast week" had dwindled into a mere public house visiting, with only a few exceptions. In the autumn of 1841, a few of our villagers determined on attempting to restore the faded jollifyings which characterized the care-despising foresters, who made this village feast in days of yore, a thing to be remembered. We began our task in a systematic way, by appointing a committee of fun, and I had the especial happiness to be allowed to sit at their board of mirth. We met in the little twelve-feet square parlour of the Jug and Glass Inn, and resolved to cater for the amusement of all who chose to visit Edwinstowe, from the 1st to the 6th of November inclusive (1841). As the sinews of mirth for the million may be furnished by the same means as the sinews of death for the million, we levied a mirthful tribute upon the inhabitants, with this trifling difference to the war tribute, that we gave the people the opportunity of saying "No, thank you," if they did not approve of the campaign! It was at one of those meetings, that I proposed we should raise the enjoyment of our annual feasts, by having an intellectual gathering on some one evening in that week. A kindred spirit animated the whole committee, and we resolved to have a gathering in honour of the worthies that had added to the renown of Sherwood Forest. There was but one question— how could we carry it out? This, at first, appeared to startle us, but we were nothing daunted—we had faith in the old adage, "Where there is a will, there is always a way," and we set to work accordingly. Our bill of fare was a strange commingling: the business of each day was set out upon a bill as conspicuously as the tricks are upon Mons. Jacobi's large posters. But a motley bill assuredly it was: ass-races, and concerts—climbing a pole for a hat, and a ramble in Birkland—jumping in sacks, and the "Sherwood Feast"—"motleys the only wear." Such a bill, that it broke the repose of our friend, Spencer T. Hall, who, it will be seen, was the chief guest at that feast; it affrighted him worse than a galvanic shock would have done. However, as I drew up the bill, all else belonging to our council of mirth was innocent,—I alone was to blame—my bump of *order* was never remarkable—I know not why, but I am often guilty of such mistakes. I remember, when a boy, my mother used to make me drink a pint-basin full of a strong solution of Epsom salts, every Sunday morning, during the spring season of the year; wry faces availed me nothing—I was forced to gulp down the saline contents; but after the nauseous draught was swallowed, I was favoured with a large slice of bread and honey as a reward. Those nasty draughts were strongly indicative of my future life, which has been a queer compound of bitter sweets. But the bill did alarm our friend, for on the 29th October, four days before our great gathering, he writes,—" Why did you link the literary feast with the donkey-races in that great bill? It was bad policy. If you have any posted in the village, or neighbourhood, pray obliterate the bottom part, before any literary strangers arrive,—it looks like a burlesque on the thing altogether."

It might look so, but we, poor simpletons in Sherwood, saw not the danger; we were alike panting for fun and food; and assuredly, on that occasion we got both!

For a long time previously, Mr. Hall and I had been brothers; he had now endeared himself to the locality by the publication of his interesting work, "The Forester's Offering:" his visits to our village had been frequent, and we felt that in spirit he was our brother forester. One day, in the summer of 1841, Mr. Hall, Mr. Trueman, and myself, were drawing towards the village, after a long ramble through Birkland and Bilhagh; Mr. Hall appeared very sad, as if overpowered with the poetry of the place—an inclination to leave the forest appeared to struggle with a desire to stay a little longer, but it only found utterance in deep and repeated sighs. In this singular mood, we slowly bent our steps to the border, each thinking of more than he knew how to tell. Mr. H. then expressed a desire to have a walking stick cut from old Sherwood; this wish Mr. T. and myself promised to see faithfully executed; the present was not time for stick-cutting, and so slowly and moodily we strolled along, wishing that the word *adieu* was not understood by brothers.

After our Sherwood feast was arranged, we decided upon making it a favourable opportunity of carrying out our promise of presenting a walking stick to Mr. Hall; certainly with more *éclat* than we thought of, when we made our promise to do so in the woodland glade; but thus does trifling sometimes grow into things of importance. We now resolved to invite him, with other literary and artistic friends, to our meeting. All things went on to our desire, and on the 3rd of November, 1841, we held our first "Gathering of Foresters." The following extracts from the newspapers will best show how our village festival was estimated by the country generally. To give a full report of the proceedings as they appeared in the newspapers on that occasion, would occupy more space than can be afforded in the pages of my humble narrative, and might also trespass too much upon the indulgence of my friends. The extracts and speeches now given, furnish an average sample of the tone and objects of our meeting :—

"GREAT GATHERING IN HONOUR OF THE SHERWOOD FOREST WORTHIES.

"We have not space at our disposal to give vent to the pleasing reflections excited by a perusal of the 'Gathering at Edwinstowe,' an event so unprecedented and interesting in its character as to form an era in the local history of this delightfully situated village—and we might add, in the history of the rural population of England. A few years ago, and Edwinstowe and its neighbourhood 'differed in no wise' from the generality of agricultural districts, and many daring and reckless characters pestered the locality: now it boasts an excellent Library, a taste for reading is displayed, and the moral condition of the population, if we may be allowed the expression, has been 'regenerated.' This pleasing and happy change is, in a great measure, attributable to the unwearied zeal and well-directed energies of that intelligent, independent, and excellent artisan, Mr. C. Thomson, with whom the Mechanics' Institution of this sequestered village of Sherwood Forest had its origin."—*Nottingham Mercury, Nov.* 12, 1841.

The *Sheffield Iris* of Nov. 9th, 1841, thus prefaces their report of our feast:—" This interesting festival, as had been previously announced, was celebrated in the Birkland and Bilhagh Lodge Room, Edwinstowe, on Wednesday last; and will hereafter be recorded in the annals of the intellectual progress of the rural population of England, as one of the most remarkable demonstrations of the kind that ever occurred in that, or perhaps in any other neighbourhood. The gathering of one hundred farmers, artisans, and labourers, from every part of Sherwood Forest, to that lovely rural village which has from time immemorial been considered its very heart; where our early Saxon kings occasionally held their court, in times when even kings were unable to read and write; where our Norman kings afterwards resorted and dwelt in all the rude splendour of the feudal ages; where Robin Hood, at the head of his brave band of Foresters, long maintained a kind of negative royal authority; and where, at this late day, remain more striking evidences of the character of those very times than any other part of England—or perhaps all England together besides can supply; we repeat, the gathering of one hundred farmers, artisans, woodmen, and agricultural labourers, purely for literary and intellectual objects—qualifies us, as journalists, in attributing to the occasion a high degree of curiosity and importance.

" The announcement stated that the principal object of the feast was to honour those worthies who, by the pen, pencil, or otherwise, had contributed to the renown of that beautiful and beloved locality; and the following very condensed summary of the proceedings will evince how far the object was carried out.

"In the early part of the day, a grey mist hung over the country, and besides obscuring its beauties, made the air somewhat chill and melancholy; but about noon all this was cleared away as if by magic: the sun stole out with softened and cheerful splendour, and laved the autumnal woods and fields—now so sublime and lovely in their many-hued array—in a subdued and harmonious glory we have seldom seen equalled, and soon were seen, one after another, dropping into the village, homely, but well dressed and intelligent-looking little knots of visitors from the neighbouring hamlets; while, as evening approached, came others, who seemed as if they had walked various but considerable distances, or anon a horse, a gig, or light cart would arrive, and be relieved of its burden, in honour of the occasion; almost every town and village of Nottinghamshire, north of Trent, furnishing its representative—to which were added several highly respectable worthies from our own good town of Sheffield, and other remote places.

"Mr. Spencer T. Hall was presented with a richly carved oak walking-stick, as a tribute of respect to his literary worth. This is one of the most singular and striking instances of the vast improvement in the tone of public opinion which is going on around us. Literary meetings and associations are certainly no rarity in our town. In fact, we are on that very account too apt to deem the entire rural population of our country as sunk in a state of gross ignorance, Our townsmen will, therefore, we are sure, be glad to see that knowledge is visiting even the recesses of the lonely village, and elevating the moral taste and feelings of what is usually, and perhaps justly, deemed the most illiterate portion of our countrymen. It was delightful to witness the deep and intelligent interest which the farmers and labourers evidently took in the addresses of the different speakers. The chair was filled with remarkable ability by an inhabitant of the village, and his speeches were all characterised by a pure and lofty tone of thought, displaying no ordinary range of reading, and breathing an enlightened and philanthropic zeal in the great cause of human improvement.

"It had been well considered that as nature has provided the feminine as well as the masculine part of the human creation with minds and hearts, and the occasion being one of a purely intellectual character, there could be no objection to the admission of ladies; and accordingly, after dinner, a considerable party attended, and appeared to take a deep interest in what passed.

"A substantial dinner having been dispatched, about eight o'clock, that truly honourable specimen of a British artisan, Mr. C. Thomson, painter, of Edwinstowe, took the chair, with Francis Fisher, Esq., of Sheffield, Mr. James Walker, and Mr. Charles Plumbe, author of 'Mornings in June,' the 'Hymn to Sunset,' and other poems, on his right, and Spencer Hall, 'the Sherwood Forester,' Messrs. Cartwright, and James Bridgeford on his left; and Messrs. Allen, Naylor, Wetton, and Ferrands, the celebrated Sherwood Minstrels, being present, and occasionally enlivening the proceedings with their effective glees.

"'The Queen,' 'Prince Albert,' 'The Princess Royal and the rest of the Royal Family,' and other loyal toasts having been duly honoured, the CHAIRMAN proposed 'The health of the Earl of Scarbrough, Lord Lieutenant of the County,' in a very appropriate speech, which was followed with three times three cheers, and the song of 'The fine old English gentleman.'

The CHAIRMAN, in an address expressive of their object in holding that meeting, concluded by a toast—'The Earl Manvers and the Duke of Portland, the noble conservators of Old Birkland and Bilhagh.'—(Three times three.)

"Glee—'Foresters sound the cheerful horn.'

"FRANCIS FISHER, Esq., was then called upon to propose 'Honour to the Memory of the Good and Mighty of Ancient Days, whose virtues yet live, though their names be forgotten.'— What an overwhelming sentiment is this, embracing the Mighty and the Good (for the good alone are mighty) of all generations! Honour to them all, and may their memories live in our 'heart of hearts.' (Cheers.) To all who in every age have striven and written, or fought for the good man, we render the tribute of our heartfelt admiration and grateful love.—(Cheers.)—Honour to the poets, philosophers, historians, and moralists of Greece and Rome, whose wisdom still enlightens us, and speaks from the tomb of ages in their deathless works!—(Cheers.)—Honour to the shades of those who have fought and bled in the sacred cause of freedom, civil or religious. Honour to all the lowly as well as the noble, who have done and dared what conscience enjoined! They have all laboured for us, and we inherit the fruits of their labours.—(Cheers.)— The modern improvements in art and science of which we are justly proud, are owing to the exertions of those who in past ages have promoted the expansion of the human mind. Ever blessed be the memories of those whose studious labours have benefited and will for ever improve mankind.—(Cheers.)—It is they who have sown the seed of those institutions for the advancement of knowledge which abound in our land. The rich legacy of wisdom inherited from the past thus enriches the present age, and gives hope of a still brighter future.—(Cheers.)—Our cheap books, Mechanics' Institutes, and public lectures, we owe to the 'Mighty and the Good of the days that are past, and whose virtues yet live, though their names be forgotten.'—(Cheers.)—Their thoughts and actions shall never die; for every noble sentiment, every truly heroic deed, each act of goodness is immortal, and its influence endureth for ever.—(Cheers.)—Other men, I repeat, have laboured, and we are entered into their labours. The *future*, then, will be entitled to some memento of *our* exertions; and I rejoice, that you, the artisans and peasants of Edwinstowe, are alive to the importance of imparting sound instruction to the youthful mind. That a Mechanics' Institute should exist and flourish in this sequestered village, is indeed a hopeful sign of the times, and highly creditable to its founders and supporters. May it long live in beauty and strength—beautiful to 'the mind's eye' as the birches of your own Birkland—strong as the storm-defying and venerable oaks, the growth of centuries, that adorn your Bilhagh! —(Loud cheers.)—Your institution may be small in its means of usefulness compared with other and larger ones, but you are adding *one* to the number of institutions whose influence and whose sure tendency for good are alike incalculable. You are labouring for ages; and *the cause alone* consecrates your service, and blesses your labour of love.—(Cheers.)—You are doing your duty; and your descendants in some future age will class *your* memories among those of the 'mighty and the good.' You are aiding to better the tone of public opinion, the improved state of which is one of the most pleasing characteristics of the present age. Outward distinctions have, to a great extent, ceased to usurp that exclusive regard which they formerly obtained. In past ages, the warrior and the oppressor were they who claimed and enjoyed the homage of man; but who are *now* becoming more and more regarded? Are they not the great teachers of wisdom, and the active benefactors of man? Who sway the destinies of nations? Statesmen alone—men of cunning and intrigue—or they of the cassock and cowl? God be thanked, no! The *many* are becoming thinking men instead of the soulless things they were of old; and is not this a heart-warming truth? Is it not a theme for unspeakable rejoicing, that knowledge is pouring its beams into the abode of the artisan and the cottage of the peasant?—(Cheers.)— Were men designed by God to be nothing better than mere 'hewers of wood and drawers of water?' Ignorance had been tried for ages, and found wanting—devoid of any power to bless, humanize, and exalt. Oppression and misrule, turbulence and crime, fanaticism and folly, have been its bitter fruits. War, with all its horrors and miseries, hath resulted from the ignorance of nations:—

> 'But war's a game which, were their subjects wise,
>   Kings would not play at.'

We have seen, yea ages have groaned under, the evils which a wrong public opinion, or at times an incapacity in a people to form any opinion at all, hath respectively engendered. What a melancholy truth is embodied in the noble poet's definition of opinion:—

> 'An omnipotence whose veil
> Mantles the earth with darkness, until right
> And wrong are accidents, and men grow pale
>   Lest their own judgments should become too bright,
> And their free thoughts be crimes, and earth have too much light.'

Now, if the moral judgment of man hath been so oft perverted by leaning to the seductive influence of a wrong public opinion, is it not a thing of unspeakable desire that this same public opinion should be a sound one, based on knowledge, enlightened by experience, characterised by forethought? Here then is a work to accomplish, a field in which we all may labour, a victory to be won more glorious than the plains of Marathon witnessed or the sword of Washington achieved.—(Loud and hearty cheers.)—If so much vice and misery have flowed from the actions of men being regulated by a bad standard, their own better judgments being warped by the multitudinous ignorance around, what may we not justly expect from a different condition of the social world, when knowledge shall become more general than ever ignorance was? Then may the general sentiment be a steady light to guide, instead of a meteor to lead astray.—(Cheers.)—Now this same general sentiment is but the conflux of individual thought—even as drops form the ocean, and atoms the material universe. It may not, perchance, be our gift directly to influence large bodies of men, nor our habit of ability even to address such; but we may exercise a less ostentatious yet beneficial sway over the minds and hearts of our neighbours, friends, and acquaintance in the hours of social converse. We may support, in some way or other, institutions adapted to promote intellectual growth and moral enlightenment. None are so powerless, but they may do something to aid the great cause of human redemption, from the slavery of soul-debasing, heart-withering, ignorance and guilt.—(Hear, hear.)—We may not be able to cast into the treasury out of our abundance, but did not Christ, the great regenerator of man, bless and sanctify with deathless record even the poor widow's mite?—(Loud cheers.)— Let us ever bear in mind what posterity is entitled to receive from us; and if we honestly do all we can, then may a member of some generation yet unborn, in celebrating, as we do now, the triumphs of mind, enrol our memories in the glorious list of 'the mighty and the good of the ages that are gone, whose virtues yet live, though their names be forgotten.'—[Mr Fisher's speech awakened throughout its delivery the warmest and noblest sensations in the meeting, and on taking his seat he was loudly applauded.]

"The CHAIRMAN then proposed, in eloquent and appropriate terms, 'The eternal renown of Robin Hood, and all other men whose patriotic deeds have consecrated Sherwood Forest to Fame.'

"The CHAIRMAN complimented those gentlemen whose regard for the locality and esteem for the objects of the gathering, had induced them to attend from remote places, and take a part in the proceedings, and gave 'Mr. Ben Hawkridge, of the Archdeaconry Office, Nottingham.'—(Cheers.)

"Mr. HAWKRIDGE was heartily cheered on rising to propose 'The Memory of Ben Jonson, Robert Dodsley, Lord Byron, Pemberton the Wanderer, and other departed writers, in whose works the woods of Sherwood wave, its plains expand and bloom, and its heroes live in immortal youth.'

"Glee—'Green thorn of the hill of ghosts.'

"Mr. SPENCER T. HALL.—Can it, then, for a moment, be supposed that the name and genius of Robert Millhouse are liable to be forgotten? Never, brother foresters! while we have heads to know and hearts to feel—never while we have a single oak left to wave, a bush to blossom, or a lark to spring from the fresh green turf, and pour its thrilling music from heaven into our bosoms.—(Cheers.)—I would that my good friend Hawkridge, whose enthusiasm in behalf of neglected genius does him honour—(Cheers)—I would he had been able to meet us an hour earlier, when the preliminaries were arranged, and then I could have told him with mingled emotions of veneration, regret, and pride, that I had myself been already appointed to propose the immortal memory of Robert Millhouse—not as one of any constellation whatever, but shining out, singly and gloriously, a star of his own bright magnitude.—(Loud cheers.)—To the very first poem I ever wrote, he kindly suggested a correction; and when on his death-bed, a few hours before his last mortal struggle, as I took my leave of him, he grasped my hand, and said, 'Farewell Spencer, farewell! go forth into the world, my lad, and may God and a dying poet's blessing go with you!'—(Hear, hear.)—Pardon my emotion, friends and brethren, for how think ye can I call these circumstances to memory without deep affection? or how can I allude, without poignant regret to the fact, that this same sweet bard, the first who ever strung with adequate power the lyre of Sherwood, has slept these three years beneath its turf, without even a little stone inscribed 'R. M.' to mark his grave?—(Hear, hear.)—But with God's help and your's, it shall be so no longer!—(Cheers.)—Robert Millhouse was a Nottingham stocking-weaver, and all the scholastic tuition he ever received was at a Sunday school, in days when artisans' libraries and mechanics' institutes were altogether undreamt of; yet, improving the scanty dole of knowledge which was dealt to him there, he qualified himself to write first a volume on the rural scenes of Nottingham Park; then another, entitled 'Blossoms;' next, the 'Song of the Patriot,' a production worthy of its title; a year afterwards, 'Sherwood Forest,' a beautiful Spenserian poem, in three cantos, descriptive and historical of our native scenes; and last of all, 'The Destinies of Man,' a work, the influence of which will be felt until the destiny of man it sings is completed! Genius has sometimes many tribulations to endure, and Millhouse had his share; and though, when I was once talking to a man of high literary reputation on this subject, he said it would be better to buy bread for the living than stones for the dead; I trust it will not be in the power of another generation to say, that the people of this day erected costly monuments to the wholesale butchers and robbers of humanity, while the peasantry of Sherwood Forest let the dead grass sigh over their sleeping bard, for want of a simple slab to guard his grave from the blast! (Cheers.)—A penny subscription from the artisans and peasantry, and the permission of the Nottingham Cemetery Company, is all that will be required to carry our object into execution; and should we, after the time he has lain without a monument, be refused the gratification of performing this duty to the memory of a bard who sprang from our own condition in society, and charmed by the music of his mind the titled and the wealthy, for a less pittance yearly than many a foreign sensualist in our metropolis gains nightly, we can still console ourselves by purchasing a yard or two of land in the Forest, and erecting a little memento of our reverence for him here.—(Loud cheers.)—As one of his personal friends—one of his sincerest, too—when this object is carried out, I would beg of you one privilege—the melancholy but affectionate one of writing his epitaph.—(Cheers.)—That epitaph must be:—

> When Trent shall flow no more, and blossoms fail
> On Sherwood's plains to scent the springtide gale;
> When the lark's lay shall lack its thrilling charm,
> And song forget the Briton's soul to warm;
> When love o'er youthful hearts hath lost all sway,
> Thy fame, O Bard! shall pass—but not till then—away!

(Loud cheers.)—Brethren, visitors, and friends, upstanding and in reverent silence we will pledge 'The immortal memory of Robert Millhouse, author of the poem of Sherwood Forest.'

"Glee—'Whose form rises.'

"The CHAIRMAN then rose and said,—Ladies and gentlemen, having paid a just tribute of respect to the departed heroes and literary worthies of Sherwood Forest, the next and most important part of my duty this evening is to present a token of our respect to one whom we consider the chief of Sherwood's living poets, and whose very prose, as he sweetly and graphically describes the favourite haunts of his youth, flushes too into poetry, and charms every reader by its simplicity, its beauty, and truth to nature. We are not going to present him with any costly plate, or splendid candelabra, or valuable purse; we have neither the ability nor the will to do that.—(Hear, hear.)—Our object is to present him with something he will value more highly—a token that shall mark the locality, and remain a substantial monument of the respect, approbation, and kind feeling of those who offer, and a genuine emblem of the heart of him who receives it—a true old English heart of oak!—(Loud cheers.)—Our dear friend and brother forester well knows, that if we have no 'garter, star, and a' that,' to invest him with, we have still a true appreciation of his merits, which must be far more delightful to him. And as in days of old, a laurel wreath was significant of the highest honour a poet could obtain; so let something as simple be equally estimated with us, whilst we from this time pledge Spencer Hall as the laureate of Sherwood Forest. The memorial of this occasion is the beatifully carved oak walking stick I hold in my hand.—(Cheers.)—It is from the heart of a very ancient oak in the neighbourhood, for any thing we can tell seven or eight centuries old.—(Cheers.)—It is made in the lower part to look knotted and gnarled, like the tree it was taken from; and on its upper part are carved the venerated emblems, the lyre and laurel. It is done, I am proud to say, by a self-taught artisan of our village, Mr. Richard Tudsbury, junior, who never lived away from this place. —(Cheers.)—The crest and shield have been most beautifully engraved in Sheffield, by Messrs. Chapman and Lowe, and could not have been more neat or appropriate—the crest bearing an old oak and birch proper, and a deer statant, surmounted by a motto of 'Home, dear home!'—(Cheers.)—The shield which crowns the head of the stick is inscribed 'To SPENCER T. HALL, author of the Forester's Offering and other works, this Walking Stick, cut from one of the Oaks of Birkland, is presented by the Artisans and Peasantry of Sherwood Forest, as a pledge of their cordial esteem, and of their admiration of his efforts to extend and perpetuate the renown of their beautiful and beloved Locality. Edwinstowe, Nov. 3, 1841.'—(Cheers.)—The stick, as you perceive, is not less stout than appropriate, and as we hope that Mr. Hall, for many, many years to come, will attend this anniversary, it will serve him both for support and defence as he walks through its parent woods.—(Cheers.)—Mr. Hall, I now present you with this walking stick, in the name of the artisans and peasantry of Sherwood Forest; accept it as a token of our friendship for your person and respect for your genius, and may it bear you on through a long and happy life to a lasting and meritorious reputation.—(Loud Cheers.)

"Glee—'Here in cool grot.'

"Mr. S. T. HALL returned thanks for the favourable notice, and in a speech of considerable length, detailed the whole history of his life, up to the present meeting. The address was listened to with intense interest, and was warmly applauded.

"A great number of other toasts of absent individuals were afterwards given and enthusiastically honoured, amongst which were the names of William, Mary, Richard, and Godfrey Howitt; Thomas Miller, John Bridgeford, Samuel Plumbe, Sidney Giles, Ephraim Brown, E. G. Pickering, &c., together with the memory of Miss Joanna Williams, authoress of a poem on Sherwood Forest; accompanied with the glees of 'Strike the Lyre,' 'Sleep gentle Lady,' and others equally appropriate.

"The CHAIRMAN then said, it became his pleasing duty to propose the health of one of the visitors, whose presence they all hailed with peculiar satisfaction; because he was sure that no gentleman could be more deserving of their best wishes and their gratitude, when the amount of good he did in the neighbourhood was considered.—(Cheers.)—After some further remarks bearing out this sentiment, he proposed 'The health of Mr. Cartwright, and thanks to him for the interest he ever evinces in the social and intellectual progress of the neighbourhood.'—(3 times 3.)

"Mr. CARTWRIGHT acknowledged the compliment in a brief, eloquent, and emphatic manner.

"Mr. S. T. HALL observed, that he had now a toast to propose which they would all gladly respond to as with one heart: it was that of their worthy, intelligent, and respectable Chairman.—(Cheers.)

"The CHAIRMAN returned thanks.

"The CHAIRMAN, in a fervent and pathetic speech, which met with a sincere response from every heart and every eye, proposed the silent memory of Mr. Reuben Trueman, one of the old inhabitants of the village, whose goodness of heart, general intelligence, and amiable social qualities, had endeared him to them all as their father and friend. [The solemn manner in which this toast was honoured, was truly affecting.]

"The succeeding toast was one which the CHAIRMAN said merited their most cordial participation. If there were men with them of whom they had reason to be proud, Mr. Charles Plumbe, postmaster of Sutton-in-Ashfield, was one of the most distinguished. —(Cheers.)—Of his refined intelligence they had many proofs; of his poetical ability, both Tait's and the Metropolitan Magazines recorded many exquisite examples; and as to his hearty good fellowship, they had only to observe the earnestness and cordiality with which he enjoyed their proceedings that night, to be convinced that no one in that quality could surpass him. He would, therefore, propose 'Health, long life, and happiness, to Mr. Plumbe, and may his success as a printer equal his merits as a writer.'—(Loud cheers.)

"Mr. PLUMBE returned thanks in a brief and witty speech.

"The CHAIRMAN next proposed 'The healths of Mr. Fisher, and Mr. Walker, of Sheffield, and all other visitors from remote places,' (to which Mr. Fisher replied;) also 'The healths of T. Desvignes, Esq. of London, M. Furniss, Esq. of Mansfield, W. P. Hadfield, Esq. of Newark, Mr. John Trueman, of Edwinstowe, and all scientific men who have endeavoured to open to the world the entomological wonders of Birkland.'—'Mrs. Spencer Hall, and the Ladies,' for which Mr. Hall returned thanks. Many other excellent toasts were given and honoured.—The sum of £2. 1s. 2d. was collected at the table towards a monument for Robert Millhouse, and a committee appointed to forward that object; and after singing the National Anthem, the company retired in evident delight with the whole proceedings."

The educational importance of our meeting was warmly applauded by the press, and we were urged to follow on the work we had so auspiciously commenced. The following, amongst other poems, approving of our exertions, is from the talented and philanthropic Miss E. Sheridan Carey:—

"LINES WRITTEN UPON READING IN THE 'SHEFFIELD IRIS,' OF NOV. 9, 1841. THE REPORT OF 'THE GREAT GATHERING' OF NOV. 3, 'IN HONOUR OF THE SHERWOOD FOREST WORTHIES:'

"*Inscribed to Spencer T. Hall, 'The Laureate of Sherwood Forest;' to his Brother Bards and Supporters; and to 'The one hundred Farmers, Artisans, Woodmen, and Agricultural Labourers,' who, with their Wives and Daughters, assisted on the occasion; by the Authoress,*

ELIZABETH SHERIDAN CAREY.

"No! not the pomp of feudal pageantry,
  Grac'd with the flow'r of Norman chivalry,
  When England's monarchs, many an age ago,
  Held court and revel in fair EDWINSTOWE;—
Not the state banquet serv'd in regal halls
Whose vanish'd splendours, ancient tome recalls;
Where cups of gold, with sparkling stones embost,
High in the air by loyal hands were tost,
As knight and noble pledg'd with joy, 'THE KING!'
And made the roof with shouts of transport ring;—
Not the proud masque where ladies' eyes shone bright
As orient gems, or stars in darkest night;
Where music floated on the perfum'd air,
And minstrels sang sweet homage to the fair;—
Not ev'n the 'gath'ring' in the blithe greenwood,
Of him—that prince of archers—ROBIN HOOD
And his brave knot of Sherwood-men
(Whose peers, those glades shall never greet again!)
When straight prepar'd with bugle, brand, and bow,
Through sylvan shades to chase the bounding roe;
Or, crown'd the sport, beneath the trysting tree
To feast and dance with all the hunter's glee,
Review the day, the daring feats detail,
Nor sink to rest till Cynthia's brow grew pale:—
Not these were more inspiring sights to see
Than EDWINSTOWE, of late beheld in thee!

"Good sooth! it was a cheering thing to trace
　Those list'ning groups of England's hardy race,
　With frames of iron, and with nerves of steel,
　Cool heads to think, and manly hearts to feel!
　Staunch tillers of the much-lov'd soil which ne'er,
　In niggard vein, defeats the rustic's care,
　But, with rich harvests of pure waving gold,
　Repays the toil that feeds the gen'rous mould!
　The bold descendants of the stalwart band
　Whose deeds are chronicled throughout the land;
　Who ev'ry oak in verdant BILHAGH knew,
　And BIRKLAND's silver birches joy'd to view;
　Hail'd 'MERRIE SHERWOOD' in all hues array'd;
　Now bath'd in sunshine, and now wrapp'd in shade;
　Now gaily prankt in Summer's brightest green,
　Now, leaf-disgarnish'd, tow'ring o'er the scene;
　Watch'd him his fringe of brilliant ferns renew,
　And from his brackens dashed the pearly dew.

"'Twas well those peaceful artisans to greet,
　Studious and mild as men whose thoughts were meet
　To commune with the Good, the Great, the Wise,
　And taste the charms that noblest natures prize.
　Well, to descry the wives and daughters there,
　With ardent wise, the mental treat to share:
　Well done, in those of sentiment refin'd
　To ope the stores of Learning to mankind;
　Well, in THE PRESS, with grateful zeal, to pay
　Spontaneous tribute to the honour'd day,
　And waft the glorious sign from Pole to Pole,
　Far as the breeze can blow or billow roll:
　And well, ye few! to quit the narrow room,
　And leave awhile the shuttle and the loom,—
　The carver's bench, the spade, the axe, the plough;
　The hearth, the field, and ev'n the forest-bough
　To homage genius, and to show that worth
　Is not, like rank, the accident of birth;
　To Knowledge seek beneath the Gospel's light;
　To worship God; and venerate the right:—
　For ends like these 'tis well to congregate,
　True to yourselves, and rev'rent to the State.

"For daily bread, to delve—to sow—to reap;
　To spin for raiment, and the right to sleep
　Beneath the thatch which industry sustains,—
　A duty this, that well rewards your pains:
　But HE who fashion'd man from out the dust,
　A *soul* committed to HIS creature's trust:
　To him, than brutes, a loftier sphere assign'd,
　And stamp'd him with the majesty of *mind!*
　Oh, then, undimm'd preserve the lucid ray,
　Nor let your God-like privilege decay!
　How blest, with books to spend the leisure hour,
　And melt or glow beneath the Muse's pow'r;

> How blest, with Science to discourse apart,
> And soften Nature with the spells of Art:
> Or, while fit toils the willing hand engage,
> In thought, to scan the pure instructive page:
> Thus shall the heart nor seek nor sigh to roam,
> And new-born pleasures glad the smiling 'HOME!'
>
> "For THEE, lov'd BARD, whose wild harmonious song,
> Of SHERWOOD's bow'rs shall mem'ry sweet prolong
> When their now royal oaks shall bloom no more,
> Nor show'r or beam, their million buds restore—
> Proud was that 'gath'ring' in blithe EDWINSTOWE,
> And dear the meed, as victor's wreath, I trow,—
> Nay, dearer far than vase of dazzling ore,
> Or laurels drench'd, alas! with human gore:
> And sweet—as fairy warblings sweet—to hear,
> The cordial strains that fill'd the Parent's ear;
> Yea, sweeter still than Senate's loud acclaim,
> Those village greetings of thy youthful fame!
> Brief are the triumphs which on faction wait,
> And false, too oft, the plaudits of the Great;
> While the fierce sword consumes as flaming fire;
> But 'raptured nations bless the soothing lyre!
>
> "What though no stone marks out the Poet's grave!
> On the bright sward shall Spring's first blossoms wave:
> There shall the Summer choicest flow'rs unfold,
> And there, the Autumn lavish burnish'd gold;
> His latest radiance there, the Sun shall throw,
> And there, the Winter drift his purest snow;
> While birds shall chant above the moss-grown bed,
> And oft, at eve, the tender tear be shed;
> For Truth shall fail, and Hope deceive us not,
> Ere 'MERRIE SHERWOOD'S' MINSTRELS be forgot!"

For some time after our meeting, letters of congratulation were sent from several eminent literary persons, which it would be sheer seeming to deny were acceptable to us, inasmuch as we could not but feel proud that our humble attempt to raise the taste of our neighbours met with response amongst our more favoured and talented labourers in social refinement. The following letter from Miss E. Sheridan Carey cannot but be interesting to the general reader, although the special occasion that called for it has passed away; the pure and humanising sentiments which breathe through almost every line of it, will make it ever new. In order that it may be the better understood, the letter addressed to that talented lady will be necessary, and no apology can be required for the reproduction, when it is considered, that unknown as we were to the lady, the preceding poem was sent in the fulness of a true Christian spirit. I, for one, was overjoyed to see the light beaming upon the hitherto dark nookings of our common country :—

"THE SHERWOOD FOREST GATHERING.

"*To Miss Elizabeth Sheridan Carey.*

"HONOURED LADY—In the name of the Associated Artisans and Peasantry of Sherwood Forest, we beg to express the gratification with which your beautiful poetical lines on our late 'Gathering,' have been read. The style in which they are written—the general tenour of the thoughts they embody—and the repository (the *Sheffield Iris*) in which they appear—are all calculated to endear them to us long—to make us treasure them in 'our heart of hearts' as words

'More dear than drops of gold.'

"To say that we do not feel proud of the attention this demonstration of our principles, views, and hopes has attracted, and of the gratulations we have in consequence received, would argue a species of insincerity or affectation in which we trust we have no part; yet, believe us, Lady, the pride of which we speak hath no kinship with vanity—and we only exult in our actions in proportion as we believe them to spring from those honest, noble motives which every human being, however humble or lofty his station, ought to cherish; or as we perceive their tendency to benefit society at large, as well as to administer to our happiness as individuals.

"Unconscious of the fact, if nature have ordained any sex of soul, we see no reason for excluding the daughters of humanity from any innocent and intellectual enjoyment which its sons are entitled to claim. It therefore delights us to see woman, true to herself, congratulating us, through your able pen, on the admission of our 'wives, daughters, and sisters' to an assembly which we hope ever to look upon with pride and joy as the first of a glorious and interminable series, at the next of which we should hail your own presence with pleasure, if it should be agreeable with your taste or convenience to attend.

"Repeating, on behalf of our rural fraternity, our thanks for the deep interest you have taken in its efforts to vindicate the Rights of Mind, and wishing you length of days, with all happiness here and hereafter,

"We remain, Honoured Lady,
"Respectfully and obediently, yours,
"CHRIST. THOMSON,
"President of the Sherwood Gathering.
"SPENCER T. HALL,
"Laureate of the Forest.
"Edwinstowe, Notts., December 3rd, 1841."

REPLY.
"London, Dec. 6th, 1841.

"GENTLEMEN—On my arrival in Town, I had the singular satisfaction to receive the address which you did me the favour to transmit to me 'in the name of the Associated Artisans and Peasantry of Sherwood Forest.'

"That you should thus cordially recognise the sympathy which, through the means of the *Sheffield Iris*, I ventured to display in the pure and ennobling object of your 'Gathering,' administers to a better feeling than the self-love which might be presumed most active on the occasion. But while I avow myself to be by no means insensible to the flattering nature of the compliment which you have paid me, I frankly admit that I regard it as a circumstance no less honourable to yourselves than to me; seeing that however defective as a composition, the 'Lines' which you have thus welcomed, are at least animated by a sound and healthful pulse.

"To Mr. John Bridgeford, the urbane and intelligent conductor of the *Sheffield Iris*, a gentleman to whom, although personally unknown, I am under much obligation for the editorial courtesy with which my desultory contributions have been indulged, I am indebted not only for the opportunity of becoming acquainted with your proceedings, but for having my attention directed to the interesting report in the *Iris* of Nov. 9th. The same generous views which impelled him to devote a large portion of his paper to the record of 'The Gathering,' induced Mr. Bridgeford to press it upon the notice of his correspondents; nor are they less his debtors for the pleasure afforded them, than you for the publicity given to your Festival.

"In common with every well-wisher to the good order, peace and happiness of society, I could not but hail with unqualified delight, the glad omens held forth by a meeting composed from the real bulwarks of the State—the 'Artisans and Peasantry' of the country,—assembled in a far rural district, from a voluntary impulse, for '*intellectual purposes only,*' and amidst innocent enjoyment *participated in by the members and their families*, breathing a tone of moral and religious sentiment which the wisest and the best must approve. On that day you put forth a bright manifestation of the graciousness of THE ALMIGHTY in showering the precious and unpurchaseable gifts of the mind, no less bounteously upon the poor man at the loom, and the peasant in the field, than upon the noble and the wealthy to whom the golden treasuries of Learning are as fountains unsealed. When the name of *Millhouse*, the bard of your own homes, shall have perished from amongst those of the poets of the land,—when the burning inspirations of *Elliott* shall be forgotten,—and '*the Laureate of the Forest*' no longer honoured,—the Lyre shall have ceased to charm, and the memory of '*merrie Sherwood*' be no more.

"You have set a glorious example, and your 'demonstration' will be greeted by every right-thinking individual. Without riches or titles—with nothing but the moral influence of your own characters, the 'zeal' in 'good works,' and the courage derived from the consciousness of a right purpose, you convened a meeting, which for its intentions and the straightforwardness and unanimity with which it was carried out, would have thrown brilliancy upon the proudest circles of rank and literature. Without neglecting a single duty, invading a single principle, or incurring a single reproach, however slight, from yourselves, or others, you have made a movement, the effects of which may, with the blessing of Heaven, be abundantly manifest in peace and joyousness long after you are gathered to repose. To ripen the understanding, to fertilize it with knowledge, to purify the heart, and to strengthen the spirit by the interchange of Christian thought, and a communion with the wonderful works of THE OMNIPOTENT; to reverence the memory of the illustrious dead, whose genius still beams on high as a shining light before men; and to offer a meet tribute to the living, by whose writings and pattern you are profited and edified;—these were the objects which you proposed and have fulfilled; and for these you are entitled to the respect—the esteem—and the gratitude of all who desire to witness the improvement of their species, to see tranquillity in every cot, and 'holiness and righteousness' throughout the land.

"Continue your happy and praiseworthy career! Share with your 'Wives, your Sisters, and your Daughters,' the means of instruction, for GOD created woman the *companion* and the *comforter* of Man; breathed into her the same spirit, dignified her with the same lofty aspirings, and endowed her with the same celestial inheritance.

"I join with you, most fully, in the hopes to which your first assembly has given rise; and in returning you my warmest acknowledgments for the invitation with which you have honoured me to be present at your next 'Gathering,' I have but to add, that I accept it with a right willing determination to be among you, if PROVIDENCE permit.

"I request that you will do me the favour to communicate this letter to 'The Associated Artisans and Peasantry of Sherwood Forest,' accompanied by my sincere wishes that health, and prosperity, and 'the peace that passeth all understanding,' may abide in, and hallow, their habitations.

"With a grateful appreciation of the kind feelings which you have expressed for my welfare 'here and hereafter,' and with best respects to your firesides. I beg to subscribe myself, Gentlemen,

"Your obliged and obedient servant,

"ELIZABETH SHERIDAN CAREY.

"To Messrs. Christopher Thomson, President of
 the Sherwood Gathering, and Spencer T.
 Hall, Laureate of the Forest."

The approbation of the public was encouragement enough to induce us to try again. We determined to hold our next Gathering in the summer season, and, if possible, in the greenwood; to the latter, however, there were several objections, and we therefore resolved to erect a large pavilion on the border of Birkland and Bilhagh. Accordingly, we announced our intention to have our second "Sherwood Gathering, in honour of Literature, Science, Art, and Moral Worth," on the 5th of July, 1842. We fitted up our tent within sight of the majestic oaks of old Sherwood, and under the shade of a group of lofty firs. To ruralise our canvas house as much as possible, we divided the inside into forest aisles, decorating the whole of it, roof, sides, and pillars, with boughs of oak, birch, and ivy; indeed, of all the leafy produce of Sherwood; enriching the various parts with floral pendants, devices, and garlands. The morning was tempestuous, a summer storm, and the rain damped our hopes as well as our coats; but early in the forenoon it cleared off, leaving us a lovely, but gleamy summer's day. Towards noon our visitors began to arrive; we had a cold collation provided, and one hundred and ten ladies and gentlemen partook of the viands; which being dispatched, those who were not so particular about the " baked meats" were admitted by ticket, to the number of three hundred. Of this meeting I had the honour to be appointed the Chairman. The addresses were, generally, of an educational character. The memory of the Poets was reverenced; the memory, and eternal renown of Robin Hood, honoured; and Science, Art, and Moral Worth were hailed on by approving sentiments.

Amongst the principal speakers were Mr. Thomas Lister, of Barnsley, the Bard of Rustic Wreath; Mr. S. T. Hall, the Bard of Sherwood; Dr. Holland, T. A. Ward, and W. Rhodes, Esqrs., of Sheffield; T. Wake, Esqr., of Worksop; Mr. John Atkin, of Muskham, author of Jonah Tink, and other poems; Mr. Wm. Wood, of Eyam, Derbyshire, the Poet of the Peak; Mr. Charles Plumbe, the poet; Dr. Mower, of Hodsock, and a number of villagers. This gathering, in honour of education and moral worth, was as mind-refreshing as the one of the previous year. A further subscription was made towards providing a stone of memorial for Robert Millhouse, and £2. 7s. 3d. was collected. As evening drew on, the whole party, preceded by a band of music, walked over the grassy carpet that skirts the forest, into the deep wood, and enjoyed themselves with a dance under the shade of the wide-spreading arms of the "Major's Oak;" and a truly enlivening sight it was, to see the mechanics from the distant towns, and the in-dwellers of the county, footing it together over the sward; the holiday groups calling up recollection to those "merrie days" when May-games and Midsummer revels were amongst the out-door recreations of the people; when peer and peasant were both human enough to join hands in the same joy-giving dance.

On this occasion, too, various poetical tributes were sent to our jubilee; amongst them was one from Miss E. S. Carey, offered, to use her own words, as " a tribute of my esteem for the object of your Gathering, and as a proof that, although prevented from witnessing your cheering festival, my thoughts and best wishes will be with you."

The contribution of Miss E. S. Carey gave a graphic description of those chivalric gatherings of olden time—

> "When gallant hearts with patriot zeal
> Beat high beneath the burnished steel,—
> When wheeling on, with thund'ring sound,
> A thousand squadrons sweep the ground,—
> When scarf, and plume, and pennon sail,
> Like storm-rent clouds upon the gale,
> And streaming on the lurid sky
> Each haughty banner gleams on high,
> Now borne aloft—now sinking low—
> Now snatch'd triumphant from the foe,
> While man and horse in stern array,
> Boom madly to the fierce melee."

Contrasting

> "The shout—the cheer—the battle-cry
> That calls to conquer or to die!"

with

> "The triumphs of philanthropy."

Then painting with a rich poetical pencil, the assembled groups at our Gathering, as vividly as if she had sketched them from the living throng, instead of the fancied, or prophetically revealed to her mind's eye; and thus concludes:—

> "The Sons of Science here commune,
> And minstrels sweet their harps attune;
> The Bard pours forth the tide of song,
> And bears the raptured mind along,—
> The sage on wisdom, virtue, dwells,
> And ev'ry heart with transport swells.
> Oh, worthy task! Oh, sacred aim!
> Oh, glorious scene! Oh, deathless fame!
>
> " A thousand years have fleeted past,
> Since Sherwood's oaks withstood the blast,
> And centuries may wane away
> Ere yet yon giant trunks decay.
> But when nor branch, nor root, is seen,
> To mark where waved the forest green—
> When the fair spot on which we stand
> Shall leave no traces in the land—

> When Sherwood shall—as Sherwood must,
> Like man, lie mould'ring in the dust,
> And time-worn pavements meet the view,
> Where now the bracken drinks the dew,
> May this our 'Gath'ring' flourish free
> In peace, in love, and loyalty!
> God speed the wish! God grant the pray'r,
> And make each 'cottage' home His care!"

It was the hard lot of the author of the following song to pine through weary days and years of sickness; yet he beguiled the pain with poetry. Even when the lamp of life was flickering, and the oil of existence nearly spent, he sang of patience, and like a soul-lover, courted the Muses until death.

This song was sent as poor Hardy's contribution to the Gathering; he was too ill to attend in person, for Death had already named the hour which he had numbered on the everlasting scroll as William's last!—

THE WILD HARP OF THE FOREST.

(Poetry and Music by William Hardy, junior, Mansfield.)

> "Away to the groves of old Sherwood, away!
>   The wild harp of the Forest is blending
> Its fairy-like notes with the wood-warbler's lay,
>   Like the music of seraphs descending
> To bless us, the beauties of nature combine:
>   The decree of Omniscience fulfilling,
> He speaks to our souls in this language divine,
>   While with rapture our bosoms are thrilling.
>   What power can bind the mighty mind,
>   Illumed by Freedom's light?
>   The potent shield of Truth we wield,
>   And Heaven still guards our right.
>
> "To the deep shady bowers of Birkland away,
>   While the sun in bright splendour is beaming:
> Creation's vast volume we now may survey,
>   The woods their rich treasures are teeming.
> Though our chalice of life be embittered with care,
>   We may drink at the fountain of gladness:
> Sweet sympathy's spirit shall rest with us there,
>   And banish all sorrow and sadness.
>   What power can bind, &c.

> "Away to the groves of old Sherwood, away!
>   The wild harp of the Forest is pouring
> Its music immortal where mild zephyrs play,
>   The Author of Nature adoring.
> Oh! while on the page of pure wisdom we gaze,
>   Each heart thrills with blissful emotion;
> Our voices shall join in the anthems of praise
>   That ascend on the wings of devotion.
>   What pow'r can bind, &c."

This song is still popular in our village, both for the sake of the author, and the sentiment it contains. It is frequently sung at our convivial meetings, and social gatherings.

It has been a subject of regret with many, that the Sherwood Gatherings have been discontinued; as such meetings for purely intellectual purposes, combined with a day's healthy recreation, must always tend to social refinement. It was intended to hold those meetings periodically, either biennially or triennially; the principal reason of their not being repeated, was the great sacrifice of time required by the directors— all of them working men, and dependent upon their labour;—the time necessary to provide accommodation upon a scale commensurate with the preparations on a former occasion, is more than their means justify in giving to the object. If, however, those meetings were held in the Odd Fellows' Lodge room, as on the first occasion, such sacrifice would not be required. Many literary friends have expressed a desire, that a reunion of friends actuated by a common wish to elevate all mankind, should again take place. If, then, objections stand in the way of gathering on the Forest, why cannot we, as before, meet in-doors, and by an interchange of mind, still make the Sherwood feast a gathering of kindred spirits? Although, at our former feasts, great numbers were naturally gathered together by the novelty of the occasion, than by a desire to promote its objects,—and many of these groups were scattered up and down in holiday knots—yet there was neither drunkenness, fighting, or other disorderly conduct, to militate against the social character of the meeting. Like its predecessor, the second "Gathering" met with the warm approval of the local press.

If the inhabitants of our village have allowed the Sherwood Gatherings to sleep, they did not forget the promise they made at them, that the grave of Robert Millhouse should have some distinguishing mark placed upon it, to note its whereabout. In the year 1841, I made a pilgrimage to the grave of Millhouse: there was no stone memorial upon it, but I found that some kind heart had *written* a notice, and had pasted it upon a board, and fastened it to the ivy-robed wall, near to the crumbling remains of the poet. Above his "narrow house" the grass was worn away, partly by the foot-fall of those who had stopped there to sigh over the ill-fated bard of "man's destiny," and partly by the curious, who mostly step aside "just to ask" who has taken the room below in the mansion of our common mother, the earth! In the year 1842, in company with my friend, Mr. Joseph Shaw, of Nottingham, I again visited the Cemetery grounds of that town, to commune with the spirit of the poet of "Sherwood Forest." The storms of the past winter had swept away the paper tribute that before attracted my attention, and with it had disappeared all the notice of Robert Millhouse. The bare-worn patch of last year was now green with rank grasses—the curious were satisfied,—Genius alone could not stay the progress of the crowds that assembled there, not even for a moment—the novelty was over, and the grass was no longer to be down-trodden. We inquired of each as they passed by, and of the officers of the place, if they could point out to us the grave we asked them for? No,—there was but one answer, " They knew there was a poet somewhere thereabouts!" We were forced to be content with their replies, vague as they were; but I left the spot with a renewed determination, that if possible, something should be done to spare the pilgrims and admirers of Millhouse's poetry, who might hereafter visit these grounds, the pain of such an equivocal answer, as that the author of " Blossoms" was entombed " somewhere thereabouts." Since that time we have redeemed our promise, and placed a commemorative stone over Millhouse's grave. Although it was at first imagined that the inhabitants of the county would join us in such a laudable endeavour—hitherto we have been but indifferently aided. The subscriptions at the Sherwood Gatherings amounted to £4. 18s. 9d. The late lamented Thomas Wright, Esq., of Upton Hall, Nottinghamshire, a gentleman whose heart and purse-strings were ever open to aid struggling genius, subscribed £1. It was at one of my short visits to Upton, where I had been kindly invited by that *Mecænas* to look over his picture gallery, and the picturesque grounds which surround his mansion, that I made known to him the desire of our villagers to show their respect for the bard of Sherwood Forest, by marking the narrow clayey bed where the poet slept; with his usual benevolence and promptitude, he rang for his butler, and desired him to see paid to me, before I left Upton, a sovereign, towards our plan. After a lecture delivered in my humble manner, before the members of the Mansfield Mechanics' Institute, the sum of £1. 2s. was subscribed towards our object. A "friend" in Nottingham contributed five shillings to our fund, and thus unitedly we raised the amount to £7. 5s. 9d. The Nottingham Cemetery Company—thanks to their benevolence—allowed us to fix the memorial in their grounds, without the usual charges being made; thus they favoured our design, and by their generosity paid their tribute of respect to the memory of a man, who, whatever his faults, was, nevertheless, an honour to the town of Nottingham, and a benefactor to his race. The bill for the monument, with the expenses of setting up and carriage, amounted to the sum of £17. 12s., leaving a balance of £10. 6s. 3d. for the committee to discharge. We have fulfilled the promise given at the first Sherwood gathering; for on the 29th of September, 1845, a monument to the memory of Robert Millhouse was erected over his grave, in the Cemetery grounds, at Nottingham. Had Robert Millhouse been born to devise plans how millions of men could be sacrificed to the Moloch of glory, and their widows and orphans immured in workhouses, and how bread-loaves and tea could be taxed to provide funds wherewith to bedeck the heroes with ribbons and medals, then the country would have risen up in their thousands to erect a monument of brass to his memory. But, as he was born poor, and forced to continue so, and devoted his time to building a mind-monument in books, to refine those who should live after him, he was doomed to short commons while living, and for aught good Christian people cared about him—as to reverence his memory would not put a shilling into their pockets—they thought it would be as well to let his bones rot quietly, and his memory perish. But, fortunately, Christian people differ about benefactors; many regarding the "heroes" as men who are no longer wanted; and hence, that bread-loaves should not be taxed to keep them. A few such thought the Nottingham poet a real hero—he wielded a quill instead of a sword; and so they erected a monument to him, leaving the sword-heroes to their friends.

One of the advantages which we have enjoyed, and still enjoy at Edwinstowe, is, the pleasure and instruction we so often receive from the companionship of the scientific and literary persons who visit us. Many of them are induced to make our village a temporary resting-place, previous to their wandering over the last vestige of the ancient Forest of Sherwood, which is but a few minutes' walk from our rural homes. To us, such visits are always beneficial; for the interchange of conversation, with thoughtful men, generally kindles up the pure fire of thought within the breasts of those who listen to them. It was our misfortune, nevertheless, to drive the poor lamented Pemberton away from us. It has been said of that child of nature, that he has been known to walk from London to Birkland, that he might enjoy but one day within the calm recesses of that leafy tenement. It was on one of those tours, in the early summer-time of 1834, that he visited our village; he expressed his desire to take up a temporary residence with us, and he was informed that he might meet with such accommodation as he desired, at the house of my friend, Mr. Robert Widdison. With this view he inquired for, and found out, the house. Mr. Widdison was from home at the time when the "Wanderer" called there: Pemberton, without making himself known to the inmates, merely asked if he could be lodged there? and an answer was returned in the negative. Poor Charles, in his usual unobtrusive manner, left the house without a word, not one of the family within having the least knowledge of the person who had called upon them. To have thus missed the opportunity of a brief acquaintance with such an exalted genius, has been, in itself, pain and mortification enough to absolve us from our seeming coldness—from the apparent churlishness of denying a quiet home to a true man, for a short time. Had Mr. Widdison been at home when Pemberton called, or had the pilgrim made himself known, the result might have been different. In either case we should have been spared an occurrence which has ever since that time been spoken of here with regret. But the poet was used to disappointment; he had many an icy "nay" from the cold world, during his course through it; and he was, therefore, prepared to receive a courteous "No" with favour. He turned his back upon my friend's house, and bent his steps toward Birkland, apparently intent upon studying the wide open book of nature, whose pages were now unfolding before him. He measured his way with the majesty of a High Priest, who had left behind him a world-babel, and had hither come to worship Nature in her far-off solitudes! The Spirit of Beauty was with him—they dwelled together in that "strange old universe." He says, it was "deeply—intensely affecting." Yes, he held communion "deep and intense," with the abiding spirit of the place; and when filled with its inspiration, he threw out his full soul of poetry into a translation of its grandeur, that will live, and be read, when every oak which on that day unbared its heart to him, shall be crumbled into the parent earth! Pemberton visited Birkland that he might give to mankind "A Peep into Sherwood Forest."* Some persons have considered that paper a mere imaginative satyr, or fairy sketch; but let those persons visit Birkland and Bilhagh in the month of August, and although the Forest has lost some of its romantic features since the "Wanderer's" picture was drawn, still, if they will go to the original, and then again to Pemberton's description of it, they will easily trace the lineaments of the brave old Saxon chieftains that rule in that leafy empire, and they may dwell upon the features of the silver-robed virgin birches that sport in their loveliness before the oaken-hearted patriarchs of the forest!

The last attempt to establish another institution of an educational and self-supporting character, in our village, has been made during the present year, 1847, by founding a society, to be called "The Association of Self-Help," which, as its name imports, is intended

---

* Published in the Monthly Repository for June, 1834, and at page 247 of "The Life and Literary Remains of Charles Reece Pemberton," edited by John Fowler, Esq., of Sheffield.

to improve the moral condition of its members. Its expressed objects are, " to accomplish, by all legitimate and moral means, support in sickness, decent interment, competence in old age, support of the widows and orphans, and the comfort of its members by association, labour, leisure, and education." This society will act as an auxiliary to the Odd Fellows' Lodges; and it is proposed to extend its advantages beyond the immediate locality of its establishment, if the public become sufficiently interested in the project to assist in its diffusion. It is an undeniable fact, that there are vast numbers of the community who would like to avail themselves of the advantages which the lodges offer, yet, as they state, they cannot do so, because they cannot, conscientiously, subscribe to all the ceremonies and observances required by the Odd Fellows' societies. Now, to an Odd Fellow, those ceremonies appear not only necessary, but they wonder why others object to try them; still there are a large number who believe that those mystic rights do not administer to any useful purpose; and, so thinking, they are predetermined not to try them. The founders of this Association to Self-Help, with but one exception, were all Odd Fellows, who had so frequently deplored the separation of so many persons from the advantages of their order. They were, moreover, desirous that privileges equal to those enjoyed by themselves, should be placed within the reach of all sects and parties. Although the lodge in our village can boast of large numbers, still there are many others who refuse to join us, yet long to avail themselves of similar benefits. Such being the case here, it was but fair to suppose, that in every town, or village, there were greater or less numbers similarly situated. Thus the founders of this institution resolved, that while they were anxious for the spread of Odd Fellows' Lodges, or any other societies that administer to the comfort of its members, they were not less ready to aid—with heart and hand—any society that proffered to elevate the working classes. Their chief regret was, that there was more work requiring to be done in the social vineyard, than there appeared to be workmen able and willing to embark in the toil of tillage. Hence their hope is, that those who refused to take up the social work in the Lodges, being now left without an excuse for their idleness, will come out and labour for Self-Help.

One peculiar feature in this new scheme is, the admission of females to the benefits of this Association. The founders of the society are sanguine that this part of their plan will prove of immense importance in their scheme of social regeneration. They are aware that there will be a loud cry made against them about the impracticability of conducting business institutions where the sexes are mixed together as members: but they do not mean to be discomfited by the wolf-cry of impracticability, without first testing it by practice. The "Lords of the creation," with all their vaunted gallantry, has too long regarded the "softer sex" as mere toys. Has not the time fully arrived, when the socializing influence of women's presence in every society where mankind in general is to be moralized and raised in independence ought to be practically recognised? And will not her presence there tend to hasten on their laudable objects? Woman has long since proved her power to battle with want and penury in the cottage; can she not, likewise, give good counsel in the social assembly, how such miseries can be best prevented? It is fully admitted, that when adversity threatens to overwhelm the household, the wife or mother can generally propose how the calamity can be best averted. In the extremes of trouble, her patience and firmness have always been equal to the trial. In our public assemblies for social pleasures, her presence is universally courted, and her attendance complimented. Has woman, then, no higher mission on earth, than to patiently drudge at home, or to dress, and go abroad for amusement? Has she not other rights, which it is high time she asserted and practised? Yes; doubt it not, woman will be as useful in our benevolent societies as she is in the cottage; her presence there will be as cheering,—her advice will be as valuable in our meetings for the sterner studies of social economy, as it has been in the hour of trial at home, or her smile been happy during the dance or the music party. Yet there are numbers ready to declare, that if you once admit females to such societies, they will be out of their place, and the society will fail. Are they justified, by experience, in so saying? or do they speak upon the credit of the old prejudiced rule, that women had no right to mingle in such assemblies? But if a few such attempts have failed, what then? Is that an argument sufficient to deter all future attempts at such a plan? Past failures generally teach a useful lesson. Try again. Let both sexes assemble, and unitedly aid in encouraging works of charity and self-dependence. It is all very well for those who never felt the keen tooth of poverty gnawing at their vitals,—it may do, perhaps, for them to proclaim, that woman's business is to boil the dumplings, and darn the stockings. Such pursuits, alike honourable and necessary, are but a part of woman's social mission; she can conceive, and execute, measures of public interest, as well as darn stockings. You, ladies, may be the regenerators of England's homes, if you like! You can help to restore the life of manliness, if you will do so. Will you longer delay? Do not you, the wives, and mothers, and sisters of the vast artisan and labouring class of England—do not you share in the want and misery occasioned by over-toil?—do you not feel the drain made from the scanty earnings of your families by the never-sparing taxes?—do you not share in the injustice which arises from the unequal distribution of the wealth which labour alone produces?—do you not share in all those, and a thousand other untold miseries? Assuredly you do. Help, then, Self-Help! Come, then, to work,—to work with your heads, as well as your hands, and better days will attend upon you! Remember, you are required to do more work in the untilled fields of humanity, than your mothers had to do. Then prepare yourselves: be not deterred by the stand-still cry, that you are out of your proper place when you meddle with social progression. You do aid the cause of benevolence by patronizing bazaars and fancy fairs, and filling up pence-cards to send missionaries to Tahiti; become missionaries of peace and plenty at home; help your friends to devise the means to send independence and true Christianity into your own cottages; unite, then, in a love-labour that shall make all mankind happy. The ladies say they cannot go to the public-houses, or they would help us at once. Thanks, kind ladies, we can manage as well in some other building. We will solicit the indulgence of schoolmasters, trustees of schools, and the managers of mechanics' institutes, for leave to commence the work in some part of their establishments, if we cannot conveniently rent appropriate rooms, or manage in private ones; we shall only require their rooms until we can build our own. So to have our own halls must be an inseparable part of our scheme; and remember, however poor we may be, this plan will help to make us richer; and as determination is the first thing required, that will lead us to the rest. Therefore, your own buildings to meet in, men of Self-Help!

Another feature of this "Association of Self-Help" is, to encourage its members to lay up their money in small sums, by regular, or *irregular* payments, until they can purchase a share of some given amount, and to receive interest upon such deposit as soon as they have purchased a quarter share. The capital acquired is to be expended in the purchase of land for gardens, so that the toiling artisan and peasant may, at a moderate rent, enjoy his garden, with the satisfaction of knowing, that some portion of it is already his own, and that every year he is purchasing a still greater share in it. It will be argued, that the Savings' Banks are already established for the good of the people, and that they can deposit their savings there, even in sums as low as a shilling. True, they might put their shillings into the Savings' Bank; hundreds of people have done so; but there is another class, and a large one too, that never think of taking their small surplus into any bank,—a class who are neither pecuniarily or morally, in a position to invest in the banks. They are prevented from various causes—such as not having a shilling to spare at the particular time required for investing, or by living a considerable distance from the banks, or by having an immediate demand for every shilling as soon as it comes, and have never studied the importance of saving the pence: these, and numberless other causes, which, unitedly, disqualify them from ranking in the banking class, have rendered such institutions as Savings' Banks as profound a mystery as the Sinking Fund, or the Exchequer Bills' process. Yet this vast mass of England's wealth-makers must be made individually rich; and until they have shillings "at once" to spare, they must make their Association Pence Banks, and become their own managers and *tellers*. A beginning must be made, and only commence right earnestly, and assuredly it will prove to be "the beginning to the end." Men, in large masses, are encouraged to do that which, isolated, they would never dream of doing, and which, indeed, they could not accomplish by individual means. Begin, then, to gather up the pence,—encourage each other by example,—fraternise together—prove your right to be "lords of the soil," by unitedly purchasing one rood of ground: that rood will make a garden for some one of your members; and if you will steadily persevere in such a course, each one may soon have his own garden plot. But you must be actuated by a far holier principle than the mere acquisition of property: every moralising influence which unity and brotherly love can generate, must pervade your meetings, and direct your conduct; your assemblies must be of a true Christian character, not a community satisfied to talk of Christian actions and love, without such love in-dwelling in your hearts; seeming has failed, seeming will ever fail to accomplish mighty consequences; be true Christian men, and your institutes will become as numerous and as popular amongst the poor, and often improvident, handicraftsmen, as the Savings' Banks and other monied societies are amongst the middle, and, so-called, rich classes. Work, then,—to work, fellow-labourers! If you have never united for such an object before, now is the time,—the very feature of this age is ASSOCIATION.

Experience has proved, that by unity and love you may become truly rich, and live in comparative comfort. The ten, twenty, and fifty pound shareholders have bought their lands, mills, mines, railroads, club houses, and churches:—try, then, the pence, shillings, five shillings, and pound shares, they will accumulate interest, and compound interest, in their humble way, and look their owners as proudly in the face as though they had cyphers added to the right-hand side of their names; and stoutly will they proclaim their power to purchase gardens, cottages, meeting halls, schools, libraries, museums, and every other associative advantage. Commence this work, and you sanctify labour to domestic happiness,—you will no longer be haunted with the night-mare of famine and potato diet: then, instead of brutal debasement, immoderate indulgence, uncharitableness, poverty, and the crime-train that fattens upon ignorance, and disunion—instead of those miseries, charity, true love, love to God and man, mutual aid, an improved and improving labour class will everywhere spring up, and those who at first stood aloof and reviled you, and sneered about wild and foolish schemes, even these will be made repentant by your perseverance, and forbearance will be constrained to cry out "See how these Christians love!"

These are some of the objects sought to be attained through this "Association of Self-Help." By self-help you will raise your class—by self-help no man was ever yet pulled downwards—none will be injured by it, all will be served: will you, then, poor half-fed labour-men, will you lend a helping hand to spread this association far and wide? In common with the existing man-making institutions that are spreading through the country, this one will raise the endeavours now used to raise the long-neglected sons of toil to that pedestal of moral worth designed for them by the Almighty; to be industrious and honest, and to enjoy the reward of labour, is God's true patent of nobility, and He waits to confer the honour upon all who, by self-help, diligently seek to deserve it.

I have thus imperfectly noted some of the educational societies in our village. The labour that has been required to establish them has been amply remunerated by the enjoyment of the social comforts that have flowed from it. We are not, however, so egotistical as to suppose that we are perfection in this woodland nook. Oh no! while the "little learning" we have received has made us proud, it has not made us vain;—no, on the contrary it has opened our eyes to the fearful danger that everywhere surrounds the semi-man; it has also shown to us the necessity of never ceasing to labour in the fields of mental improvement, revealing to us the spiritualizing influences of virtuous actions, and the hideousness of vice. Rejoicing, then, that we are living in the sun-rise of an intellectual day, we cannot shut our eyes to the fact, that there are hundreds of our fellow men who are not yet awake to the necessity of raising themselves out of the slough of unlettered degradation; and we would fain encourage all to partake of the refining enjoyment of self-instruction and social converse. We ask you, therefore, to become men instead of thoughtless animals,—take as much of our plan as gives promise of bringing you nearer to God's image; what you see deficient in our rural community, supply to yourselves by your knowledge of our defects, and what is bad in us, carefully avoid. By such a course, we shall likewise be benefited through your observations. Give us the use of your prescription, and we will purge ourselves of our besetting sins.

Feeling it to be our sacred duty to labour side by side with all those who desire to see our toiling masses happy, we are earnestly solicitous that our rural population should cast aside their apathy, and labour as zealously in the work of social regeneration as some of our intelligent neighbours of the cities and towns have already done.

I have felt the leaden weight which oppresses the yearning mind, that with scarcely one twinkling ray has had to grope its way through the grim valley of unlettered night; and it gladdens my heart to know, that within a few short years, the sun-beams of literature and science have rent the gloomy pall of prejudice that enveloped the soulless anatomies that stalked blindly through the earth. Thanks to the spread of education, and free thoughts, which have now turned thousands "from darkness to light," and given us goodly promise that better days await us. Thanks to the spread of knowledge—the uprising generation will not have to encounter the blind worms that half-a-century back denied the right of thought to the poor tanned-faced horny-handed labourer, who wasted his strength that England might be commercially great. Thanks to the Press, that has scattered the powers of mind into every corner of the civilized world, the toiler may at last be allowed to think; and yet a little while, and he shall eat! The antagonism of parties is exploded—the potency of shams and cants are disputed,—and man and mind alone shall rule in

"The good time coming."

CHAPTER IX.

BIRKLAND AND BILHAGH.

As I have imperfectly sketched some of the intellectual features of the village of Edwinstowe, and drawn the manners of its inhabitants, I would fain try with my crude pencillings to describe some of the landscape beauties that surround us. What if rugged Utility demands the sacrifice of two-thirds of our life-time, and that toil-worn and weary, he forces us to bed soon after our day's work is ended—we can still love Nature. Although we are forbidden to walk abroad in the green fields on the Sabbath, lest we peril our souls by finding a religion without a creed, we have still a Sabbath of the heart, and can feel pure and holy thoughts dwelling with us, while we are talking with God in Nature's calm solitudes; and happy are we to hear the "still small voice" of inward peace whispering to our heart of hearts that God is there! Iron men, who worship ledgers, may talk cosily about political economy, and how steam mills must clash and clang full eighteen hours per diem, as it would be found impossible to transmute hearts-blood into brass in ten short hours, and so disqualify them from erecting a golden calf within their counting-houses. Partisan law-makers may, in their wisdom, have day-dreams about a class created by proudness of heart to carry logs and draw water, and make bricks, whilst, Pharaoh-like, they refuse the necessary straw. All these things they may propound,—and for the time, they may believe them to be good, as they, too often, leave Humanity's claims out of their abstractions; but God and Nature are eternal; "seed-time and harvest" come and go, as the Creator willed they should—the flowers blossom, the streams sing aloud, the trees kiss the breeze, and God be thanked,

"The lark still warbles flying!"

A kind man, in his soul-fulness, exclaimed "thank God for books!" and who does not answer, "Amen"? And reverently do I exclaim, "God be thanked for His abundant store of untaxed beauties,—for trees, streams, birds, flowers, bees, for sunlight, storm-clouds, zephyrs, and sou'-westers! for these and goodness untold, God be thanked!" If the luxuries of life, and some of its substantials be denied to us, still we are rich, luxuriantly rich, for the God of Nature has unsealed His Universal Treasury, and bidden the lowest take out of it freely, "without money and without price."

"The men
Whom nature's works can charm, with God himself
Hold converse; grow familiar day by day,
With his conceptions; act upon his plan,
And form to His the relish of their souls."

Come, then, we will have one day in the woods, and let us go out determined to be charmed! It is a fine midsummer's day; just such an one as we could desire. The sun shines brightly, a slight breeze from the west stirs the air, the deep ultra-marine sky is chequered over with clouds of a light grey colour, and their pearly edges are bordered with a pure silvery white; and how carelessly they trail over the realms of space! Those very clouds make the face of day more lovely; for see how far-off hills and distant woods lie basking in a sea of etherial gold; these couriers have for a moment veiled, to us, Sol's lustrous eye, with their fleecy train, and they have thrown their mantle of shadow over the green-sward at our feet, and around yon upland wood, making the distant light more celestial, and the fore-gloom mysterious and solemn. Farewell, for a time, to the village: we are now leaving the brick, tile, and thatched-roofed cottages behind us:—but we cannot travel fast; nature, and art, together, crowd over every square inch of earth, and every atom, or drop, has a spirit within it! It may be that we are panting for greenery, but we must not hasten to it; already we are forced to pause, and look into the church. We cannot pass a village church without stopping to admire it—no matter about its decorations, whether it be Saxon or florid Gothic—we cannot pass it unheeded: these churches are hallowed by all that we love. While we gaze reverently upon them, memory opens her flood-gates, and departed friends—perhaps a mother, or a brother, or the companions of boyhood, are there, and sweep past us on recollection's tide. Time, too, has sanctified these old churches, and we never gaze upon them but an indescribable reverence steals over, and subdues us. Like many others of our old village churches, this one appears to have been built at various periods, judging from its mixed parts of Anglo-Norman and later Gothic. That graceful spire, with its regular ashlar courses and decorated crochets, and niches, appears much younger than the irregular coursed tower, and circular-headed arches, which ornament it. Some of the dark age restorers, probably, ashamed of the rough, rubble-handed masons of Stephen's day, have charitably spared future antiquarians the blush for those early bunglers, and have, consequently, pebble-dashed the old tower, and made it "neat and respectable." Father Time witnesses strange mutations; who knows but in these transition days, he may yet see some leather-aproned men, with dressing-tools and mallets, stripping the neat pebble-dashing off again with a fair-play gusto, and grumbling out their determination to let the old tower stand upon his own merits, even though he has to support a spire of the third Edward's? With all its irregularities—which, after all, may constitute its charm—our church is an interesting structure. The present vicar—the Rev. J. B. Cobham, has had the interior renovated, the "genteel pews" have been taken out, and stalled seats introduced, whose character corresponds with the mixed architectural style of the building. Some centuries hence, when the new oak has become browned with age, the stalls will assimilate with the architectural decorations, and may pass off as the work of ancient days,—or what will be still better, reflect credit upon the modern restorers. There is but little in or about this church to enrapture the antiquary; no ancient brasses, crosses, or remarkable monuments. There are the remains of a nearly-forgotten tradition here, which goes on to state, that in the forest-days, the patriot ranger, Robin Hood, had been apprised, that on a certain day, some lordling, whose " might was right," was going to marry the lovely maid Marion, against that lady's will, and that the outlaw had determined upon rescuing her from his fangs; he accordingly ambushed his band near to the church, and when the ceremony had fairly commenced, the " merrie men" entered the church, and took the damsel under their especial protection: and the tradition further declareth, that the said Lady Marion rewarded the chivalry of bold Robin Hood with her hand; and that soon afterwards, the very pious chaplain, Friar Tuck, officiated at the same altar from which the lady was rescued, and joined them together by the rites of "holy church." Another tradition, not less veritable than the former one, married Will Stukely—one of Robin's bold archers—in a similar adventurous manner, at the parish church of Eakring.* The churchyard of Edwinstowe, is well-conditioned, but yet contains nothing remarkable, except a specimen of mediæval tombstone writing—

> " Robert Rockley body here is laid,
> Its for him these lines are made,
> That we all here may remember
> He died the 19th of September,
> Robert Rockley son be he,
> His age is near to 23.
>   1742."

---

* The village of Eakring is five miles S.W. of Edwinstowe, and the place where the benevolent Mompesson, who distinguished himself during the plague, at Eyam, in Derbyshire, lies buried.

Again our route is onward, and under the boughs of that fine aspen-tree which overhangs the garden wall. Is it not a beautiful tree? A picture in itself, and not an every-day specimen of the species,

> "That with silver lines his leaf."

Majestically he throws his ashy-grey arms around us. His tremulous leafage is full of music, ever mirthful; the louder the storm blows, still the louder he sings. In the stillness of night, when no voice, save the nightingale's, wakes the calm even there, like the lone lover who invokes the moon, he untiringly sings on.

Before we climb the hill, let us rest awhile under the shade of this group of old firs, and through their lancet windows look out upon the scene around us. Many a tug these old firs have had with the west wind; old Boreas has puffed away at them for a hundred years; he has shaven some of their limbs, but he has failed to up-root them; they have waxed strong with age. Here is a boll, seventy feet high, and ten feet in circumference; we need not fear to lean against him, he has taken care of himself: how his roots are meshed, and plaited, for yards around us;—what cares he for winds! In common with his brotherhood, this little fraternity have colonized themselves at a respectable distance from the old oaks, on the upland; they are the porters to Birkland—the path lies through their enclosure. These ever-green sentinels have been amused with oft-repeated love stories, told in audible whispers, by many a rustic youth and artless maiden, without a witness, save the "blessed moon," who coyly stole down through the few loop-holes left by the matted foliage, and by these old firs, which feigned sleep, yet laughed to hear the mad-capped lovers

> "Embrace, and kiss, and take ten thousand leaves."

How cool and refreshing it is to sit here and look out upon the emerald plot before us, and to listen to the happy children who are gathered there! See how the plump and ruddy-faced youngsters are rolling topsy-turvy upon the grass. Happy souls! Care has not made himself acquainted with you yet. We remember when we were as happy as you are now; we sometimes sigh, but in vain, for your joyous state. Twice a child? Alack! bleached hair, and wrinkled already; by-and-by a treble squeak, and then—senility. Yet we remember the days when our juvenile love-labour was its own reward, even as your's is now. How actively the urchins are employed! years of apparent labour is, to them, but the work of an hour; the building of a palace, a church, or a village is begun, altered, demolished, and re-commenced with never-tiring industry. One juvenile mason has scooped out a portion of the sand-bank, and is about to fashion his little mansion; and he has, perhaps, unwittingly, broken up the homes of thousands of mining bees, which are colonized along that bank side. Yonder little girl appears to be studying the housemaid's mysteries,—her constructive powers have been called into action to make herself a broom, which she has accomplished by binding together a bunch of heather; how dilgently she trims up the supposed room; in her endeavour to clean the floor, she sweeps up the very foundation of it. She has contrived a pier glass out of the bottom of a broken dish, which my lady's scullion had thrown away, under the old hawthorn hedge, by the roadside. They have proclaimed the baby of two years old—the youngest in their train—the Queen of May; they have placed her upon a throne of turf, and twined a coronal of bind-weed and lady's fingers together, and wreathed them around her infantile brows; they have linked up a regal collar of dandelion stalks, and jewelled it with daisies, and have given her a long bracken-stalk for a sceptre. Hark to their coronation anthem! It was set to music by Wilderspin :—

"If your lesson will not do, try, try, try again!"

Farewell, thrice happy souls, enjoy your heaven of earthly bliss while you may. Life is to you but as one long holiday. Soon—very soon, you will be glad to snatch a few hours out of Time's weary moil, even as we do now!

We must leave this road, which is dignified by the title of turnpike-road. Half a century ago it was only known here as the Swinecote-road, and its old name was descriptive of its use; then, its chief service was to lead to the forest, and the villagers' swine were, by ancient right, free wood-rangers! This somewhat beaten track, through the pine-clump, is our road. See how the way-side is bespangled with wild flowers; here is the golden lady's finger, and the trailing potentilla; wild thyme, in purply patches, interspersed with shining green bilberry plants; extensive beds of sage-green heath, which, in autumn, will be one mass of purple bells, making gay the face of nature, and filling nectar-cups for legions of honey-bees, and troops of iris-tinted butterflies. Did you ever see such a field of gorse before? For two miles in length it is one waving sea of gold, every green leaf being completely buried in the vast profusion of the papilinaceous flowers; their perfume floats on the breeze, and its lusciousness reminds one of the scent of newly ripened cocoa-nuts—if, indeed, it can be likened to anything but itself—it is so powerful, that we can drink it in with our nostrils. Tourists, and admirers of nature, who have frequently visited here, declare that its beauty is superior to anything of the kind, either in England or Scotland. We must keep right onward through this garden of furze, which is so picturesquely fringed with tall palmy brackens, and coral-belled foxgloves: we leave the little reedy pond to our left hand. The smoke which you observe coming up the valley, at about two miles' distance, is from the cottages of the little town of Ollerton. The river Maun runs along the valley, and then, meeting with the river Idle, they unitedly flow on to the Trent. You perceive the river Maun flashing up like ribbons of silver about a mile to the right hand, the distant woods of Wellow Park, and the billowy brecks of Boughton close in the view. Now, the "last vestige of Sherwood's right to renown" is before us. What associations it conjures up! Here a dense mass of umbrageous foliage; there, a wreck— "the ruined Palmyra of a Forest." Yet, here, in the forest days, when kings and nobles gave up their whole life-time, as as it were, to the chase,—in those days, when Saxons, Danes, and Normans, followed the velvety antlered deer adown the entangled glades of "merrie Sherwood,"—then this "ruined Palmyra" was a perfect temple. There stand a cluster of lightning-scathed columns, bereft of pediment and entablature; silent memorials of the march of time; dumb mouths, preaching to us of the nothingness of human life; moralizing, with a philosophy peculiarly their own, upon the ages which they have seen

"Come like shadows,—so depart."

Although they are old, scathe-looking, and nearly leaf-dismantled, yet they look down upon us with a cynical smile, saying to the poor admirer, "Vain babbler, talkest thou of deeds done of life-long years, and renowned days of Egypt, Spain, and Waterloo? Where wert thou when Cressy and Agincourt were won? Where didst thou live when Ascolon fell, and Palestine was conquered? Didst thou ever see the Roman's Eagles 'flout the air'? Wert thou at all acquainted with Arthur, or Wessex, Egbert, or Albert?" "I remember them all! I was a grown man when that said Robin Hood you boast about, was driven to take shelter amongst us. By my reckoning, a few years ago, he was hunted from your cities by armed men, spurred on by wicked laws. He found a sanctuary amongst us; bravely we screened him from ruffianly vengeance; outcast, foodless, houseless, we found him a bowery home, gave him all Sherwood to range over, and with his long bow he procured himself food from the red deer; meal he took from those who had a superabundance, and no man knew better how to provide himself with sack, and other needful sauces, than did that same Robin Hood. Here he reigned a Green-wood King, maintained himself, chastised the oppressors, and succoured the defenceless and weak, and ruled long a patriotic and liberty-loving chief over this vast domain. I could fill up all the years of thy life with such tales; I could tell thee of Druids' fires, of Scots and Picts, of "roses white and red," of plumed knights and beauteous ladies, of liberty-fired Cavaliers, and Roundheads. I could tell thee stories of all ages, from the very day the Romans* were encamped at my feet, even up to the date of thy birth; and with all thy grey-bearded wisdom, our brotherhood hope to live to see the days when war shall be no more, and man be to man a friend and a brother."

We are now on the threshold of this leafy temple; already the woodland portals open to us, and invite us to their pillared cathedral aisles. Mark you: on our right hand stands a dwarfed, time-blanched, grim-looking sentinel; how he frowns upon us, and menaces us to halt. Just such an elfin I well remember my old dame schoolmistress told me roamed the woods at night, carrying with her a long-toothed comb, to scratch and tear up the flesh of bad boys and girls, who roamed out after sun-set. Had I met this same wood-demon when I was fourteen years of age, instead of forty-four, I should have had a fit of my own. His grinning phiz is somewhat startling; his monster eyes glare upon us, and an out-stretched paw appears ready to pounce upon us, should we dare to advance. As terrible as he looks, we may venture to approach him; "there is no speculation" in his large eyes. This very

---

* Major Rook, the celebrated Antiquarian, and others, have given their opinions, that Roman encampments were held in Birkland and Bilhagh, or *Bellehagh*, near to the village of Edwinstowe. The author has in his possession a Lupercilian Medal, struck at the feast of Rome, which was dug up in 1845, while excavating the earth, for the foundation of a building, in this village. The medal is rather corroded on one side, but distinct enough to show the head and inscription of Romulus; and on the obverse, there is the wolf suckling Remus and Romulus, with S. 1. G. struck in Gaul.

fellow would furnish a study for our Gothic decorations,—a fine corbel, or water-tank head; and could we but insert a leaden pipe in his huge mouth, we should fancy that we had seen him before, copied in stone, and oak, at York, Lincoln, and Peterborough cathedrals. Farewell, ghostly friend! let those who choose be alarmed at thy scowling face, to us there is beauty in your grimness.

Slowly let us descend this slope; quietness is here. This is no sight-seeing place; no trim borders, or neatly cut verges, are here. This is a relic of the past: for the hour, then, we will, if we can, live in the past. One short hour of meditation with Nature has assured us that "God made the country," whoever made the town.

We are in *Birkland*, or the land of birches. Oaks of ten centuries' growth are assembled amongst thousands of graceful birches. A sisterhood of silver-robed and auburn-tressed wood-nymphs here live in happy communion, in a realm of their own; for they are, peculiarly, the birches of ancient Birkland. Were you ever in such a landscape garden before? You have read of sylvan groves, and Tempe's bowers; here is the verdure of one, and the redolence of the other; and in England, too, in the heart of Nottinghamshire. Here, Rhine *voyageurs*, is an *English* scene, as magical with wild beauty as when it was first called into existence by the Omnipotent. Within these woods Nature holds her high festival throughout the year: they are always full of beauty. In summer, they are embowered in sheeny green, and troops of chatting daws, perched on the old oaks, "tines and randlepipes" caw over their comical stories; cooing ring-doves, with a melancholy pleasure, tell their love-tales; choirs of merry song-birds carol there throughout the long days; and the the music-hearted nightingales make glad the night with their songs. These glades are lovely, too, when fruit-bowed Autumn paints them with her pencil of molten gold, tawny orange, deep vermilion, and mellow brown, which are rendered still more mysterious by the blue mists, and showers of falling leaves, peculiar to this season. Old Sherwood is not less beautiful, sublimely grand, when ice-crowned winter visits it. Then the age-gnarled, time-bleached oaks bare their venerable heads to the fury of the black, belching storm, and, like old Lear, they bravely defy its pitiless spite, daring it to "rumble its belly full." Now and then their white heads are singed with an "oak-cleaving thunder-bolt," and they are prostrated with a tremendous crash; sometimes they are riven by the fatal bolt into ten thousand times ten thousand shivers: but, nothing dismayed, the patriarchal host bide out the pelting storm, stretching forth their whitened arms into the leaden-tinted storm-clouds, as if to bid them welcome, while the scared owls flap the murky air with heavy wings, and utter hideous shouts in the wild night-day! Still, winter has its woodland grandeur. When the Titan oaks, all leaf-dismantled, stand grimly forth in the sickly December's sun-rays, with their massy bolls and serpentine branches all studded over with myriads of icy-rimed diamonds, each crystal ball glancing back the sun-beams in interminable lines of dazzling silver, then the effect is indescribably grand. Then, too, the dropping locks of the disrobed sylphide birches hang dishevelled, all powdered by the hoared frost, and stiffened like stalactites in a storm-king's hall; and the crisped brackens, and weeping mosses, are shrouded beneath a billowy sea of snow-flakes, while the winds, in their tortuous mirth, have writhed into numberless petrific caves, and strewn them over with the icy-skeleton forms of satyrs and wood-gods, which old Winter has sacrificed in his stormy sport. The seasons have their several beauties, and Nature has ever a charm for those who love her.

The fitful clouds had been silently stealing along the heavens, and mysteriously deepening the gloom which surrounded us, and its solemnity well accorded with our meditation; but, suddenly, the fiery-eyed sun burst out, and rained down a shower of gold through the chinks in the forest. We had now rambled along the narrow foot-path, which is fringed with tall palmy brackens, and we find ourselves in an open clearing— the fine old " Major's Oak" is before us, waving his broad leafy green head in the sun's dazzling lustre. The view up the long broad glade is enchanting. Through the loop-holes of Birkland and Bilhagh we catch glimpses of the blue horizon, and distant woods: a group of dark bushy pine-trees interlines the sweeping moorlands, contrasting, in picturesque beauty, with the purple heather, and golden furze. The Saxon-hearted oaks are scattered up and down, in a thousand diversified forms,—knotted, time-riven, white, grey, and lichened over with many-hued beauties. The summer-dressed lady-birches, in their kirtles of white, flaunt their long ringlets gracefully in the gentle breeze, and the whole scene is one of sylvan beauty. We will now turn along this closely scythe-shorn glade, towards yon famous oak. This glorious old fellow is called by the villagers the "Major's Oak," in honour, it is said, of Major Rooke, the antiquarian: with him, this oak was an especial favourite; he imagined that a Roman encampment was held near to it; and report states, the Major had search made around it, for Roman coins, &c.; but whether he was rewarded for his trouble, by adding to his museum, we have not been informed; however, the Major's name sticks closely by this tree, and it is more honourable than its former one of "Cock-pen Tree"—for such was the oak's name,—and by the old inhabitants living here, it is still known by that name. At one period, no place within the county was more notorious for their breed of game-cocks, than the village of Edwinstowe, and to keep their fowls free from contamination with the more humble, and not less despised, dunghill breed, "the pure blood" was kept within the hollow carcase of this tree. There was another advantage, too,—not only did they enjoy their " own walk," but by being stowed up in this sequestered spot, they were out of the reach of those marauders, who "thought it no trouble to go fifty miles to steal a good fowl, when a great main was to be fought." The old adage of " honour amongst thieves," did not form any part of the cock-fighters' creed; for although they might fraternize together to prosecute their heart-withering sport, they had no objection to rob each other, when, by so doing, they could adminster to their own intemperance, or supposed gain. It was not an uncommon thing for those heroes of the cock-pit to have their "roosts" watched for several nights previous to Shrove-Tuesday, and other remarkable cock-battle holidays. But, thanks to the progress of mind, and honour to humanity, the "Major" does not allow the game-fowls to congregate within his time-honoured carcase now-a-days. As you approach the Major, you fancy you have passed finer specimens already; but note him carefully as you near the veteran,—look well at his broad and age-furrowed flanks,—see his antique roots thrown firmly into the soil, and observe, that by actual measurement, his boll grips the earth with a circumference of *ninety feet;* a little higher up, six feet from the ground, his girth is thirty feet; and of "his fifty arms," which he throws so majestically around, one alone is twelve feet in circumference, while, unitedly, he waves his oaken wreath over a diameter of two hundred and forty feet! Like the rest of his green-wood brethren, the storms of a thousand winters have shaven his locks and shortened his manly proportions, but they have only scathed— they have not killed him; although time has disembowelled him, there is still sap in his old carcase, and he gives fair promise of delighting ages yet unborn. When pale-hearted King John, and the proud Edwards, claimed him as their own, they branded, with their initials and imperious "broad arrow," this once free Saxon heart. In olden time, the woodwards, and forest rangers, badged these forest-kings with iron brand, each tree, on its southernmost side; and the old Major, like many others of his race, scorned to wear the slave-mark. This very badging struck deep into the old Saxon's vitals, and he determined, even at the loss of his bowels, to throw off the brand. On the south side he has gradually opened his stout sides, and the aperture is now large enough to admit one person at once into his hollowed carcass. It was, within my notice of this tree, much wider; and it is curious to observe, that in many of these Birkland oaks, which, to outward appearance, are hastening to decay, numbers are enwrapping themselves in a new coating of bark, and sending out young branches, covered with heathy foliage, which, in their season, are ripe with fruit. These furnish another proof of the benevolence of a care-wise Providence, who covereth with beauty all His works. On one occasion, seven of our villagers took breakfast within the age-scooped trunk of this old oak, and we had plenty of room for all the necessary furniture of coffee, kettles, and cups. On many occasions, our village choir has stepped aside in their woodland rambles, and sheltered themselves within the Major's heart, to the number of twelve, and sometimes more—there we have joined in singing praises to God, for filling the earth with goodness! Glorious remnant of the primæval forest! Long, long mayest thou survive the blasts of Time, that future generations may sing of God's greatness within, and around, thy glorious crown! Mighty monarch of the woods, live on, secure from the utilitarian's axe. May thy green locks deck the forest glade, that has hitherto yielded utilitarian beauties to the poor labouring sons of men, who were too poor to purchase the luxuries of pleasure grounds, or to roam abroad for recreation! To the poor men, the hays of Birkland and Bilhagh have been more valuable, more *utilitarian*, than if every acre had been "inclosed," and corn-waving; aye, more utilitarian—I say it advisedly—in these days of threatened famine, more truly, and morally, useful, than if it had been the property of half-a-dozen "large farmers," and its grandeur had been stubbed, and burned, to swell their rick-yards and granaries. In what botanical garden, or Arboretum, could we have found thy compeer, brave old Major? They sing of England's wooden walls—let them sing of thee. Shall we petition "Boz," who has immortalized the ivy that twines around thy brethren, to immortalize thee in musical verse? A song to thy wooden walls! Thou art a first-rate tower of defence, calmly anchored in an emerald sea,—thy innumerable yards manned with myriads of waving leaves,—anon thou wilt be stored with millions of acorns, to raise up a forest of successors to adorn the groves, or build up countless fleets for all coming time, if need be! He gives us a significant nod, and shakes his green locks at the bare mention of "fleets," as much as to say,—"I have seen blood enough spilt before now." Neither wars, however, nor rumours of wars, affect him—he rides peacefully upon his beloved turfy home, blessed, and blessing! Farewell, old Major, thou type of manliness, and perseverance, and endurance.

The old Major's Oak is not the only remarkable tree amongst the thousands that still adorn this remnant of Sherwood's pride. Every tree is a picture, and one whose antique character stamps it as peculiarly one belonging to ancient Birkland or Bilhagh. The most remarkable of them have, however, received local names, from some partial circumstance;—hence, the "Millhouse Oak," so called in consequence of the Bard of Sherwood Forest, who, after he had written his poem, made a pilgrimage to this last remnant of the ancient forest, and being overtaken by a terrible storm of rain, took refuge within the hollow oak, now dedicated to him. The "Shamble's Oak," or "Hooton's Shambles," is not less a remarkable specimen of this hoary forest. In this tree, a butcher of the name of Hooton, used to conceal the carcasses of sheep which he had stolen, until he could find a market for them. At the time he carried on his nefarious trade, this tree was in the thick and embowered forest, and, to all appearances, a very unlikely place for a sheep stealer to inhabit, and the retreat served to elude suspicion. Three carcasses, it is said, were hung up within the oak when he was taken. There are persons, still living, who remember the beam, and the hooks, being in the tree. This patriarchal tree is upwards of thirty feet in circumference, and the hollow trunk is capable of holding fourteen persons within it. There are others, such as the "Hottentot Venus,"—the "Imperial Master's Oak,"—"Togo-Dubeline,"—the "Brazen Serpent in the wilderness," &c., &c., which, from the sports of Nature, and other remarkable peculiarities, are endeared to the villagers, by associations connected with their friends, or remarkable visitors, who have, from time to time, localized these trees by distinctive appellations.

There are, also, other oaks, not less remarkable, which, although without the boundary line of modern Birkland, are still within its ancient limits. Amongst them may be noted the "Parliament Oak,"—"Duke's Walking Stick"—"Greendale Oak,"—"Seven Sisters' Oak," &c. The Parliament Oak is within the ancient park attached to Clipstone Palace; in the high chase days, the palace was a retreat for the royal sportsmen. This wreck of time still exists, and stands in a little dell close by the road side, midway between Mansfield and Edwinstowe. Tradition says, that whilst the first Edward, and his princely retinue, were merrily chasing the panting deer, through the entangled paths of Shirewood, that a messenger arrived in breathless haste, bearing intelligence to his majesty, that his new subjects in Wales were in open revolt. The king instantly summoned his knights around him, and held an urgent council under this tree. The knights, with brief resolve, cried out for war, prompt suppression, exterminating war! Their departure was immediate, and history supplies us with the sequel. This tree is supposed to be above one thousand years old. It is time-tinted, age hewn, and lightning-topped. His Grace the Duke of Portland, has it propped and supported by poles; but, although Time is at work upon it, its worst destroyers are men, who, to their shame be it spoken, cannot visit this tree without carving their names, or, still worse, to taking off "wood enough to make a snuff-box." What cares this old oak to have their puny initials carved upon him? He who has seen whole generations of men come and go, may well exclaim with Emerson, "So hot? my little sir."

The Greendale Oak is a very remarkable remnant of ancient Sherwood. It stands in a bowery dell, within the finely wooded park of Welbeck. A strange sepulchral mass truly! all propped and stayed with large poles, to keep him up. We cannot gaze upon it without a feeling of wonder, how such a weather-whitened pile could stand the uprooting blasts of centuries, and when, to all human foresight, his dissolution was near, that he should again take a new lease of life, send out a vigorous stem, and gem it with a coronal of shining green! This tree is now forty feet high, and is fifty feet in girt at the base. A century and a half ago, a carriage-road was cut through his tough heart; this aperture is ten feet six inches high at the entrance, and six feet three inches wide. This Pandeon-archway is now planked diagonally with oak, and otherwise ribbed and supported. For thirty feet upward, Father Time has been trying his hand at open-roofing, and he has chisselled the dome into quaint pendants, and fanciful ribs; and the sombre brown of the over-head vaulting is dashed with streams of light which pour in through the shattered loop-holes that once were filled with vigorous branches. Nine feet on one side, at the bottom of the tree, is covered with bark, which climbs upwards, and at twenty feet from the ground, encircles the whole; from thence, a new tree towers aloft, spreading over a diameter of forty-five feet. Like unto many of his fellows, the Greendale Oak presents a visible translation from the jaws of death, to glorious new life! As I gazed upon his large time-whitened boll, methought it was the natural tomb of some wood-god of a past poetical age, and the large black spectral cavities, from which the lusty arms had fallen, aided the illusion. As the sun rushed past with precipitated step, and in an instant was gloomed again; and as the wind piped, now a solemn symphony, then a long, low, and faint moan, shrouding the green vale in sublime wildness,—and when, again, the wind-swept lute piped a time-honoured pastoral, my fancy's eye saw a whole troop of Satyrs dance out of an adjoining thicket, and chaunt a requiem to the wood-spirit entombed within the bowels of this mighty oak.

To the lovers of simple nature, in all its phases, old Sherwood presents a peculiar charm. To the entomologist, Birkland offers a fine field of research. Mr. Trueman, of Edwinstowe, a scientific and devoted lover of that branch of natural history, has enriched the cabinets of the curious, as well as our national collection in the British Museum, by his recent discoveries. His cabinet of British insects, may be ranked amongst the best in our county, containing, as it does, some of the rarest specimens, particularly so in coleopterous branches of the science.

Farewell, old Birkland! long may thy picturesque glades flourish in wild beauty; and as the varied seasons roll over thee, may they fill us with the hope, that but a little longer, and we, the sojourners of earth, shall be called by the Great Father of all things, to enjoy an Eternal Summer in the God-lit glades of Heaven!